Background Practices

Background Practices

Essays on the Understanding of Being

Hubert L. Dreyfus

EDITED BY
Mark A. Wrathall

OXFORD
UNIVERSITY PRESS

OXFORD
UNIVERSITY PRESS

Great Clarendon Street, Oxford, OX2 6DP,
United Kingdom

Oxford University Press is a department of the University of Oxford.
It furthers the University's objective of excellence in research, scholarship,
and education by publishing worldwide. Oxford is a registered trade mark of
Oxford University Press in the UK and in certain other countries

© Hubert L. Dreyfus & Mark A. Wrathall 2017

The moral rights of the authors have been asserted

First Edition published in 2017

Published in the United States of America by Oxford University Press
198 Madison Avenue, New York, NY 10016, United States of America

British Library Cataloguing in Publication Data
Data available

Library of Congress Control Number: 2017930947

ISBN 978-0-19-879622-0

Contents

Acknowledgments   vii

Credits   ix

Introduction: Background Practices and Understandings of Being   1
Mark A. Wrathall

Part I. Authenticity and Everydayness

1. Interpreting Heidegger on *das Man* (1995)   19

2. Could Anything Be More Intelligible than Everyday Intelligibility? Reinterpreting Division I of *Being and Time* in the Light of Division II (2000)   27

3. Foreword to *Time and Death* (2005)   45

Part II. Hermeneutic Realism

4. Defending the Difference: The Geistes/Naturwissenschaften Distinction Revisited (1991)   77

5. Heidegger's Hermeneutic Realism (1991)   94

6. How Heidegger Defends the Possibility of a Correspondence Theory of Truth with Respect to the Entities of Natural Science (2001)   109

Part III. Historical Worlds

7. Heidegger's Ontology of Art (2005)   125

8. Between Technê and Technology: The Ambiguous Place of Equipment in *Being and Time* (1984)   141

9. On the Ordering of Things: Being and Power in Heidegger and Foucault (1989)   155

Part IV. Nihilism and the Technological Age

10. Heidegger on the Connection between Nihilism, Technology, Art, and Politics (1992)   173

11. Highway Bridges and Feasts: Heidegger and Borgmann on
    How to Affirm Technology (1997)   198
    Hubert L. Dreyfus and Charles Spinosa

12. Nihilism on the Information Highway: Anonymity versus
    Commitment in the Present Age (2004)   218

13. Christianity without Onto-Theology: Kierkegaard's Account of
    the Self's Movement from Despair to Bliss (2003)   231

Bibliography   247
Index   255

Acknowledgments

As was the case with the first volume of Bert's collected papers, an immense debt of gratitude is owed to Genevieve Dreyfus, who has worked patiently and tirelessly to help bring this book to fruition.

M.A.W.

Credits

Chapter 1 originally published in *Inquiry*, vol. 38, no. 4 (1995), pp. 423–30. The journal can be found online at www.tandfonline.com. Reprinted by permission of Taylor & Francis.

Chapter 2 originally published in *Appropriating Heidegger*, edited by James E. Faulconer and Mark A. Wrathall (Cambridge University Press, 2000). Reprinted by permission of Cambridge University Press.

Chapter 3 reprinted by permission of the Publishers from "Foreword," in *Time and Death* by Carol J. White, edited by Mark Ralkowski, foreword by Hubert L. Dreyfus (Ashgate, 2005), pp. ix–xxxvi. Copyright © 2005.

Chapter 4 originally published in *Einheit der Wissenschaften: Internationales Kolloquium der Akademie der Wissenschaften zu Berlin* (Walter de Gruyter, 1991). Reprinted by permission of Walter de Gruyter GmbH.

Chapter 5 originally published in *The Interpretive Turn: Philosophy, Science, Culture*, edited by David R. Hiley, James F. Bohman, and Richard Shusterman (Cornell University Press, 1991). Reprinted by permission of CORNELL UNIVERSITY PRESS in the format Book via Copyright Clearance Center. This paper is a slightly revised version of chapter 15 of Hubert Dreyfus, *Being-in-the-World: A Commentary on Division I of "Being and Time"* (Cambridge: MIT Press, 1991) and appears with the permission of MIT Press.

Chapter 6 originally published in *The Practice Turn in Contemporary Theory*, edited by Theodore R. Schatzki, Karin Knorr Cetina, and Eike von Savigny (Routledge, 2001), pp. 151–62. Reprinted by permission of Taylor & Francis Books.

Chapter 7 originally published in *A Companion to Heidegger*, edited by Hubert L. Dreyfus and Mark A. Wrathall (Blackwell, 2005). Reprinted by permission of John Wiley & Sons Ltd.

Chapter 8 originally published in *Tulane Studies in Philosophy*, vol. XXXII (Tulane University, 1984). Reprinted by permission of the Philosophy Documentation Center. A French translation of this essay appears in *Martin Heidegger*, edited by Michel Haar (L'Herne, 1983), and this version appears by permission of Cahier de L'Herne.

Chapter 9 originally published in *Michel Foucault, Philosophe* (Rencontre internationale Paris 9, 10, 11 janvier 1988, © Editions du Seuil, 1989). Reprinted by permission of Editions du Seuil.

Chapter 10 originally published in *The Cambridge Companion to Heidegger* (Cambridge University Press, 2006). Reprinted by permission of Cambridge University Press.

Chapter 11 originally published in *Man and World*, vol. 30 (1997), pp. 159–77. Reprinted with permission of Springer Science+Business Media.

Chapter 12 originally published in *Community in the Digital Age*, edited by A. Feenberg and D. Barney (Rowman & Littlefield Publishers, 2004). Reprinted by permission of Rowman & Littlefield Publishing Group.

Chapter 13 originally published in *Religion after Metaphysics*, edited by Mark A. Wrathall (Cambridge University Press, 2003). Reprinted by permission of Cambridge University Press.

Introduction

Background Practices and Understandings of Being

Mark A. Wrathall

The essays in this volume exemplify a distinctive feature of Hubert Dreyfus's approach to philosophy, namely the way his work inextricably intertwines the interpretation of texts with his own analysis and description of the phenomena at issue. In fact, these two tasks—textual exegesis and phenomenological description— are for Dreyfus necessarily dependent on each other. In approaching philosophy in this way, Dreyfus is an heir to Heidegger's own historically oriented style of phenomenology.

In describing his own approach to the interpretation of Nietzsche, for instance, Heidegger observed that "description and interpretation are meshed in such a way that it is not always and immediately clear what is taken from Nietzsche's words and what has been added to them."[1] He then went on to explain:

> Of course, every interpretation must not only take things from the text but must also, without forcing the matter, be able quietly to give something of its own, something of its own concerns. This something extra is what the layman, comparing it to what he takes to be the content of the text devoid of all interpretation necessarily deplores as interpolation and sheer caprice.[2]

Dreyfus could easily describe his work in a similar way. When he interprets Heidegger and other thinkers in the existential-phenomenological tradition, he meshes description and interpretation, "quietly giving something of his own" to

---

[1] Martin Heidegger, *Nietzsche*, vol. 3, trans. David Farrell Krell (New York: Harper & Row, 1987), 192.

[2] Heidegger, *Nietzsche*, vol. 3, 192–3.

the text. "How does one go about clarifying and applying a thinker like Heidegger?," Dreyfus asks. He answers:

Since Heidegger, unlike contemporary analytic philosophers who attempt to give a logical analysis of concepts, always attempts to anchor his discussion in the phenomena, I try to use his text to draw attention to pervasive phenomena that are often overlooked, and then use an elaboration of these phenomena to cast exegetical light on the text.   (Chapter 2)

For Drefyus, as for Heidegger, it is always the phenomena that are ultimately determinative for an interpretation. At the same time, Dreyfus seems as committed as Heidegger to the thought that "one cannot think without thinking historically."[3] Thus Dreyfus always philosophizes in a kind of dialogue with thinkers in the history of philosophy. Their texts direct him to the phenomenon in question, but it is ultimately his own understanding of the phenomenon that drives his reading of their works. At times, this leads Dreyfus to discard certain aspects of a thinker's work—those that stray from the phenomenon of primary interest—in favor of others that allow him to achieve a more perspicuous grasp of the phenomena. And he holds open the possibility that the text is itself "genuinely confused" (Chapter 1)—a judgment he arrives at when every attempt to make sense of it in light of the phenomena fails.

For Dreyfus, as for Heidegger, it is more important to relate a text to "current concerns rather than freezing the text in the past" (Chapter 1). "It has always seemed to me," Dreyfus explains, "that the text of a thinker is only worth studying if reading it makes a significant difference in how we see the world and ourselves. Our job as commentators is to clarify the text and bring out its relevance" (Chapter 2). On Dreyfus's approach, a text is best understood when we share in the questions that it addresses, and answering those questions is ultimately more important to him than fidelity to the "original" meaning of the text. Moreover, unlike many philosophers working in the Continental tradition in philosophy, Dreyfus throughout his career has tried to engage with the problems that motivate contemporary work in the analytic mainstream of philosophy. He sees it as a criterion of the significance of his interpretation of a Continental thinker that he can "show the relevance ... to issues of current concern,"[4] and his interpretations of these figures thus contribute to the ongoing philosophical conversation. Critics can be

---

[3] Martin Heidegger, *Seminare*, *Gesamtausgabe* vol. 15 (Frankfurt: Vittorio Klostermann, 1986), 427.

[4] Chapter 2. Of course, Dreyfus is quite critical of analytic methodology in other respects as missing the phenomena by focusing too narrowly on the logical analysis of concepts. See "The Primacy of Phenomenology over Logical Analysis," Chapter 7, *Skillful Coping*, ed. Mark Wrathall (Oxford: Oxford University Press, 2014).

surprised or even offended that Dreyfus reads such figures as Heidegger, Merleau-Ponty, Foucault, and Kierkegaard as if they are directly relevant to contemporary analytic disputes, and as if their works belong to the same canon of philosophical texts as Wittgenstein's *Philosophical Investigations*, Davidson's *Essays on Actions and Events*, or Searle's *Speech Acts*. As a result, Dreyfus (like Heidegger before him) is sometimes accused of indulging in violent and willful interpretations of the philosophers he takes as his interlocutors. "The attempt to enlist Heidegger in contemporary projects," the objection goes, "can blind one to the specific European dimensions of his thought."[5] But both Dreyfus and Heidegger would see such complaints as symptoms of an overly narrow view of what good historical philosophizing should aspire to.

For instance, in dismissing as nonsensical the idea that we could arrive at an account of "*the* Kant," of "Kant as he is in himself," Heidegger insisted that "the actuality of the historical . . . resides in its possibility. The possibility becomes in each case manifest as the answer to a living question."[6] One can think of different approaches to philosophy as falling on a spectrum. At one extreme, philosophy is practiced as the interpretation of historical texts, with a regulative ideal of perfect exegetical fidelity. At the other extreme, philosophy is practiced as "problem solving"—as taking up timeless philosophical problems, and working out solutions to the challenges they pose (or at least a dissolution of the appearance of a problem). There are good reasons to doubt the viability of a position at either extreme. Every philosophical problem is indelibly shaped by the historical conditions under which it arises, and by the forms of life and patterns of thought that make it a salient issue. It's naive to try to treat questions in philosophy without at least some appreciation for the history that generates them. At the other end of the spectrum, it's equally naive to think that we could get access to the meaning of a philosopher's words without ourselves taking a look at the matter that provoked his reflection. By orienting his interpretation of a text toward "living questions," Heidegger situated his own approach more toward the "problem solving" end of the spectrum.

Moreover, Heidegger understood that true fidelity to a philosophical text requires the interpreter to go beyond the thinker's own understanding of his works. Heidegger insisted that "the wish to understand a thinker in his own terms is something else entirely than the attempt to take up a thinker's quest and to

---

[5] Richard McDonough, "Review of *Being-in-the-World*," *The Journal of Speculative Philosophy*, vol. 9, no. 4 (1995): 312.

[6] Martin Heidegger, *The Metaphysical Foundations of Logic* (Bloomington: Indiana University Press, 1984), 71–2.

pursue it to the core of his thought's problematic. The first is and remains impossible. The second is rare, and of all things the most difficult."[7]

For Heidegger, the most interesting "core of a thinker's problematic" is his or her understanding of being. Dreyfus shares Heidegger's view on this. But Dreyfus's contribution to reading the historical canon of philosophy comes from his recognition that an understanding of being is embodied in the "background practices" of a culture. "In order for things and people to be intelligible at all," Dreyfus claims, "there must always be a clearing—background practices containing an understanding of being." Yet, Dreyfus argues, background practices are all too often overlooked completely, or else their importance is misunderstood. This is in part because the practices themselves cannot be adequately described using the analytic tools with which philosophers are most familiar: "there are no beliefs to get clear about; there are only skills and practices. These practices do not arise from beliefs, rules, or principles, and so there is nothing to make explicit or spell out. We can only give an interpretation of the interpretation already in the practices."[8] Dreyfus reads philosophers as engaged in this project of giving a phenomenological interpretation of the interpretation of being embodied in the practices.

Each chapter in this volume is an exercise in the kind of hermenutic methodology that characterizes all of Dreyfus's work. In these essays, we see Dreyfus entering into a productive dialogue with such thinkers as Heidegger, Foucault, and Kierkegaard. In the process, he illustrates how a broad range of philosophical topics—for instance, scientific realism, authenticity, the technological character of contemporary life, the nature of art, nihilism, and the history of being, to name a few—can only be properly understood when we recognize how they are grounded in the background practices that shape our lives and give meaning to our activities, our tasks, our normative commitments, our aims and our goals.

So what is a background practice? Let me start with a discussion of practices in general. In expressions like "skills and practices," Dreyfus's use of the word "practices" might sound pleonastic—as if the word "practice" is synonomous with "skill." And he does at times use the words interchangeably. But there is a distinction to be drawn between skills and practices—a distinction Dreyfus usually respects. Skills, one might say, enable us to participate in a practice fluidly. But a practice is not reducible to a skill. It is rather the standing condition of the possibility of acting skillfully in a domain. To be more precise, a practice is a complex structure that sustains action. This structure is a particular way of

---

[7] Martin Heidegger, *What Is Called Thinking?* (New York: Harper & Row, 1968), 185.
[8] Hubert Dreyfus, *Being-in-the-World: A Commentary on Heidegger's Being and Time, Division I* (Cambridge, MA: MIT Press 1991), 22.

organizing the world and agents into settings within which normatively articulated purposive activities can be pursued coherently. The structure (a) is embodied in skillful dispositions to act, (b) is incorporated concretely into the equipmental contexts of the surrounding world, and (c) involves an element of social recognition.

For example, the practice of soccer is a complex structure that involves:

(a) embodied agents, over whom are distributed the broad variety of skills involved in playing soccer and staging soccer matches—skills for dribbling, passing, heading, and shooting the ball; skills for tackling; skills for running the offside trap, and so on. In acquiring these skills, agents also acquire the ability to perceive and respond appropriately to soccer situations;

(b) concrete equipmental contexts that include soccer pitches, uniforms, boots, balls, whistles, flags, goal posts, and so on. Each item of equipment has its specific style, dimensions, and features in virtue of the fact that it is part of the practice of soccer; and

(c) socially shared vocabulary for talking about soccer, socially constituted roles (like goalie, striker, midfielder, manager, referee, linesman, etc.), and a shared sense of good and bad, exciting or boring, and proper or improper ways of performing soccer activities.

A practice, then, is not an action nor reducible to a set of actions. While an ongoing practice necessarily gives rise to lots of particular actions, the practice is found not in those actions, but in the skills, objectifications, and shared meanings that support and give structure to those actions. In defining the concept of a practice, I focus on this structure rather than the actions sustained by the structure for a couple of reasons. First of all, a practice can continue to exist, even when there are no actions being performed in furtherance of the practice. The practice of soccer continues even at those moments, as rare as they might be, when no one is playing or watching soccer (or engaging in the many other activities—tending the pitch, training, strategizing, signing contracts, etc.—that are sustained by the practice of modern soccer). The practice continues just so long as there are people who possess the skills to put on a soccer match, and there are fields and balls and all the other equipment needed to play soccer. Second, I focus on the structure rather than activities because there is a sense in which someone can perform the same action as practitioners do without participating in the practice. A baseball player who kicks a stray soccer ball while shagging fly baseballs during batting practice is not engaging in the practice of soccer. Conversely, one *can* be involved in a practice, even while performing an action that does not properly belong to the practice in question. If a midfielder catches a soccer ball during a soccer match, this counts as a (bad) movement in the practice of soccer, even though it is an action that is explicitly precluded by the rules of soccer. So, the practice itself is the structure in virtue of which certain actions will "belong to" or "express" or "instantiate" the practice. And an action expresses the practice well when it furthers the ends or purposes of the practice while drawing on the skills and equipment that embody the practice. The practice itself resides in the intertwining of bodily skills, equipmental contexts, and social meanings that form the background and basis of the actions.

Practices are purposive because there is an end or goal in view when one engages in the practice. Or, more typically, there are a set of interrelated goals or ends in view. In playing soccer, one aims at winning the game. But one can also participate in the practice with the aim of being entertained, of earning money, of getting fit, or of winning the esteem of others. The full rich character of most practices comes from the way that they support the pursuit of multiple aims. To say that a practice has ends or goals in view, however, does not mean that the practice will cease once the goal is attained. Practices tend to be open-ended in the sense that there may not be some final performance that will eliminate the desire to continue with the practice in question. Practices persist beyond any particular successful performance of the actions that belong to the practice.

Because a practice is purposive, the actions that instantiate a practice are subject to the normative order sustained by the practice. To say that a practice has a normative order or that it is normatively articulated means simply that there are better or worse ways to engage in the practice, and the actions that belong to a practice can be done well or badly, properly or improperly. Being subject to the normative order of a practice is a criterion by which we can tell if an action belongs to a practice. For instance, the baseball player who kicks a stray soccer ball is not criticizable if he kicks it badly by the standards of soccer. By the same token, the soccer midfielder who handles the ball is blameworthy, no matter how well or elegantly he executes a catch. As Joseph Rouse explains, "actors share a practice if their actions are appropriately regarded as answerable to norms of correct or incorrect practice."[9]

Because practices are ingrained into bodies in the form of skillful dispositions to act and discriminatory capacities, the practice persists independently of our current involvements and gives us standing possibilities for action. I can still be involved in the practice of soccer, even at those times in which I am fully absorbed in cooking dinner—provided, that is, I retain the skills and dispositions that would

---

[9] "Two concepts of practices," in Karin Knorr Cetina, Theodore R. Schatzki, and Eike von Savigny, *The Practice Turn in Contemporary Theory* (New York: Routledge, 2001), 199.

allow me to play soccer. This standing, skillful disposedness is an important way in which practices bring intelligibility to the world. My ability to understand what would otherwise be a chaotic whirl of events depends on having skills for discriminating meaningful features and responding appropriately to what happens around me. For instance, it is because I have skills for gauging the flight of a soccer ball and chesting it, trapping it, kicking it, and so on, that a soccer pitch makes sense.

There is an unmistakable social dimension to most if not all practices. This social dimension is perhaps most visible in the shared language and vocabulary we have for talking about the practice. An important part of being initiated into a practice consists in learning how one speaks about the activities that belong to the practice. But at a more profound level, the social dimension of the practice is found in the way that to participate in a practice is to join together with others in a common undertaking. Indeed, many actions cannot even be performed without the recognition of other participants in a practice—namely, their acknowledgment that an action of such and such a type belongs to or is an expression of such and such a practice. In engaging in a practice, I am taking upon myself a particular status. Social recognition of this status is often a constitutive condition for being able to participate in practices. Consequently, gatekeeping mechanisms are frequently employed to protect that status. Without social recognition of one's status as a legislator, for instance, saying "yea" in the legislative chamber is not an action of voting within the practice of lawmaking. The enthusiastic fan who runs onto a soccer pitch during the game cannot score a goal, no matter how many times he kicks a ball into the net. Practices are also social in the sense that they are typically learned from, or learnable by, others. Inauguration into practices is an essential part of coming to belong to a broader community. In being so inaugurated, we acquire a shared social sense of appropriateness—of not just what constitutes a proper or improper performance within a practice, but also what constitutes a good and worthwhile life. "It is this distinction" between the proper and improper performance of a practice, Dreyfus notes, "that makes possible the coordination of equipment and roles in the human world" (Chapter 1). Practices are thus social in the sense that they involve coordination with others, or the sharing of aims and intentions in the pursuit of a common goal.

As a result of the social dimension of practices, there is an inherent tendency toward the average, universal, and general in practices.[10] As socially constituted, practices must be in principle accessible to and communicable to everyone. This generalizing tendency is reinforced by the way that practices are partially incorporated into the built environment. The equipment that sustains the practice

---

[10] Of course, the strength of this tendency varies from practice to practice and world to world.

stands as something ready to be taken up by anybody, or at least anybody who acquires the skills and dispositions required to engage in the practice.

The generality built into practices is an important aspect of the intelligibility they produce. Their generality allows me to share with others a feel for the sense things have, and to communicate this sense to others through a word or gesture. But it also, as Dreyfus notes, "both make[s] *conformity* inevitable . . . and make[s] possible the flight from anxiety into the slavish *conformism* which Heidegger calls making *the one* one's hero" (Chapter 1). Because each of us makes sense of the world by playing a role in some set of practices, and because those roles are themselves defined and organized by shared social senses of propriety and impropriety, we understand ourselves at a fundamental level as beholden to shared public norms.

We can see, then, the shared practices are absolutely central to our ability to understand ourselves and the things and people around us. From birth on we are initiated into a variety of practices (and take up roles within those practices). This initiation generally takes the form of providing me with exemplary demonstrations of *how to act*, rather than giving me detailed instructions on *what to do*. As I imitate others, I acquire skills that make me aware of and capable of discerning projectible connections between entities and events. The practices I participate in thus orient me to my world. Because I encounter situations in terms of practices, I understand in advance how situations could and should unfold. The practice, with its purposive orientation to ends and goals, also determines what's important and unimportant, relevant and irrelevant. It gives me reasons and motivations for acting by giving me an identity or status that comes from the role I play in the furtherance of the practice. Thus, the practice makes it possible for me to make sense of myself. I know who I am, what I should do, what would count as progress or regress—namely, getting better and better at performing those actions that will advance the ends of the practice.

So much for an account of practices in general, and a review of the way specific practices make particular domains of activities intelligible to us. What, now, is a *background* practice? In some sense, all practices form a kind of background to actions, withdrawing from consideration as we are engaged in the action. The soccer player can execute a pass in a game of soccer only because she is participating in the practice of soccer. But as she is executing the pass, she need not have any sense at all that she is acting *in order to* perpetuate the practice of soccer. Ordinarily, what will be salient for her are the affordances of the current situation—the players to whom she can pass the ball, the defenders positioning themselves to intercept the pass or tackle her, and so on. The practice itself becomes transparent in favor of the entities and tasks that are most pressing at the moment. Thus, practices in general tend to withdraw into the background of our concern.

But the practices that Dreyfus targets with the name "background practices" are not merely operating in the background. They also form the background against which a large number of other practices makes sense. These are the practices that, at the deepest level, form the background to any other practice at all in a particular world because they "embody pervasive responses, discriminations, motor skills, etc., which add up to an interpretation of what it is to be a person, an object, an institution, etc."[11] Ordinary practices make a limited domain of entities and actions intelligible to us. Background practices make the world in general intelligible to us. They help us make sense of what it is to be a thing, an event, a person, a meaningful aim or goal, and so on. Like other practices, a background practice is not a mental representation of what it is to be a person or object: "Such an understanding is contained in our knowing-how-to-cope in various domains rather than in a set of beliefs that such and such is the case. Thus we embody an understanding of being that no one has in mind."[12] We embody this understanding through a particular structure of (a) skillful dispositions to act, (b) concrete equipmental contexts, and (c) forms of social coordination that together shape, constrain, and normatively articulate the actions we perform with respect to people, objects, and institutions in general. As Dreyfus puts it, "our practices are needed as the place where an understanding of being can establish itself." He explains:

our understanding of Being...is embodied in the tools, language and institutions of a society and in each person growing up in that society. These shared practices into which we are socialised provide a background understanding of what counts as objects, what counts as human beings, and ultimately what counts as real, on the basis of which we can direct our actions toward particular things and people. Thus the understanding of Being creates what Heidegger calls a clearing.   (Chapter 9)

Take, for example, modern technological practices for dealing with animals. For most of us, this involves:

(a) skillful dispositions to act, including "our skill in buying pieces of them, taking off their plastic wrapping, and cooking them in microwave ovens" (Chapter 10);
(b) concrete equipmental contexts such as supermarkets, kitchens, and factory farms;

and

---

[11] Dreyfus, *Being-in-the-World*, 17.   [12] Dreyfus, *Being-in-the-World*, 18.

(c) forms of social coordination, including such roles as "consumer" and "producer," and such shared values as efficiency and availability.

We don't ordinarily attend to these practices, or even recognize our activities and built environment as being organized into a coherent practice because, Dreyfus argues, "these practices can function only if they remain in the background." He explains:

our cultural practices and the understanding of being they embody allow us to direct our activities and make sense of our lives only insofar as they are and stay unarticulated, that is, stay the atmosphere in which we live. These background practices are the concealed and unmastered that Heidegger tells us give seriousness to our decisions.   (Chapter 10)

Although they are concealed from our focal attention, we are all "socialized" into them nonetheless, and they "provide the conditions necessary for people to pick out objects, to understand themselves as subjects, and, generally, to make sense of the world and of their lives."[13]

Because practices like these—practices for dealing with animals, objects, and other people—are so fundamental, they give a coherence to the culture as a whole. They "provide a background understanding of what matters and what it makes sense to do, on the basis of which we can direct our actions" (Chapter 10). But because our understanding of being is grounded in practices like these, it is no more coherent, stable or necessary than the practices themselves. Thus an understanding of being, Dreyfus points out, is historically contingent and variable because "our practices can never be grounded in human nature, God's will, or the structure of rationality":[14]

human beings...live in a world that is made intelligible by their shared background practices and...these background practices cannot and need not be made explicit and justified.... [T]he practices that make people and things intelligible can be pointed out and their general structure described but...the understanding of being in those practices cannot be spelled out in detail and given a transcendental or metaphysical grounding.

(Chapter 3)

Once we recognize how background practices play a constitutive role in grounding an understanding of being, a number of important questions open up. For instance, we have seen already how thoroughly social the background practices are. Our understanding of the world is articulated by these practices, and thus we grow up in the first instance into a shared way of understanding everything.

---

[13] Dreyfus, *Being-in-the-World*, 4.   [14] Dreyfus, *Being-in-the-World*, 37.

"We do not say what we see," Heidegger explains of our immediate everyday experience of the word, "but rather the reverse, we see what one says about the matter."[15] But, one can ask, is this social articulation essential, so that all of our activities are inescapably determined by a shared form of intelligibility? Or is it possible to be authentic—to break out of slavish conformism to shared norms and standards, and act instead in ways that make sense without being generally intelligible? The essays in the first section of this volume explore such questions. In Chapter 1, Dreyfus offers an interpretation of Heidegger's account of "the one" or "the anyone" (*das Man*). In the activities of everyday existence, Heidegger argued, I am not my own self but an "anyone-self" (*Man-selbst*). As an "anyone-self," "I do what anyone ought to do in this situation," or "I think what every one thinks." The "anyone" on Dreyfus's reading names the way our practices encourage an "essential tendency to minimize the distance between ourselves and others by subtle coercion or co-option, especially when we are not aware of doing so. We constantly and unconsciously shape up others' pronunciation, the distance they stand from us, and how they use their knives and forks, and the like; they shape us up in the same way." Thus, Dreyfus concludes, we are structurally disposed by our practices to "reduce . . . difference and so perform . . . the ontological function of establishing norms and thus opening up a shared human world." In Chapter 2, Dreyfus describes two different forms of authenticity that are possible, despite the inevitable dependence of our understanding of being on shared social practices. The first form of authenticity—authenticity as *phronesis*—is a rejection of efforts to codify and regulate the practices through explicit rules and standards. The *phronimos* recognizes that there's a sense to the practices that can never be captured in a rule-bound way. Through "the gradual refinement of responses that grows out of long experience acting within the shared cultural practices," the *phronimos* learns to preserves what is most essentially at stake in the shared practices—even when this requires her to act in a way that is contrary to conventional rules for acting. "Such a person's understanding of his society is richer and deeper than the average understanding," Dreyfus argues, and thus it has a kind of authenticity to it, even if this understanding of the situation is fundamentally constituted by the shared background practices. But Dreyfus also sees that there is a higher form of authenticity—one that responds not to what is essential in the shared social practices, but rather to what is essential to being a human being. What is essential to human existence is our "homelessness." We don't belong uniquely to any set of practices, and thus we experience (at some

---

[15] Martin Heidegger, *The History of the Concept of Time* (Bloomington, IN: Indiana University Press, 1985), 56.

level—usually far removed from reflective consciousness) every possible form of life as contingent. This is a negative characterization of human existence; viewed positively, what is most definitive of us is our capacity to disclose new ways of being in the world:

According to Heidegger our nature is to be world disclosers. That is, by means of our equipment and coordinated practices we human beings open coherent, distinct contexts or worlds in which we perceive, act, and think. Each such world makes possible a distinct and pervasive way in which things, people, and selves can appear and in which certain ways of acting make sense.   (Chapter 11)

This points to a higher form of authenticity. We are authentic when we live in a way that owns up to our nature as world disclosers. On this picture, the most authentic person is the "cultural master," who reconfigures the world, stepping out of existing background practices into a changed set of practices. In Chapter 3, Dreyfus further deepens our understanding of the ideal of authenticity by cataloguing a variety of ways in which interpreters have tried to make sense of Heidegger's claim that authenticity involves "anticipatory resoluteness" in the face of death. But death, Dreyfus points out, "has both an individual and a cultural instantiation": "cultures, like the people and the things that focus their style, must die if new worlds are to be disclosed." In both Chapters 2 and 3, Dreyfus develops a model of cultural transformation that is consistent with the idea that all intelligibility is ultimately grounded in social practices. "In a histor-ical change," Dreyfus explains, "a historical figure makes history by retrieving some practices from the past and giving them a new central role in the present." With that change in background practices, "human beings and things show up differently" (Chapter 3).

In the papers in the second section, Dreyfus explores a very special set of background practices—those that allow scientists to encounter objects that are apparently constituted independently of our social practices. Scientists, Dreyfus contends, are "background realists," meaning that their background practices "take the independent existence of their domain of objects for granted." Dreyfus argues for a kind of "hermeneutic realism" about the entities discovered by the natural sciences. His position is "hermeneutic" in the sense that he recognizes that our access to reality is grounded in interpretive practices, and he aims to spell out what those practices take for granted. But he is a "realist" in the sense that he argues that the conditions of access to entities do not determine or constitute those entities as such. Instead, Dreyfus argues that the realist self-understanding of scientific practices is "internally coherent and compatible with the ontological implications of our everyday practices." In Chapter 4, Dreyfus shows that being a realist about natural entities is compatible with pluralism or, as he calls it, "plural realism." If intelligibility is always grounded in our practices, Dreyfus points out, then there is no point of view from which one can ask about or provide an answer to the one true nature of ultimate reality. "Different understandings of being," Dreyfus concludes, "reveal different realities or domains of intelligibility, and since no one way of revealing is exclusively true, accepting one does not commit us to rejecting the others." In Chapter 6, Dreyfus argues against the view that grounding intelligibility in background practices will lead to a deflationary account of the reality of the entities discovered by the natural sciences. The deflationary realist holds that objects appear to be independent of us only relative to a particular set of practices, but in fact their existence is dependent on the practices that disclose them. Dreyfus argues instead for the coherence of a robust realism. "The independence claim makes sense," Dreyfus maintains, and "science can in principle give us access to the functional components of the universe as they are in themselves in distinction from how they appear to us on the basis of our daily concerns, our sensory capacities, and even our way of making things intelligible." To support the coherence of such a claim, Dreyfus draws a distinction between access practices and constitutive practice. Human artefacts and equipment are *constituted* by the practices for using them. But scientific practices, by decontextualizing objects from the way they are encountered in everyday life, are "contingent practices for identifying objects," and thus give us *access* to the objects in a way that allows us to recontextualize and reinterpret them in theoretical terms.

The essays in section three further explore what it means to posit the existence of a plurality of worlds; they offer an account of how new worlds arise, and they describe the succession of worlds that have characterized Western history. A world, on the Heideggerian understanding that informs Dreyfus's work, is a

> whole context of shared equipment, roles, and practices on the basis of which one can encounter entities and other people. So, for example, one encounters a hammer as a hammer in the context of other equipment such as nails and wood, and in terms of social roles such as being a carpenter, a handyman, and so forth. Moreover, each local cluster of tools, the skills for using them, and the roles that require them constitutes a sub-world such as carpentry, or homemaking, and each, with its appropriate equipment and practices, makes sense on the more general background of our one shared, familiar, everyday world.   (Chapter 3)

In other words, a world is not just a haphazard grouping of practices, equipment, and roles, but a "total system"[16]—a whole ordered and coherent way of

---

[16]   Dreyfus, *Being-in-the-World*, 90.

coordinating and aligning and orienting practical contexts—that gives substance to an understanding of being. The world we grow up into consequently gives us the possibilities for action and self-determination that end up determining our lives: "embodied, everyday practices produce, perpetuate, and delimit what people can think and do" (Chapter 9). In Chapter 7, Dreyfus argues that the coherence of all the foreground practices that make up a world is grounded in a style that characterizes the background practices of that world:

> Style is the way the everyday practices are coordinated. It serves as the basis upon which old practices are conserved and new practices are developed. A style opens a disclosive space and does so in a threefold manner: (a) by coordinating actions; (b) by determining how things and people matter; and (c) by being what is transferred from situation to situation.   (Chapter 7)

But how is it that a new style can arise and establish itself, thereby reconfiguring the background practices and ushering in a new world? One way in which Heidegger accounted for this was through great works of art manifesting, articulating, and glamorizing a world's style. "A culture's practices tend to gather so as to open and illuminate a world," Dreyfus explains, "and they use the artwork to do so." In Chapter 8, Dreyfus illustrates several distinct world styles by contrasting Greek, industrial, and technological practices for using equipment.[17] And he shows how Heidegger's own account of equipment in *Being and Time* helped set the stage for technology by encouraging an understanding of being that "leaves open, indeed encourages, the kind of attack and reordering of nature that encounters natural objects as *Bestand* [resources]." In Chapter 9, Dreyfus more fully illuminates the style of the background practices of our current technological world by comparing Heidegger's account of *Gestell* with Foucault's account of bio-power. Heidegger's emphasis on the signification contexts within which people and things show up and encounter each other is complemented by Foucault's emphasis on the way embodied practices perpetuate, delimit, and produce what people are capable of saying and doing. Foucault's regimes of power, like Heidegger's epochs of being, are clearings which open up a finite field of possibilities that govern action. And both Heidegger and Foucault are especially concerned with the current clearing, with its pressure toward ever greater optimization and normalization.

The review of the totalizing, technological ordering of the world in Chapter 9 sets up the fourth and concluding section of essays, which explore ways to resist the nihilism implicit in totalizing practices. Dreyfus defines nihilism as the leveling

---

[17] Dreyfus provides a more complete review of six distinct worlds in Chapter 11.

of all meaningful differences, as a result of which existence no longer has inherent meaning. Human existence loses its goal or direction, and thus nothing can have authority for us, make a claim on us, or demand a commitment from us. In Chapter 10, Dreyfus follows Heidegger in arguing that modern nihilism is ultimately rooted in background practices that subject everything—including our moral knowledge—to detached reflection. "The more our know-how is formulated and objectified as knowing-that," Dreyfus argues, "the more it is called up for critical questioning, the more it loses its grip on us." We rightly "celebrate our ability to get everything clear and under control"—an ability fostered by foreground practices as diverse as power stations, the fast food industry, and global information technologies. But these practices for the total organization of the world depend on our background practices revealing everything as a resource to be optimized and controlled. In Chapter 11, Dreyfus and Spinosa ask whether it is possible to "relate ourselves to technology in a way that not only resists its devastation but also gives it a positive role in our lives." They argue that we can affirm technological things provided that they can play a role in giving us an identity, rather than merely dispersing or decomposing us into a contingent set of disaggregated skills. If we could become aware of ourselves as "active world disclosers" with a repertoire of different background practices available to us, they argue, then we could affirm the technological style as one way among many others of opening up possibilities for action. In Chapters 12 and 13, Dreyfus turns from the late Heidegger to Kierkegaard's very different way of responding to the threat of nihilism posed by our technological background practices. For Kierkegaard, we cannot overcome nihilism on our own. We instead need to experience ourselves as gripped by or summoned by something that gives birth in us to an infinite passion. If we respond to that summons with a passionate, unconditional commitment, the world will once again be articulated into meaningful distinctions between the important and trivial, the good and bad, the worthwhile and pointless.

PART I

Authenticity and Everydayness

1

Interpreting Heidegger on
das Man (1995)

In their debate over my interpretation of Heidegger's account of *das Man* in *Being and Time,* Frederick Olafson and Taylor Carman agree that Heidegger's various characterizations of *das Man* are inconsistent. Olafson champions an existentialist/ontic account of *das Man* as a distorted mode of being-with. Carman defends a Wittgensteinian/ontological account of *das Man* as Heidegger's name for the social norms that make possible everyday intelligibility. For Olafson, then, *das Man* is a privative mode of *Dasein,* while for Carman it makes up an important aspect of *Dasein*'s positive constitution. Neither interpreter takes seriously the other's account, though both acknowledge that both readings are possible. How should one choose between these two interpretations? I suggest that we choose the interpretation that identifies the phenomenon the work is examining, gives the most internally consistent account of that phenomenon, and shows the compatibility of this account with the rest of the work.

The controversy in several past issues of *Inquiry* concerning my interpretation of Heidegger's *Being and Time* has not only illuminated the text but has also revealed important inconsistencies in Heidegger's *magnum opus.* It thus raises the question, how should one interpret a philosophical text that is genuinely confused? It would seem obvious that one should first determine whether the inconsistencies stem from the juxtaposition of two or more distinct views. If so, one has either to show that these views are consistent or, if they cannot be reconciled, one will have to foreground one and assimilate as much as one can of the other. But which should one choose? This issue comes up in a sharp and illuminating way in the debate between Frederick Olafson and Taylor Carman on Heidegger's account of the relation of the individual to the social world, that is, on the nature and status of the anonymous and impersonal dimension of social life that Heidegger calls *das Man.*[1]

---

[1] Since the issues to be discussed hinge on the exact meaning of *das Man,* I will translate the term literally as *the one.*

In *Being and Time* Heidegger says both that "authentic self-being is an existentiell modification of *the 'one'*... as an essential existentiale,"[2] i.e., that the individual supervenes on an impersonal, structural feature of human being, and that "the oneself is an existentiell modification of the authentic self,"[3] i.e., that the individualized self is basic, and the impersonal supervenes on it. Olafson, in conformity with the second claim, maintains that *the one* is "a distorted modality of *Mitsein* (being-with)." He sees *the one* as a transitory stage of socialization in which the human infant is dependent upon the social and holds that this deformation is corrected when an authentic *Dasein* "breaks out" of the one and assumes responsibility for its beliefs and actions. Carman counters this existentialist reading with a Wittgensteinian one, citing Heidegger's claim that *the one* is an essential existentiale to support his contention that *the one* denotes the anonymous social norms that give equipment and human roles their intelligibility. Authenticity on this view would be a specific way of taking up these constitutive norms, not a way of breaking out of them.

There is evidence in the text to support each view. Heidegger does advance a Kierkegaardian account of the public in which everyday social life is described as a disburdening and leveling concealment of the truth of the human condition. This description of *the one* is paired with an account of what Heidegger calls fleeing. Olafson describes this motivated cover-up in psychological terms: "[I]n the public and anonymous mode of being that Heidegger calls *das Man* we try quite elaborately to steer clear of... individuatedness in our thoughts about ourselves. But that is the kind of effort that, like the avoidances induced by post-hypnotic suggestion, presupposes an understanding of the very fact that is being steered clear of."[4] Since, on this reading, *das Man* is not an existential structure but an existentiell mode or style of existence, it can be overcome. As Olafson says:

In Division II... Heidegger... describes a *Dasein* that awakens out of [its] tranquilized state and reclaims its responsibility and power of individual choice in a very radical way. Heidegger describes this recasting of *Dasein*'s life into the mode of authenticity as "choosing choice" and it issues in a state of resoluteness in which we accept our true situation.... This is the existential Heidegger that Sartre drew on... It clearly shows that, as Heidegger understands it, *Dasein* has options that are independent of Das Man.[5]

---

[2]   Martin Heidegger, *Being and Time*, trans. J. Macquarrie and E. Robinson (New York: Harper & Row, 1962), 168.

[3]   Heidegger, *Being and Time*, 365.

[4]   Frederick A. Olafson, "Individualism, Subjectivity, and Presence: A Response to Taylor Carman," *Inquiry* 37 (1994), 332.

[5]   Frederick A. Olafson, "Heidegger *à la* Wittgenstein or 'Coping' with Professor Dreyfus," *Inquiry* 37 (1994), 63.

But here we are not in the realm of the existential or structural but of the existentiell or psychological. Heidegger himself says as much when criticizing Kierkegaard: "Soren Kierkegaard explicitly seized upon the problem of existence as an existentiell problem, and thought it through in a penetrating fashion. But the existential problematic was...alien to him."[6]

None the less, Olafson's existentialist reading is, as he would say, secure. It fits the majority of passages in the text and places *Being and Time* in the historical context of the criticism of mass society typical of Mandarin German professional philosophy. This way of reading *Being and Time* has been widely accepted. It is the understanding of Heidegger that influenced Sartre and, through him, a whole generation of students, writers, and philosophers in the fifties.

Carman and I reject this accepted reading. Focusing on Heidegger's claim to be doing ontology and his claim that *the one* is an essential structure of *Dasein*, we make the case that *das Man* denotes the shared norms that determine both equipmental use and the point of such use, which Heidegger calls significance. Olafson notes that animals have skills and use things that are functionally appropriate for achieving certain ends, but Taylor adds that only human beings distinguish between the proper and improper use of equipment. (A hammer is for pounding in nails not for opening paint cans.) It is this distinction that makes possible the coordination of equipment and roles in the human world, so Heidegger can conclude that "*the 'one'* itself articulates the referential context of significance."[7]

Looking at the phenomenon of *das Man* as Carman and I do credits Heidegger with developing an account of *Mitsein* that shows where the sharedness of our tasks and comportments comes from. Since for Olafson individualized *Dasein* is basic, *Mitsein* must arise from some positive agreement among the individuals, not from already socialized *Dasein*, which he takes to be a privative state. And, since Olafson finds no account of how such agreement could emerge, he claims that there is here a serious gap in Heidegger's argument. In his book Olafson tells us:

Heidegger never worked out an account of the way in which the agreement among human beings...implicitly orders the relationships of human beings to one another.[8]

If a theory that does justice to...*Mitsein* [being-with] were to be developed, it would have to take into account such facts as that what I uncover as a hammer, say, has been previously used (and thus uncovered) as a hammer by others and that it is normally from these others that I have learned what a hammer is and how to use one.[9]

---

[6] Heidegger, *Being and Time*, 494.   [7] Heidegger, *Being and Time*, 167.

[8] Frederick A. Olafson, *Heidegger and the Philosophy of Mind* (New Haven, CT: Yale University Press, 1987), 242.

[9] Olafson, *Heidegger and the Philosophy of Mind*, 147.

Carman's and my Heidegger offers just such an account, pointing out that the equipment and goals of a society are defined by norms that apply to *anyone*.

When entities are encountered, *Dasein*'s world frees them for a totality of involvements with which *the one* is familiar, and within the limits which have been established with *the one's* averageness.[10]

Heidegger's basic point is that the background familiarity that underlies all coping and all intentional states is an agreement in proper ways of acting and judging into which human beings are "always already" socialized.[11]

By "others" we do not mean everyone else but me—those over against whom the "I" stands out. They are rather those from whom, for the most part, one does *not* distinguish oneself—those among whom one is too. This being-there-too with them does not have the ontological character of a being-present-at-hand-along-"with" them within a world.... "With" and "too" are to be understood *existentially*.... By reason of this with-like being-in-the-world, the world is always the one that I share with others.[12]

But Olafson finds talk of social norms "potentially very misleading."[13] While he might allow that the everyday norms for using equipment properly are shared by both authentic and inauthentic *Dasein*, he holds that the everyday norms for dealing with people would not be followed by an authentic *Dasein*. He is right that how one deals with particular other people is an existentiell issue. On the structural level, however, equipment is in the service of social roles. "One is a shoemaker, tailor, teacher, banker. Here *Dasein* is something which others also can be and are."[14] And we must in our everyday activity understand ourselves and others in terms of these roles, whether or not we also relate to particular people authentically. Presumably this is why Heidegger says:

[The] everyday way in which things have been interpreted is one into which *Dasein* has grown in the first instance, with never a possibility of extrication. In it, out of it, and

---

[10] Heidegger, *Being and Time*, 167.

[11] Olafson is right in pointing out that I was mistaken in my commentary in claiming that, according to Heidegger, a baby becomes *Dasein* through socialization. His citation shows that Heidegger holds that "a child can learn from its mother through imitation only because it is itself an In-der-Welt-sein" (Olafson, "Heidegger à la Wittgenstein or 'Coping' with Professor Dreyfus," 64). This does raise a problem, however. If the infant is being-in-the-world from birth then it presumably is born with existence (in Heidegger's sense) as its mode of being, that is, its being is already an issue for it. But neither my nor Olafson's account can make sense of such a claim. Perhaps before the baby can have *Dasein* in it, and so imitate its mother, it must be subjected to some sort of social training.

[12] Heidegger, *Being and Time*, 154–5.

[13] Olafson, "Heidegger à la Wittgenstein or 'Coping' with Professor Dreyfus," 61.

[14] Martin Heidegger, *History of the Concept of Time*, trans. Theodore Kisiel (Bloomington, IN: Indiana University Press, 1985), 244.

against it, all genuine understanding, interpreting, and communicating, all re-discovering and appropriating anew are performed.[15]

By devaluing this passage, read in conjunction with the one that claims that *das Man* articulates the world, Olafson makes the gap he finds in Heidegger's thinking appear even more outrageous. "If *das Man* were really a necessary condition for the intelligibility of our world and not just the principal modality of our being at the time when we are learning our basic skills, it should follow that to the extent that we break out of *das Man* these forms of intelligibility must become unavailable to us."[16] This would, indeed, be a huge problem for Heidegger if he did in fact believe that authentic *Dasein* breaks out of *das Man*, but Heidegger is clear that "in no case is a *Dasein* untouched... by the [everyday] way in which things have been interpreted, set before the open country of a 'world in itself' so that it just beholds what it encounters."[17] Even authentic *Dasein* must in some sense do what one does. Perhaps, when *Dasein* experiences anxiety, it finds itself and others unintelligible. But as soon as it resolutely acts on the basis of this anxiety it must do so in conformity with public norms of intelligibility. The impersonal norms into which we are socialized both make *conformity* inevitable (except for those who are insane) and make possible the flight from anxiety into the slavish *conformism* that Heidegger calls making *the one* one's hero.[18] What we break out of, Heidegger tells us, is this conformism, i.e., being so dominated by our sense of what is normal and proper that we respond to the general rather than the specific situation.[19]

Just how conformism is supposed to arise is not very clear in *Being and Time*, but it somehow is made possible by what Heidegger calls *Abständigkeit*. Olafson seems to me right in interpreting *Abständigkeit* in its everyday ontic sense as a concern with how one differs from one's neighbors.

There are evidently respects in which we are better or worse off than our fellows; and the fact of such differences—what [Heidegger] calls *Abständigkeit*—becomes a focus of concern for each of us individually.[20]

Heidegger says as much:

In one's concern with what one has taken hold of, whether with, for, or against, the Others, there is a constant care as to the way one differs from them, whether that

---

[15] Heidegger, *Being and Time*, 213.
[16] Olafson, "Individualism, Subjectivity, and Presence: A Response to Taylor Carman," 336.
[17] Heidegger, *Being and Time*, 213.   [18] Heidegger, *Being and Time*, 422.
[19] Heidegger, *Being and Time*, 346.
[20] Olafson, "Heidegger *à la* Wittgenstein or 'Coping' with Professor Dreyfus," 56.

difference is merely one that is to be evened out, whether one's own *Dasein* has lagged behind the Others and wants to catch up in relationship to them, or whether one's *Dasein* already has some priority over them and sets out to keep them suppressed.[21]

Carman's account of *Abständigkeit* is less plausible. While Heidegger says that *Abständigkeit* is "constant", by treating it as a breakdown of norms that makes those norms conspicuous, Carman makes *Abständigkeit* an infrequent phenomenon.

[W]here as ordinarily we conduct ourselves by unconsciously adapting to the various normalizing pressures around us, in standoffishness [Carman's translation of *Abständigkeit*] it is normality and abnormality as such that become the focus of our concern.[22]

I agree with Olafson that there is no textual basis for this reading. But this is merely a disagreement over what Heidegger has in view as the existentiell phenomenon in question.

Heidegger makes clear, however, that as an existentiale *Abständigkeit* is an ontological phenomenon that is primordial and works inconspicuously in the background.

If we may express this existentially, such Being-with-one-another has the character of *Abständigkeit*. The more inconspicuous this kind of Being is to everyday *Dasein* itself, all the more stubbornly and primordially does it work itself out.[23]

This ontological sense of *Abständigkeit* I take to be our essential tendency to minimize the distance between ourselves and others by subtle coercion or co-option, especially when we are not aware of doing so. We constantly and unconsciously shape up others' pronunciation, the distance they stand from us, and how they use their knives and forks, and the like; they shape us up in the same way. As an existentiell, then, *Abständigkeit* denotes an ontic concern *Dasein* has with its distance from its neighbors, which is overcome in authenticity; as an existential, however, *Abständigkeit* denotes an essential structure of all *Dasein*'s activity that inconspicuously reduces difference and so performs the ontological function of establishing norms and thus opening up a shared human world.

Although differing existentiell accounts might well be reconciled by a careful reading of the text and a description of the relevant phenomenon, there is no way to reconcile an interpretation that takes *das Man* to be a surmountable, ontic, existentiell deformation of authentic *Dasein* with one that takes it to be an existential, ontological structure upon which authentic *Dasein* is grounded.

---

[21] Heidegger, *Being and Time*, 163–4.
[22] Taylor Carman, "On Being Social: A Reply to Olafson," *Inquiry* 37 (1994), 220.
[23] Heidegger, *Being and Time*, 164.

Heidegger cannot consistently claim both that *the one* is a privative form of *Mitsein*, and that "*the one* belongs to *Dasein*'s positive constitution."[24] Yet, there are enough passages on each side so that neither claim can be dismissed as a simple lapse.

Both interpreters recognize the contradiction. The question then arises, how should an interpreter proceed? Surely, to begin with, one should develop each of the views in all their relevant consequences for a reading of the text. But then what? It seems to me that one then has a choice. Following the preponderance of textual evidence and the accepted interpretation, one can attribute to Heidegger an ontic/existentialist position that emphasizes the danger of conformism and the importance of responsible choice, while admitting this position's shortcomings and the glaring gap it leaves in the overall argument. This reading reinforces Heidegger's emphasis on the foundational character of the individual subject (no matter how subject is construed) and thereby locks him into the deviation into subjectivity that he says ultimately led him to abandon *Being and Time*.[25] This is Olafson's approach.

Or one can try to help Heidegger remain true to his goal of writing an ontological interpretation of *Dasein* in which its essential structures are laid out and shown to account for the fact that human beings are able to disclose entities.[26] This amounts to taking one aspect of Heidegger's task to be to develop a phenomenology of the role of social norms in forming the background of intelligibility, even though he finds such norms degrading and dangerous. It shows him to be more original than Sartre, Habermas, and others, and has the further advantage of bringing out his stand on those questions concerning the background and how it works that currently concern both continental and

---

[24] Heidegger, *Being and Time*, 167.

[25] Heidegger says of *Being and Time*, "[T]he path taken terminates abruptly at a decisive point. The reason for the disruption is that the attempt and the path it chose confront the danger of unwillingly becoming merely another entrenchment of subjectivity" (Martin Heidegger, *Nietzsche*, vol. 4 (New York: Harper & Row, 1982), 141).

[26] Later Heidegger explicitly rejects a psychological reading of *Being and Time*. In "The Origin of the Work of Art" he says that resoluteness (*Entschlossenheit*) never meant decisiveness but (*Ent-schlossenheit*) opened-up-ness to Being: "The resoluteness (*Entschlossenheit*) intended in *Being and Time* is not the decisive action of a subject, but the opening up of *Dasein*... to the openness of being" (Martin Heidegger, "The Origin of the Work of Art," in *Poetry, Language, Thought* (New York: Harper & Row, 1971), 67). Olafson worries about the objection that his interpretation has no place for Heidegger's ontological concerns. He claims that his Heidegger "could very well be ontological in the only sense that really counts—that of recognizing the special character of *Dasein* in all its manifestations" (Olafson, "Heidegger *à la* Wittgenstein or 'Coping' with Professor Dreyfus," 59). One wonders why this is the only sense of "ontological" that really counts. I would have thought that the only sense of ontological that counts for Heidegger is recognizing whatever makes disclosedness possible.

analytic philosophers. This form of interpretation leads to the view defended by Carman.

Finally, which account should we prefer? I don't think the usual Gadamerian and Davidsonian appeal to charity can help us here. Heidegger does not want us to choose the interpretation of the phenomenon that accords best with common sense. After all, what he admires in Aristotle is his ability "to continue to force inquiry back to the phenomena and to the seen and to mistrust from the ground up all wild and windy speculations, no matter how close to the heart of common sense."[27] Rather, I think the reasons for choosing one interpretation over another depend upon our goals. If one wants to understand perennial human pathologies, the initial reception of *Being and Time*, and Heidegger's failure to finish it, Olafson's foregrounding of the phenomena of conformism and authenticity is invaluable. If, in contrast, one wants to focus on a phenomenon that brings out an essential structure of human being as well as showing the depth and consistency of Heidegger's ontological project, then it seems to me Carman's approach and mine is to be preferred. This account attempts to interpret Heidegger out of the phenomenon of world disclosure that motivated his thinking at the time of writing *Being and Time* and throughout his life.

So where Olafson encounters crucial gaps in Heidegger's account, Carman finds inconsistencies that arise when the matter of Heidegger's thinking pushes him beyond his elitist prejudices. For Olafson is right; Heidegger never liked his findings regarding the importance of *das Man*. Indeed, he avoided any mention of *the one* if he could make his point without it as, for example, in *Basic Problems* in his brief account of being-in-the-world as the foundation of intentionality. But he never gave up his claim that *the one* governs everyday intelligibility, which is the only intelligibility we've got.[28] Carman's and my interpretation has the advantage of asking the reader to understand *Being and Time* by joining Heidegger on his path of thinking about the phenomenon of disclosing. This approach has the happy consequence of engaging the reader in how *Being and Time* relates to current concerns rather than freezing the text in the past.

---

[27]   Martin Heidegger, *The Basic Problems of Phenomenology*, trans. Albert Hofstadter (Bloomington, IN: Indiana University Press, 1982), 232.

[28]   In 1946 in "Letter on Humanism" he repeats his claim that "the dictatorship of the public realm...decides in advance what is intelligible and what must be rejected as unintelligible" (Martin Heidegger, *Basic Writings* (New York: Harper & Row, 1977), 197).

2

Could Anything Be More Intelligible than Everyday Intelligibility?

Reinterpreting Division I of *Being and Time* in the Light of Division II (2000)

Introduction

It has always seemed to me that the text of a thinker is only worth studying if reading it makes a significant difference to how we see the world and ourselves.[1] Our job as commentators is to clarify the text and bring out its relevance. But how does one go about clarifying and applying a thinker like Heidegger? Since Heidegger, unlike contemporary analytic philosophers who attempt to give a logical analysis of concepts, always attempts to anchor his discussion in the phenomena, I try to use his text to draw attention to pervasive phenomena that are often overlooked, and then use an elaboration of these phenomena to cast exegetical light on the text. Finally, I test the significance of the result by seeking to show the relevance of Heidegger's insights to issues of current concern. The following remarks are meant to demonstrate this approach.

Average versus Primordial Understanding

Heidegger says that division I of *Being and Time*[2] provides a phenomenology of average everydayness and so will have to be revised in the light of the authentic way of being he describes in division II. My attempt to write a commentary

---

[1] This chapter is based on a paper presented at the inaugural meeting of the International Society for Phenomenological Studies, Asilomar, California, July 19–23, 1999. I would like to thank the participants for their helpful suggestions. I would also like to thank Wallace Matson for his help in sorting out the New Testament Greek.

[2] Martin Heidegger, *Being and Time*, trans. John Macquarrie and Edward Robinson (New York: Harper & Row, 1962). All parenthetical references are to this edition. Some translations have been modified.

exclusively on division I[3] was, therefore, criticized on the ground that I presented as Heidegger's view theses that were taken back in division II. None of the critical reviewers, however, said what my exclusive concentration on division I led me to get wrong. And, as far as I could tell, none of the claims made in division I was taken back in division II.

I now see, however, that focusing exclusively on division I did, indeed, lead me to make at least one serious mistake. I overlooked warnings, scattered about in division I, that the average intelligibility described there would later be shown to be an inferior form of understanding, in contrast to a richer more primordial kind of understanding described in division II.

In my commentary, I spelled out Heidegger's basic theses that (1) people have skills for coping with equipment, other people, and themselves; (2) their shared everyday coping practices conform to norms; (3) the interrelated totality of equipment, norms, and social roles form a whole, which Heidegger calls "significance"; (4) significance is the basis of average intelligibility; (5) this average intelligibility can be further articulated in language. As Heidegger puts it, "We have *the same thing* in view, because it is in *the same* averageness that we have a common understanding of what is said" (212).

In spite of the obvious irony, in Heidegger's conclusion, that "publicness proximally controls every way in which the world and Dasein get interpreted, and it is always right" (165), I concluded that, for both Heidegger and Wittgenstein, the source of the intelligibility of the world and of Dasein is the average public practices articulated in ordinary language.

This interpretation still seems right to me, but I went on, mistakenly, to conclude from the *basis* of intelligibility in average understanding and ordinary language that for Heidegger, as for Wittgenstein, there was no other kind of intelligibility. I noted Heidegger's claim that "by publicness everything gets obscured, and what has thus been covered up gets passed off as something familiar and accessible to everyone" (165), but I went on, nonetheless, to argue that there could be no higher intelligibility than the public, average, intelligibility provided by the social norms Heidegger calls *the one*. Any higher intelligibility, like Plato's ideas, Descartes's mathematical relations among bits of extension, or Hegel's self-transparent *Geist*, I claimed, would necessarily be metaphysical, so Heidegger would surely have rejected any such idea. Likewise, any sort of private intelligibility that was not, at least in principle, shareable would seem to be a sort of *unintelligibility*. The whole point of intelligibility is that it is shared or at least shareable, if not by all rational

---

[3]   Hubert L. Dreyfus, *Being-in-the-World: A Commentary on Heidegger's Being and Time, Division I* (Cambridge, MA: MIT Press, 1991).

creatures, at least by all those brought up in a given culture or form of life. So, I simply denied that for Heidegger there could be any higher intelligibility than that in the public practices and the language that articulates them.

I have since come to see that I was wrong. Heidegger clearly holds that there is a form of understanding, of situations, on the one hand, and of Dasein itself, on the other, that is superior to everyday understanding. He calls this superior understanding "primordial understanding" (212). I still hold, however, that this primordial understanding cannot be some radically different way of making sense of things, since, for Heidegger, this higher intelligibility must somehow be based on and grow out of the average intelligibility into which everyone is socialized. So, although such higher intelligibility may in fact be accessible only to the few, as a form of shared intelligibility it must in principle be available to everyone. What could such a more primordial form of understanding be?

To get a clue, it helps to recall what we learn from Ted Kisiel's researches into the sources of *Being and Time*. According to Kisiel, the book grows out of Heidegger's work on Aristotle: division I elaborates on *techne*, everyday skill, and division II on *phronesis*, practical wisdom.[4] So we would expect Heidegger to present his own version of the mastery of the cultural practices that, according to Aristotle, enables the *phronimos* to "straightway" "do the appropriate thing at the appropriate time in the appropriate way." But just what phenomena do Aristotle and Heidegger have in mind with *techne* and *phronesis*? The way to find out is to let these phenomena show themselves as they are in themselves, so I will take a moment to describe, in a very abbreviated way, four stages one goes through in acquiring a new skill in any domain, as well as what one has when one has become an expert, especially an expert in social situations, Aristotle's man of practical wisdom.[5]

A Phenomenology of Skill Acquisition

Stage I: Novice

Normally, the instruction process begins with the instructor decomposing the task environment into context-free features that the beginner can recognize

---

[4] Theodore Kisiel, *The Genesis of Heidegger's Being and Time* (Berkeley, CA: University of California, 1993). Kisiel says: "The project of *BT* thus takes shape in 1921–24 against the backdrop of the unrelenting exegesis of Aristotle's texts ... from which the pretheoretical models for the two Divisions of BT, the *techne* of *poesis*, for the First, and the *phronesis* of *praxis* for the Second, are derived" (9). Greek has been transliterated.

[5] For a more detailed account of the model of skill acquisition, see Hubert L. Dreyfus and Stuart E. Dreyfus, *Mind over Machine* (New York: Free Press, 1988).

without the desired skill. The beginner is then given rules for determining actions on the basis of these features.

The student automobile driver learns to recognize such domain-independent features as speed (indicated by the speedometer), and is given the rule, "Shift when the speedometer needle points to 10."

The child who is learning how to act ethically in his or her culture might be given the rule "Never tell a lie."

Stage 2: Advanced Beginner

As the novice gains experience actually coping with real situations, he or she begins to note, or an instructor points out, perspicuous examples of meaningful additional aspects of the situation. After seeing a sufficient number of examples, the student learns to recognize them. Instructional *maxims* can then refer to these new *situational aspects*.

Of course, if the beginner follows the rule "Shift at 10 miles an hour," the car will stall on a hill or when heavily loaded. So the advanced beginner learns to use (situational) engine sounds as well as (non-situational) speed in deciding when to shift. He learns the maxim: "Shift up when the motor sounds like it is racing and down when it sounds like it is straining."

Likewise, the policy of not lying will get a child into fights and excluded from important events so, with the coaching of the parents, children learn to tell their friends when leaving their homes that they had a good time, regardless of the truth. Thus the child learns to replace the rule "Never lie" with the maxim "Never lie except in situations when making everyone feel good is what matters."

Stage 3: Competence

With more experience, the number of potentially relevant elements that the learner is able to recognize becomes overwhelming. At this point, since a sense of what is important in any particular situation is missing, performance becomes nerve-wracking and exhausting, and the student may well wonder how anyone ever masters the skill.

To cope with this overload and to achieve competence, people learn through instruction or experience, to devise a plan or choose a perspective that determines which elements of the situation must be treated as important and which ones can be ignored. By restricting attention to only a few of the vast number of possibly relevant features and aspects, such a choice of a perspective makes decision-making easier.

A competent driver leaving the freeway on an off-ramp curve learns to pay attention to the speed of the car, not whether to shift gears. After taking into account speed, surface condition, angle of bank, etc., the driver may decide he is going too fast. He then has to decide whether to let up on the gas pedal, take his foot off the pedal altogether, or step on the brake, and precisely when to perform any of these actions. He is relieved if he gets through the curve without being honked at, and shaken if he begins to go into a skid.

A young person learns that there are situations in which one must tell the truth and others in which one lies. Although this is daunting, the adolescent learns to decide whether the current situation is one of building trust, giving support, manipulating the other person for his or her own good, harming a brutal antagonist, and so forth. If, for instance, trust is the issue, he then has to decide when and how to tell the truth.

The competent performer, then, seeks rules and reasoning procedures to decide upon a plan or perspective. But such rules are not as easy to come by as are the rules and maxims given to beginners. There are just too many situations differing from each other in too many subtle ways. More situations, in fact, than are named or precisely defined, so no one can prepare for the learner a list of types of situations and what to do in each. Competent performers, therefore, must decide for themselves what plan or perspective to choose without being sure that it will be appropriate.[6]

Such decisions are risky, however, so one is tempted to seek the security of standards and rules. When a risk-averse person makes an inappropriate decision and consequently finds himself in trouble, he tries to characterize his mistake by describing a certain class of dangerous situations and then makes a rule to avoid them in the future. To take an extreme example, if a driver pulling out of a parking space is side-swiped by an oncoming car he mistakenly took to be approaching too slowly to be a danger, he may make the rule, never pull out if there is a car approaching. Such a rigid response will make for safe driving in a certain class of cases, but it will block further skill refinement. In this case it will prevent acquiring the skill of flexibly pulling out of parking places. In general, if one seeks to follow general rules one will not get beyond competence.

But without guidelines, coping becomes frightening rather than merely exhausting. Prior to this stage, if the rules do not work, the performer, rather than feel remorse for his mistakes, can rationalize that he has not been given adequate rules. Now, however, the learner feels responsible for his choices. Often choice leads to confusion and failure. Of course, sometimes things work

---

[6] Such a decision as to what matters in the current situation, i.e., what sort of situation it is, requires that one share the sensibility of the culture and have the ability to respond to the similarities recognized by one's fellows.

out well, and the competent performer experiences a kind of elation unknown to the beginner. Thus, learners at this stage find themselves on an emotional roller coaster.

As the competent performer becomes more and more emotionally involved in his task, it becomes increasingly difficult for him to draw back and adopt the *detached* rule-following stance of the beginner. While it might seem that this involvement would interfere with rule-testing and so would lead to irrational decisions and inhibit further skill development, in fact just the opposite seems to be the case. If the detached rule-following stance of the novice and advanced beginner is replaced by involvement, one is set for further advancement, while resistance to the acceptance of involvement and risk normally leads to stagnation and ultimately to boredom and regression.[7]

Stage 4: Expertise

With enough experience with a variety of situations, all seen from the same perspective but requiring different tactical decisions, the competent performer seems gradually to decompose this class of situations into subclasses, each of which shares the same decision, single action, or tactic. This allows an immediate intuitive response to each situation.[8]

The expert driver, generally without paying attention, not only feels in the seat of his pants when speed is the issue; he knows how to perform the appropriate action without calculating and comparing alternatives. On the off-ramp, his foot just lifts off the accelerator or steps on the brake. What must be done, simply is done.

Also, with enough experience and willingness to take risks, some children grow up to be ethical experts who have learned to tell the truth or lie spontaneously, depending upon the situation, without appeal to rules and maxims. Aristotle would say that such a person has acquired the virtue of truthfulness. Some people grow up to be experts capable of responding appropriately to a wide range of interpersonal situations in their culture. Such social experts could be called virtuosi in living.[9]

---

[7] Patricia Benner has described this phenomenon in *From Novice to Expert: Excellence and Power in Clinical Nursing Practice* (Menlo Park, CA: Addison-Wesley, 1984), 164.

[8] [MW: Dreyfus has omitted here one stage from his usual account of skill acquisition—the stage of "proficiency," which comes between "competence" and "expertise." For a description of proficiency, and for a more detailed account of the skills model, see Hubert L. Dreyfus, *Skillful Coping*, ed. Mark A. Wrathall (Oxford: Oxford University Press, 2014).]

[9] This description poses a problem, however. How come many people grow up to be expert drivers but only a few become social virtuosi? The answer seems to be that there are at least two kinds of skills: simple skills, such as crossing the street and driving, and subtle skills, such as music,

As a result of accepting risks and a commitment to being better than average, the virtuoso in living develops the capacity to respond appropriately even in situations in which there are conflicting concerns and in which there seems to those looking on to be no appropriate way to act. Pierre Bourdieu describes such a virtuoso:

Only a virtuoso with a perfect command of his "art of living" can play on all the resources inherent in the ambiguities and uncertainties of behavior and situation in order to produce the actions appropriate to each case, to do that of which people will say "There was nothing else to be done," and do it the right way.[10]

This is obviously Aristotle's *phronimos*. Of course, there may be several wise responses. Indeed, on my account, the idea of a *single* correct response makes no sense since other virtuosi with different funds of experiences would see the matter differently, and even the same *phronimos* would presumably respond differently once he had had more experience and therefore could discriminate a richer repertoire of situations.

The *Phronimos* as a Socially Recognized Virtuoso versus the History Maker as World Transforming Master

We can now generalize this account of skill acquisition and return to *Being and Time* to see whether the virtuoso's increasingly refined sense of the social situation is, perhaps, the more primordial understanding Heidegger has in mind. We can do this by seeing how Aristotle's *phronimos* is related to Heidegger's resolute Dasein. Heidegger is clear that the average way of acting is to obey standards and rules. He describes "Dasein's lostness in the one" as following "the tasks, rules, and standards...of concernful and solicitous being-in-the-world" (312). In contrast, Heidegger's resolute individual deviates from the banal, average, public standards to respond spontaneously to the particular situation.

---

sports, and social interaction. It makes little sense to speak of a virtuoso everyday driver, whereas one can be a virtuoso musician or a champion in some sport. Acquiring simple skills requires only that one face risks and uncertainty without falling back on rules or fleeing into detachment, whereas acquiring hard skills requires, in addition, a motivation continually to improve—then, one needs both the willingness to take risks and a commitment to excellence that manifests itself in persistence and in high standards for what counts as having done something right. One also must be sensitive to the distinctions in the relevant domain. (Such sensitivity in an extreme form in music is perfect pitch.) Such sensitivity is a component of what we call talent. Talent in this sense is a necessary condition for becoming a virtuoso in any field.

[10] Pierre Bourdieu, *Outline of a Theory of Practice*, trans. Richard Nice (Cambridge: Cambridge University Press, 1977), 8.

In Heidegger's terms, irresolute Dasein responds to the general situation (*Lage*), whereas resolute Dasein responds to the concrete Situation (*Situation*). As Heidegger puts it: *"for the one . . . the Situation is essentially something that has been closed off.* The one knows only the '*general situation*'" (346), while "resolute Dasein" is in touch with the "'concrete Situation' of taking action" (349). The distinction between these two kinds of situation seems to come out of nowhere in *Being and Time* but they clearly have their origin in Heidegger's detailed discussion of *phronesis* in his 1924–5 lecture course. There he says:

> Dasein, as acting in each case now, is determined by its situation in the largest sense. This situation is in every case different. The circumstances, the givens, the times, and the people vary. The meaning of the action itself, i.e., precisely what I want to do, varies as well . . . It is precisely the achievement of *phronesis* to disclose the respective Dasein as acting now in the full situation within which it acts and in which it is in each case different.[11]

Given the phenomenology of skill acquisition, it should be clear that the concrete Situation does not have some special metaphysical or private kind of intelligibility cut off from the everyday. Rather, intelligibility for the *phronimos* is the result of the gradual refinement of responses that grows out of long experience acting within the shared cultural practices. Thus, in discussing *phronesis* Heidegger quotes Aristotle's remark that "Only through much time . . . is life experience possible."[12] And in *Being and Time* he is explicit that the intelligibility of the Situation disclosed by resolute action is a refinement of the everyday:

> Authentic disclosedness modifies with equal primordiality both the way in which the "world" is discovered . . . and the way in which the Dasein-with of Others is disclosed. The "world" which is ready-to-hand does not become another one "in its content," nor does the circle of others get exchanged for a new one; but both one's being toward the ready-to-hand understandingly and concernfully, and one's solicitous Being with Others, are now given a definite character . . .   (344)

Thus, "Even resolutions remain dependent upon the one and its world" (345–6).

Moreover, as Aristotle already saw, expert response is immediate, and Heidegger agrees that "resoluteness does not first take cognizance of the Situation . . .; it has put itself into the Situation already. As resolute, Dasein is already *taking action*"

---

[11] Martin Heidegger, *Plato's Sophist* (Bloomington, IN: Indiana University Press, 1997), 101. In the *Sophist* course, Heidegger has not yet made a clear distinction between *Lage* and *Situation*. In this lecture course, he uses both terms interchangeably to refer to the concrete situation. See, for example: "out of the constant regard toward that which I have resolved, the situation (*Situation*) should become transparent. From the point of view of the *proaireton*, the concrete situation (*konkrete Lage*) . . . is covered over" (102).

[12] Heidegger, *Plato's Sophist*, 97.

(347). Or, as Heidegger already put it in his 1924–5 lectures: "in *phronesis*... in a momentary glance (*Augenblick*) I survey the concrete situation of action, out of which and in favor of which I resolve myself (*ich mich entschließe*)."[13]

Also, according to Aristotle, since there are no rules that dictate that what the *phronimos* does is the correct thing to do in that *type* of situation, the *phronimos*, like any expert, cannot explain why he did what he did. Heidegger, of course, agrees:

The Situation cannot be calculated in advance or presented like something occurrent which is waiting for someone to grasp it. It only gets disclosed in a free resolving which has not been determined beforehand but is open to the possibility of such determination.   (355)

So when Heidegger asks rhetorically, "But on what basis does Dasein disclose itself in resoluteness?" he answers:

Only the resolution itself can give the answer. One would completely misunderstand the phenomenon of resoluteness if one should want to suppose that this consists simply in taking up possibilities which have been proposed and recommended.   (345)

All the virtuoso can do is stay open and involved and draw on his or her past experience.[14] The resulting resolute response defines the Situation. As Heidegger puts it, "the Situation *is* only through resoluteness and in it" (346).

Like the *phronimos*, the resolute individual presumably does what is retro-actively recognized by others as appropriate, but what he does is not the *taken for granted*, *average* right thing—not what *one* does—but what his past experience leads him to do in that particular Situation. Moreover, as we have seen, since the Situation is specific and the *phronimos*'s past experience unique, what he does cannot be *the* appropriate thing. It can only be *an* appropriate thing. Still, unlike Kierkegaard's Knight of Faith suspending the ethical, who can only be under-stood by himself and others as a madman or a murderer, "Resolution does not withdraw from 'actuality,' but discovers first what is factically possible; and it does so by seizing upon it in whatever way is possible for it as its ownmost ability-to-be in the 'one'" (346). Thus, in responding to the concrete Situation the resolute individual is recognized as a model; not of what *general* thing to do,

---

[13] Heidegger, *Plato's Sophist*, 114.

[14] I'm following Heidegger in reading *Ent-schlossenheit* as openness not determination. See "The Origin of the Work of Art," in *Poetry, Language, Thought*, trans. Albert Hofstadter (New York: Harper & Row, 1971). "The resoluteness [Ent-schlossenheit] intended in *Being and Time* is not the deliberate action of a subject, but the opening up of human being... to the openness of Being" (67).

but of *how* to respond in an especially appropriate way. In this way, "when Dasein is resolute, it can become the 'conscience' of others" (344).

It should now be clear that Kisiel's claim—that Heidegger, in his account of resolute Dasein in division II, is working out Aristotle's phenomenology of practical wisdom—helps make sense of Heidegger's cryptic remarks about the resolute Dasein's response to the concrete Situation. But Kisiel's plausible way of understanding the passages in question is complicated by another group of interpreters who point out that Heidegger's account of authenticity is also deeply influenced by his early interest in the account of radical transformation in St. Paul, Luther, and Kierkegaard. These interpreters focus on Heidegger's use of the term *Augenblick*.

We have already seen that, indeed, in the 1924–5 lecture course Heidegger uses the term *Augenblick* to describe the *phronimos*'s instant of insight. This reading is confirmed by *Basic Problems*, where the *Augenblick* is equated with Aristotle's *kairos*, the moment of appropriate skillful intervention. "Aristotle saw the phenomenon of the instant (*Augenblick*), the *kairos*," Heidegger says.[15] But *Augenblick* is also Luther's translation of St. Paul's moment in which we shall be changed in a "twinkling of an eye." So John van Buren claims that "Heidegger took this movement that concentrates itself at the extreme point (*eschaton*) of the *kairos* to be the kairological time that he had already discovered in the Pauline eschatology."[16]

Unfortunately, the evidence van Buren cites for this claim does not seem to establish it or even suggest it, but rather suggests the contrary, viz. that Heidegger

---

[15] Martin Heidegger, *Basic Problems of Phenomenology* (Bloomington, IN: Indiana University Press, 1982), 288.

[16] John van Buren, *The Young Heidegger: Rumor of the Hidden King* (Bloomington, IN: Indiana University Press, 1994), 231. The whole discussion of *kairos* and *Augenblick* is hard to follow since, as I understand it, the term *kairos* is never used in New Testament Greek to mean the time of transformation that later came to be called kairological time. The term translated *Augenblick* occurs in 1 Corinthians 15:52 to describe what will happen when we are raised from the dead: "We shall all be changed in a moment (*atomos*), in the twinkling of an eye (*ripei en ophthalmou*)." But the term gets extended by Kierkegaard to cover all the ways that one's identity and world are suddenly and radically transformed. Kierkegaard goes even further. The Greek for what is normally translated by "the fullness of time" when Jesus returns to transform the world is *pleroma*, while the term for the transformation in which the Christian is reborn as a "new creation" is *metanoia*, but both crucial moments are subsumed by Kierkegaard under the notion of an *Augenblick* as the moment of a decisive transformation. Finally, not too surprisingly, all the terms that refer to a total transformation of identity and/or world get lumped together and identified with the Greek moment of decisive action or kairos. What is surprising is that those concerned with the use of these terms in Heidegger do not bother to sort out the various phenomena to which they refer. For example, van Buren blurs all distinctions when he tells us that, "Following St. Paul, as well as Aristotle, Heidegger stresses that particular *kairoi*, situations, are always 'new creations' that come 'like a thief in the night'" (283).

uses *kairos* to refer not to *religious time*, but to secular action *in a concrete situation*.

Van Buren says that in the 1924–5 lecture course, Heidegger connected *kairos* in Aristotle with the Pauline theme of *kairos* as "the twinkling of an eye": "*Phronesis* is the glancing at the this-time, at the this-time-ness of the momentary situation. As *aisthesis*, it is the glance of the eye, the *Augen-blick*, toward the concrete at the particular time..."[17]

Van Buren seeks further support in a passage from Heidegger's lectures, *Phenomenological Interpretations with Respect to Aristotle*, but this passage, too, supports the Aristotelian reading.

Phronesis is the illumination of *dealings* that temporalizes life in its *being*. The concrete interpretation shows how this being, *kairos*, is constituted...It goes toward the *eschaton*, the extreme, in which the determinately seen *concrete situation* intensifies itself at the particular time.[18]

Although the translation leaves things rather murky, clearly Heidegger is here describing the cultural virtuoso's resolute dealing with the concrete Situation, not the moment of rebirth of the Christian in which he gets a new identity, nor the moment of the coming of the Messiah when the world will be transformed and the dead raised in the twinkling of an eye.

But, in spite of these blatant misreadings of the texts, the interpreters who want to give Heidegger's use of *Augenblick* a Christian interpretation are onto something important. There is a surprising moment where Heidegger introduces the *Augenblick* in a way that seems clearly to refer to the *phronimos*'s daily dealings with things and equipment. He says:

To the anticipation which goes with resoluteness, there belongs a Present in accordance with which a resolution discloses the Situation...That *Present*...we call the *Augenblick*... The *Augenblick* permits us *to encounter for the first time* what can be "in a time" as ready-to-hand or present-at-hand.   (387, 388)

So far, this is no surprise, but then Heidegger appends a footnote saying, "S. Kierkegaard is probably the one who has seen the *existentiell* phenomenon of the *Augenblick* with the most penetration..." (497 iii). What can this mean?

Heidegger seems to want to describe the phenomenon of the response to the concrete Situation at a level of formality that covers any decisive moment in which Dasein, as an individual, breaks out of the banality of the one and takes

---

[17] Van Buren, *The Young Heidegger*, 229.
[18] Van Buren, *The Young Heidegger*, 231. My addition of italics. Unfortunately, van Buren does not give a page reference to the source of this quotation.

over its situation, whether that be the Greek act of seizing the occasion or the Christian experience of being reborn.[19] For Heidegger, either type of decisive moment is an *Augenblick*. In a course given shortly after the publication of *Being and Time*, the Greek and Christian views, their radical difference, and their formal similarity are spelled out together. Heidegger first speaks in general terms of "Dasein's *self-resolution* (*Sich entschliessen*) to itself...to what is given to him to be, this self-resolution is the *Augenblick*."[20] He then fills this out in Aristotelian terms, explaining, "The *Augenblick* is nothing else than the *glance of resoluteness*, in which the full Situation of an action opens up and is held open."[21] But he also suggests that this Aristotelian moment of decisive action falls short of the kind of radical transformative *Augenblick* Kierkegaard had in mind. "What we here indicate with 'Augenblick' is what Kierkegaard was *the first to really grasp in philosophy*—a grasping, which *begins the possibility of a completely new epoch in philosophy* since Antiquity."[22]

Although Heidegger's view is difficult to sort out, if we hold onto the phenomena in question we can be sure that Heidegger did not simply identify the Greek understanding of *kairos* with the Christian understanding of *Augenblick*, although he did see each as manifesting a *resolute*, i.e., *open, way of being* which was a precondition of a *special moment of decisive action*. One thing is sure, one cannot even begin to make sense of Heidegger if, like Kisiel, one simply cites lecture texts to argue that Heidegger's account of resolute Dasein in *Being and Time* is an adaptation of Aristotle's *phronimos*, or, like van Buren, one cites other lecture texts to argue that *Augenblick* in *Being and Time* must be understood in the light of Christian kairological time. Without first seeing that Aristotle and St. Paul are describing two genuine, but seemingly irreconcilable, *phenomena*, the challenging exegetical questions do not even arise.

Once we focus on the phenomena, however, we can see that each interpretation has something right, but each mistakenly claims to have the whole story. A satisfactory interpretation requires clearly distinguishing two experiences of the source, nature, and intelligibility of decisive action—the Greek experience, arising from *a primordial understanding of the current Situation*, which makes possible *virtuoso coping* in the current world, and the Christian experience, arising from *a primordial understanding of Dasein itself*, which makes possible

---

[19] Which Kierkegaard calls becoming a new creation, see Søren Kierkegaard, *Fear and Trembling* (New York: Penguin, 1985), 70.

[20] Martin Heidegger, *Die Grundbegriffe der Metaphysik: Welt, Endlichkeit, Einsamkeit* (Frankfurt am Main: Klostermann), 224.

[21] Heidegger, *Die Grundbegriffe der Metaphysik*, 224.

[22] Heidegger, *Die Grundbegriffe der Metaphysik*, 225 (my italics).

a transformation of self and world. Heidegger seems to be distinguishing Dasein's primordial understanding of the current Situation from Dasein's experience of its most primordial way of being, and yet trying to subsume them both under the *Augenblick* when he says, "Dasein gets ... brought back from its lostness by a resolution, so that both the current Situation and therewith the primordial 'limit-Situation' of being-towards-death, will be disclosed as an *Augenblick* that has been held on to" (400).

At other places in the text, moreover, it seems clear that the two different forms of understanding are disclosed by two different forms of resoluteness. The first is discussed in chapter 2 of division II. There Heidegger defines resoluteness as *"self-projection upon one's ownmost being-guilty, in which one is ready for anxiety ... "* (343). This kind of resoluteness arises from facing one's thrownness and the consequent anxiety that comes with the realization that one's average understanding with its rules and standards has no intrinsic authority. Holding on to this anxiety makes possible the openness, involvement, and willingness to take risks that, in turn, make possible the acquisition of expertise. Resoluteness thus makes possible the virtuosity of the Heideggerian *phronimos* who, because he has held on to anxiety and so no longer takes for granted the banal public interpretation of events, can see new possibilities in the most ambiguous and conflicted situations and so can do something that all who share his world will retroactively recognize as what was factically possible at the time. Such a person's understanding of his society is richer and deeper than the average understanding and so he is generally more effective. But he is not yet fully authentic.

Besides the *effective coping* of the *phronimos*, made possible by an expert grasp of the *concrete Situation*, there is a fully *authentic* way of acting made possible by Dasein's understanding of *its own way of being.* This authentic way of acting is a more complete form of resoluteness in which Dasein not only faces the anxiety of guilt, viz., the sense that its identity and social norms are thrown rather than grounded and thus have no final authority, but, furthermore, faces the anxiety of death, viz., that Dasein has to be ready at all times to die, i.e., give up its identity and its world altogether. In such an understanding, Dasein manifests "its authenticity and its totality" (348).

Heidegger seems to be distinguishing and ranking the two ways of holding on to anxiety and the kind of resoluteness each makes possible by holding that only the second is authentic and whole. In chapter 5, when he turns to the "authentic historizing of Dasein" (434), he says:

We have defined "resoluteness" as a projecting of oneself on one's ownmost being-guilty ... Resoluteness gains its authenticity as *anticipatory* resoluteness. In this, Dasein understands itself with regard to its ability-to-be, and it does so in such a manner that it will go right under the eyes of Death in order thus to take over in its thrownness that entity which it is itself, and to take it over wholly.   (434)[23]

Thus, anticipatory resoluteness makes possible an even more primordial form of intelligibility than the pragmatic understanding evinced by the *phronimos* or social virtuoso.

To be innovative in this religious sense requires *anticipatory* resoluteness—anxiously facing both death and guilt. The resolute *phronimos* merely experiences his thrownness and so has the sense that the social norms are not rules to be rigidly followed. He therefore gives up a banal, general understanding of social norms and responds to the concrete Situation, but he can still be understood by his peers to have effectively solved a shared problem. In anticipatory resoluteness, however, anxiety in the face of death has freed Dasein even from taking for granted the agreed-upon current cultural issues.

Repetition makes a *reciprocal rejoinder* to the possibility of existence that has-been-there ... But when such a rejoinder is made to this possibility in a resolution, it is made *in an Augenblick*; *and as such* it is at the same time a *disavowal* of that which in the "today," is working itself out as the "past".   (438)

Here the *Augenblick* does name the inception of a new creation. In the moment of decisive action, authentic Dasein can take up a marginal practice from its cultural heritage.

[Fate] is how we designate Dasein's primordial historizing, which lies in authentic resoluteness and in which Dasein *hands* itself *down* to itself, free for death, in a possibility which it has inherited and yet has chosen.   (435)

Dasein can then act in such a way as to take over or repeat the marginal practice in a new way and thus show a form of life in which that marginal practice has become central and the central practices have become marginal. Such an innovator is so radical that he transforms his generation's understanding of the issue facing the culture and produces a new authentic "we." He thus goes beyond not only the banal general understanding of his peers, but even beyond the

---

[23] It is hard to reconcile this claim that *only anticipatory* resoluteness reveals Dasein authentically and fully with the claim in the earlier discussion of the resoluteness of facing guilt that "we have now arrived at that truth of Dasein which is most primordial because it is *authentic*" (343). I think Heidegger was simply confused as to how he wanted to relate the two kinds of resoluteness. Generally, he sticks to the view that anticipatory resoluteness is the most complete kind of resoluteness because it involves facing death.

Situational understanding of the *phronimos*.[24] We could call such a fully authentic history-making Dasein a cultural master.[25]

Ethical and Political Implications

The phenomena of the social virtuoso and the cultural master have ethical and political implications. For example, Heidegger's account of the resolute response to the factical situation offers a way out of the antinomy presented by Dworkin's and Derrida's account of legal decision-making. Dworkin holds that "judges must,...so far as possible, regard the existing legal practice as expressing... a coherent conception of justice and fairness, and so are charged to uncover this

---

[24] Heidegger sensed that such an authentic Dasein's reinterpretation of what his generation stands for—how the shared social practices hang together and have a point—allows him to transform his culture, but in *Being and Time* Heidegger could not yet see how radically a culture could be transformed. Only when he had understood that the style of a culture—its whole understanding of being—could change, could he fully grasp what it would be like for a cultural master to disclose a new world. Heidegger presumably would include such cultural masters among the statesmen, gods, and philosophers who disclose new worlds. They are all instances of "truth establishing itself." See Martin Heidegger, "The Origin of the Work of Art," 61, 62.

[25] The most extreme form of the transformation such a history-making Dasein brings about is a cultural version of the *Augenblick* of Christian conversion. This, for Kierkegaard, is the *Augenblick* as the fullness of time. The whole culture is reborn into a new world. Since the new world has new standards of intelligibility, the cultural master, like Kierkegaard's Abraham, cannot explain himself and so cannot be recognized by his peers as having done something appropriate as the *phronimos* can. But, unlike Abraham suspending the ethical, who is totally repulsive to his contemporaries and even himself, the history-maker, because he draws on a shared heritage, is not totally unintelligible. He is a charismatic figure who can *show* a new style and so be *followed*, as Jesus was followed by his disciples, even though they did not understand the meaning of what they were doing. He will not be fully intelligible to the members of the culture, however, until his new way of coordinating the practices is articulated in a new language and preserved in new institutions. The phenomenon of world disclosing is described and illustrated in Charles Spinosa, Fernando Flores, and Hubert L. Dreyfus, *Disclosing New Worlds* (Cambridge, MA: MIT Press, 1997).

These accounts of the special way the social virtuoso can seize the moment and the way the historical innovator can transform the culture seem to be correlated with Heidegger's two-stage account of the present dimension of Dasein's authentic temporality. *Primordial* temporality makes possible world-time and thus the *phronemos*'s experience of being solicited, on the basis of past successes, to respond to the current Situation so as to open up new possibilities for dealing with available and occurrent entities. (Heidegger's account of how primordial temporality makes possible pragmatic temporality has been analyzed by William D. Blattner in his excellent book, *Heidegger's Temporal Idealism* (Cambridge: Cambridge University Press, 1999).)

Authentic temporality, by contrast, is a secularization of the Kierkegaardian account of Christian temporality in *The Concept of Anxiety*, in which the temporal structure makes possible the decisive instant of individual conversion and world transformation. Heidegger seems to have wanted to recover both the Greek and the Christian understanding of temporal transformation, but did not have time to work out how the two kinds of non-successive temporality (primordial temporality and authentic temporality) were related to each other and to his ontological project.

conception and to make decisions in specific cases on the basis of it."[26] Thus, according to Dworkin, an explicit sense of the principles involved should actually guide a judge when she applies the law as well as when she justifies her decision.

Derrida is enough of a Heideggerian to sense that there is no theory behind a judge's practice and no single right decision, so he rightly sees that the judge's justification could not be the basis of her decision and must therefore be, at best, a rationalization. Thus he rejects Dworkin's rationalism. However, without an understanding of the phenomenon of skillful coping behind Heidegger's claim that a resolute way of being makes possible a richer more primordial kind of understanding, Derrida wrongly concludes that in making a decision the judge must be making a leap in the dark: "the instant of the just decision...is a madness."[27] I suspect that three different sorts of cases are lumped together by Derrida.

(1) There is the case of extrapolating the law to new situations that are similar but never identical to previous cases and for which there is no set of features in terms of which one can justify one's judgments of similarity. Here Derrida is right, there can be no *theory* of how to proceed, but Heidegger would presumably analyze an expert judge's decisions on the basis of the phenomenon of expert coping and so hold that the judge, like any resolute *phronimos*, neither acts on principle nor makes a leap in the dark, but rather straightway engages in "*the disclosive projection and determination of what is factically possible at the time*" (345). With an eye to the phenomenon, we can see that the judge would be acting as a social virtuoso, led by her past experience to respond to the subtle similarities between the current situation and situations in which she had already made what were recognized as appropriate responses. Even when such a *phronimos* reflects, she does not reflect on abstract principles but stays involved and reflects on her expert sense of the concrete situation.

As Derrida sees in such cases, there cannot be one right decision as Dworkin assumes. Two different judges, with different past experiences and different ways of having entered the current situation, may well see the situation differently. Remember, Heidegger says: "The Situation cannot be...presented like something occurrent which is waiting for someone to grasp it. It only gets disclosed in free resolving..." (355). But even then, one of the several possible

---

[26] See Gerald J. Postema, "Protestant Interpretation and Social Practices," *Law and Philosophy* 6 (1987), 283–319. Postema presents a critique of Dworkin based on Bourdieu and Wittgenstein which is similar to the one I am suggesting here.

[27] Jacques Derrida, "Force of Law: The 'Mystical Foundation of Authority,'" *Cardozo Law Review*, part 2 (1990), 967.

wise decisions need not be chosen arbitrarily. The virtuoso judges can talk to each other about the way they entered the current situation and relate the situation to other situations in the hope of getting their colleagues to see things the way they do. This may work to produce agreement, but even if it does not, the choice between the remaining candidates is not the arbitrary imposition of power; it is a choice between possible wise decisions.

Still, Derrida is right that, since similarity cannot be reduced to certain shared features, any justification that tried to explain the judge's decision in terms of *classes* of situations would have to be a rationalization that drew either on principles like those the expert judge followed when she was only competent or, at best, more refined principles the expert had abstracted from many cases. But Heidegger would want to add, I hope, that, although such principles could not capture the judge's expertise, they need not be arbitrary. That is, they could serve as convincing justifications for a *competent* decision even though they could not be used to determine what counted as the relevant similarities in the next case, and thus could not serve as the basis for a genuinely wise decision.

(2) There is the decision of a legal *innovator* who brings to bear a whole new way of looking at the role of the law in some domain. Such a decision would be even further from being rationalizable, but, if Heidegger is right, it would not be a leap in the dark but a masterful response to marginal practices. The marginal practices do, indeed, make a "leap from the wings to center stage,"[28] but the innovative master does not make a blind leap in responding to them; rather, thanks to his openness, he has a subtle sense of the marginal practices that are moving into the center.

(3) The nearest thing to a Derridian leap in the dark occurs where there are two or more conflicting sets of values. These are the kinds of cases that reach the Supreme Court, such as pornography cases in which the court must decide between the well-being of the community and the right to free speech. In such cases there does not seem to be any non-arbitrary way of deciding which way to understand the situation. Each judge will decide on the basis of his or her own set of values and past experience, but the decision will be imposed by the majority. This does seem to be a case, if not of a leap in the dark, at least of an arbitrary imposition of power.

Only this third type of case fits Derrida's analysis, but Derrida mistakenly holds that *all* decisions that extrapolate to a new situation have the arbitrariness

---

[28] Michel Foucault, "Nietzsche, Genealogy, History," in *Language, Counter-Memory, Practice*, trans. Donald F. Bouchard and Sherry Simon (Ithaca, NY: Cornell University Press, 1977), 150.

found only in type-three cases. He claims that either a decision is guided by cognitive rails and thus is mechanical but uninteresting, or else it is arbitrary. He thus misses the relevance of the two types of primordial understanding that Heidegger describes. By in effect denying the way a resolute person's past experience can feed into a sense of what is factically possible and thus make possible a wise or even an innovative decision that is not dictated by principle but is not arbitrary either, Derrida gives support to the nihilism of the legal realists.

Conclusion

In summary, according to division II of *Being and Time*, public, average, everyday understanding is necessarily general and banal. Nonetheless, this leveled average understanding is necessary both as the background for all intelligibility and in the early stages of acquiring expertise, and so it is both ontologically and genetically prior to any more primordial understanding. Once, however, an expert has broken out of the banal, thanks to the anxious realization of his thrownness and, by repeated risky experience in the everyday world, has mastered the discriminations that constitute his skill, he can respond to the situation in a more subtle way than a non-expert can. This primordial understanding of the concrete Situation has no special content—no source of intelligibility other than everyday intelligibility—but it, nonetheless, makes possible the social virtuoso's successful responses to the most difficult social situations. Furthermore, by facing the anxiety of death and so seeing that the issues of his culture and even his own identity could be radically changed, a fully authentic Dasein can manifest an even higher kind of primordial understanding. As a cultural master he can take up marginal possibilities in his culture's past in way that enables him to change the style of a whole generation and thereby disclose a new world.

3

Foreword to *Time and Death* (2005)

There are already hundreds of books on Heidegger, why add one more? Because no one has successfully employed Carol White's strategy of interpreting *Being and Time* in the light of Heidegger's later works. White has taken up the most fundamental and difficult aspect of Heidegger's thought and has presented a coherent and plausible retrospective reading of his development. Her approach turns out not only to cast new light on the origin of Heidegger's later ideas but also to illuminate *Being and Time* as groping toward them. Thus, her account enables White to relate what *Being and Time* says about *human time* to Later Heidegger's talk of *the time of being*,[1] thereby reconstructing for us the phenomenon, from beginning to end, Heidegger was struggling to describe. As White says:

I quote freely from the whole chronological range of Heidegger's works since one of my basic premises ... is that he spent his life saying, to use his term, "the Same."[2]

Of all the books written on his work, Heidegger would probably have preferred this one, since he himself was constantly reinterpreting his earlier works as attempts to articulate the one thought he was all his life trying to put into words.

White shows that, from his unfinished first attempt in *Being and Time* to the late essay *Time and Being*, Heidegger is trying again and again to find the right way to describe the basic structure of finitude that makes possible our access to the world and to everything in it. Her book follows Heidegger's path of thinking by showing how he worked out the structure of finitude in terms of death and time. White argues convincingly that Heidegger's thought is unified by the insight,

---

[1] In translating Heidegger's technical terms, I've followed the recommendations of the editor of Carol White, *Time and Death: Heidegger's Analysis of Finitude*, ed. Mark Ralkowski (Burlington, VT: Ashgate, 2005). I've also modified all quotations from Heidegger's texts to make them consistent with this decision.

[2] "Preface" to White, *Time and Death*.

elaborated in detail in this book, that being human is historical, and that, in the West, being itself has a history.

White's basic insight is that in *Being and Time* Heidegger already had a dim sense of what he was later to call the history of being, even though in *Being and Time* the history of our understanding of being is presented simply as a decline from the pre-Socratics' understanding of being as *presencing* through a series of metaphysical (mis)understandings of being as pure *presence*. Heidegger already had the idea that Parmenides' understanding of being was an originating leap that defined the history of the West, but he later saw that this originating leap gave rise, not just to a gradual loss of the pre-Socratics' insight but, rather, to a series of radically reconfigured worlds. That insight, White contends, led him from an analysis of the finite timeliness of human being to the finite temporality of being itself.

Readers will, I hope, be able to find their own way through White's lucid reconstruction of Heidegger's deepening account of temporality. In this preface, I want to concentrate on what I consider one of the most important rewards of White's retrospective reading. I hope to show how her approach enables her to explain and fit together Heidegger's lifelong series of seemingly inconsistent pronouncements concerning death and finitude, and that this in turn enables her to give an original and convincing interpretation of the controversial section on death in *Being and Time*—an interpretation that is closer to the phenomenon and to the text than any interpretation so far presented in the many books and articles on this subject. Her ability to use the unifying thread of Heidegger's thinking (read back to front) to make sense of Heidegger's understanding of death is proof of the power of her approach.

But first, to prepare to understand White's masterful analysis of death and finitude, we need to turn to her account of what Heidegger means by being and how being can itself have a history.

The Phenomenon of Being

White is able to see Heidegger whole in spite of his constantly changing neologisms and higher and higher levels of abstraction, because, through it all, she keeps her eye on the phenomenon—the "matter for thought," as Heidegger would say. She sees that, from the start, what Heidegger means by being is not some super entity, nor some general property of all entities, but the intelligibility that makes entities accessible. And that, as he later saw, for us in the West, what counts as intelligibility depends upon the style of each particular cultural epoch.

As Heidegger first puts it in *Being and Time*, "Being is that on the basis of which entities are already understood."[3] He spells this out through a description of the intelligibility of the everyday world. World is the whole context of shared equipment, roles, and practices on the basis of which one can encounter entities and other people. So, for example, one encounters a hammer as a hammer in the context of other equipment such as nails and wood, and in terms of social roles such as being a carpenter, a handyman, and so forth. Moreover, each local cluster of tools, the skills for using them, and the roles that require them constitutes a sub-world such as carpentry, or homemaking, and each, with its appropriate equipment and practices, makes sense on the more general background of our one shared, familiar, everyday world. Heidegger calls the way the shared background practices are coordinated to give us access to things and to ourselves our understanding of being. He says:

> That wherein Dasein already understands itself . . . is always something with which it is primordially familiar. This familiarity with the world . . . goes to make up Dasein's understanding of being.   (119)

Heidegger sees that this familiarity is so pervasive that it is easily passed over. As he puts it, it is nearest to us and so furthest away. White and I share the idea that to begin to see our own sense of familiarity and how it works we need a contrasting case of the style of another culture.

As White notes, sociologists point out that mothers in different cultures handle their babies differently and so inculcate the babies into different styles of coping with themselves, people, and things. To get a feel for the phenomenon—the way the background practices work to grant intelligibility—I'll elaborate her suggestive example in further detail. As long as we can use it to get a sense of how a cultural style works, we need not be concerned as to whether the sociological account is accurate or complete.

Let us suppose, as we are told by the sociologists, that American mothers tend to put babies in their cribs on their stomachs, which encourages the babies to move around effectively, while Japanese mothers tend to put their babies on their backs so they will lie still, lulled by the mothers' songs. As the infants develop, American mothers encourage passionate gesturing and vocalizing, while Japanese mothers are much more soothing and mollifying. In general, American mothers situate the infant's body and respond to the infant's actions in such a way as to promote an active and aggressive style of behavior, while Japanese mothers, in contrast, promote a greater passivity and sensitivity to harmony.

---

[3] Martin Heidegger, *Being and Time*, trans. I. Macquarrie and E. Robinson (New York: Harper & Row, 1962), 25, 26. Henceforth page references to this translation appear in parentheses after the quotation.

The babies, of course, imitate the style of nurturing to which they are exposed. It may at first seem puzzling that the baby successfully picks out precisely the gestures that embody the style of its culture as the ones to imitate, but, of course, such success is inevitable. Since *all* our gestures and practices embody the style of our culture, the baby will pick up that pervasive style no matter what it imitates. Starting with a style, various practices will make sense and become dominant, and others will either become subordinate or will be ignored altogether.

The style, then, determines how the baby encounters himself or herself, other people, and things. So, for example, no bare rattle is ever encountered. For an American baby, a rattle-thing is an object to make expressive noise with and to throw on the floor in a willful way in order to get a parent to pick it up. A Japanese baby may treat a rattle-thing this way more or less by accident, but generally we might suppose a rattle-thing is encountered as serving a soothing, pacifying function like a Native American rain stick. In general, what constitutes the American baby as an *American* baby is its cultural style, and what constitutes the Japanese baby as a *Japanese* baby is its quite different cultural style.

Once we see that a style governs how anything can show up *as* anything, we can see that the style of a culture does not govern only the babies. The adults in each culture are shaped by it as they respond to things in the way they show up for them. The style of coping with things, out of which all conceptualizing grows, determines what it makes sense to do, and what is worth doing. It should come as no surprise, given the picture I have just presented of Japanese and American culture, that Japanese adults seek contented social integration, while American adults are still striving willfully to satisfy their individual desires. Likewise, the style of enterprises and of political organizations in Japan serves to produce and reinforce cohesion, loyalty, and consensus, while what is admired by Americans in business and politics is the aggressive energy of a laissez-faire system in which everyone strives to express his or her own desires, and where the state, business, or other organization's function is to maximize the number of desires that can be satisfied without destructive instability.

The case of child-rearing helps us see that a cultural style is not something in our minds but, rather, a disposition to act in certain ways in certain situations. It is not in our beliefs but in our artifacts, our sensibilities, and our bodily skills. Like all skills, it is too embodied to be made explicit in terms of rules.[4] Therefore it is misleading to think of a cultural style as a scheme, or conceptual framework.

---

[4] For an argument to this effect, see Hubert Dreyfus and Stuart Dreyfus, *Mind over Machine: The Power of Human Intuitive Expertise in the Era of the Computer* (New York: Free Press, revised paperback edition, 1988).

Our cultural style is invisible both because it is manifest in everything we see and do, and so is too pervasive to notice—like the water to the fish—and because it is in our comportment, not in our minds. And this is not a disadvantage or limitation. Like the illumination in a room, a cultural style normally lets us see things just in so far as we don't see *it*. That is, like the background in perception, the ground of intelligibility must recede so we can see the figure.[5] As Heidegger puts it, the mode of revealing has to *withdraw* in order to do its job of revealing us and things, and it is the job of phenomenology to make it visible. In *Being and Time* he says:

What is it that phenomenology is to let us see? What is it that must be called a "phenomenon" in a distinctive sense?...Manifestly, it is something that proximally and for the most part does *not* show itself at all: it is something that lies *hidden*, in contrast to that which proximally and for the most part does show itself;...but at the same time it is something that belongs to what thus shows itself, and it belongs to it so essentially as to constitute its meaning and its ground.   (59)

Style, while remaining hidden, is what makes everything intelligible and is what Heidegger calls being. Each specific style is a specific mode of intelligibility and so is a specific understanding of being. Being never fully reveals *itself*, at least not *as* itself, so it turns out that, for Heidegger, being is the phenomenon that is the proper subject of phenomenological study:

[T]o lay bare the horizon within which something like being in general becomes intelligible is tantamount to clarifying the possibility of having any understanding of being at all—an understanding which itself belongs to the constitution of the entity called Dasein.   (231)

Heidegger is still saying the same thing in his last work: *Time and Being*.[6] Being holds itself back "in favor of the discernability of the gift," that is, of being in regard to the grounding of what-is.[7] As White puts it: "The contribution of the background practices recedes unnoticed in favor of the things that are."[8]

We come a step closer to White's analysis of death when we see how she draws on this account of being to explain human finitude. One of White's most original and valuable insights is to see that our inability to spell out the understanding of being in our background practices is one important aspect of what Heidegger

---

[5] The exception, according to Heidegger, is cultural works of art such as temples and cathedrals, the acts of great statesmen, and the writings of thinkers, each of which shows the style by articulating and glamorizing it. See Martin Heidegger, "The Origin of the Work of Art," in *Poetry, Language, Thought*, trans. Alfred Hofstadter (New York: Harper & Row, 1971).

[6] Martin Heidegger, *On Time and Being*, trans. Joan Stambaugh (New York: Harper & Row, 1972).

[7] Heidegger, *On Time and Being*, 9.   [8] White, *Time and Death*, 5.4.

means by human finitude. Heidegger calls this condition ontological guilt, which he defines as the structural condition that Dasein cannot get behind its thrownness.[9] White glosses this as the claim that "our finitude prevents us from ... turning the background practices into explicit knowledge."[10] And she adds:

> [T]he finitude of knowledge is a matter of its grounding in an understanding of being which cannot be taken up in conceptual judgments. We should give up our quest for not only an absolute knowledge of things in themselves, as Kant thought, but also for explicit knowledge of the source of our knowledge.[11] The goal of knowing the presuppositions of our knowledge, so devoutly pursued by Kant, Hegel, Husserl, and every other metaphysician, is unattainable.[12]

But, as Heidegger insists, there is nothing wrong with this structural condition that we can't make the background of our thought and action explicit; indeed, it serves a positive function in enabling us to make sense of things at all.

From this "limitation" there follows a second important aspect of finitude. Already in *Being and Time* Heidegger stresses that the practices on the basis of which entities are understood cannot themselves be justified or grounded. Once a practice has been explained by appealing to what one does, no more basic justification is possible. As Wittgenstein later puts it in *On Certainty*: "Giving grounds [must] come to an end sometime. But the end is not an ungrounded presupposition: it is an ungrounded way of acting."[13]

This view is antithetical to the philosophical ideal of *total* clarity and *ultimate* intelligibility. Heidegger in *An Introduction to Metaphysics* suggests that there can be no such metaphysical grounding:

> It remains to be seen whether the ground arrived at is really a ground, that is, whether it provides a foundation; whether it is an ultimate ground [*Urgrund*]; or whether it fails to provide a foundation and is an abyss [*Ab-grund*]; or whether the ground is neither one nor the other but presents only a perhaps necessary appearance of foundation—in other words, it is a nonground [*Un-grund*].[14]

To relate this point to her account of finitude, White quotes a crucial but little-noticed remark of Heidegger's published five years after *Being and Time*:

---

[9] Heidegger, *Being and Time*, 330.   [10] White, *Time and Death*, 5.1.

[11] Martin Heidegger, *Kant and the Problem of Metaphysics*, trans. Richard Taft (Bloomington, IN: Indiana University Press, 1997), 245/Martin Heidegger, *Kant und das Problem der Metaphysik* (Frankfurt am Main: Klostermann, 1991), 229f.

[12] White, *Time and Death*, 5.1.

[13] Ludwig Wittgenstein, *On Certainty*, edited by O. E. M. Anscombe and G. H. von Wright and translated by Denis Paul and G. E. M. Anscombe (New York: Harper & Row, 1969).

[14] Martin Heidegger, *An Introduction to Metaphysics*, trans. Ralph Manheim (New York: Anchor Books, Doubleday, 1961), 2, 3.

So profoundly does finitude entrench itself in existence that our ownmost and deepest limitation refuses to yield to our freedom.[15]

This understanding of finitude leads White to take Dasein, Heidegger's technical term referring to us, not as naming individual human beings, but as referring to a way of being of all human beings, in other words that they live in a world that is made intelligible by their shared background practices and that these background practices cannot and need not be made explicit and justified. White, therefore, warns against all individualistic readings of *Being and Time*. For her, Heidegger is not an existentialist emphasizing subjectivity and personal choice, nor is he a romantic holding that there is a deep inner self to which Dasein is called to be true. Heidegger is an ontologist interested in the conditions of the possibility of intelligibility, and he understands that the practices that make people and things intelligible can be pointed out and their general structure described but that the understanding of being in those practices cannot be spelled out in detail and given a transcendental or metaphysical grounding.

The History of Being

In the published part of *Being and Time*, Heidegger attempted to work out an ontological account of the universal structures of worldhood and thus ground a "science of being." He was, therefore, not interested in what he called ontic accounts of specific sub-worlds, other cultures, nor epochs in our own culture's understanding of being. It was only in the early 1930s that Heidegger was struck by the idea that, in our Western culture at least, the understanding of being has a history that is more than a story of decline. As he puts it:

[I]n the West for the first time in Greece what was in the future to be called being was set into work . . . : the realm of what there is as a whole thus opened up was then transformed into entities in the sense of God's creation. This happened in the Middle Ages. These entities were again transformed at the beginning and in the course of the modern age. Entities became objects that could be controlled and seen through by calculation. At each time a new and essential world arose.[16]

It follows that each time a culture gets a new understanding of being, human beings and things show up differently. For the Greeks, what showed up and solicited attention were heroes and followers along with beautifully crafted things; for the

---

[15] Martin Heidegger, "What is Metaphysics?" in *Pathmarks*, ed. William McNeill (Cambridge: Cambridge University Press, 1998), 108/Martin Heidegger, *Wegmarken* (Frankfurt am Main: Klostermann, 1996), 118, quoted in White, *Time and Death*, 5.1.
[16] Heidegger, "The Origin of the Work of Art," 76, 77.

Christians, it was saints and sinners, and things showed up as temptations and allegories of God's plan. There could not have been saints in ancient Greece; at best there could only have been weak people who let others walk all over them. Likewise, there could not have been Greek-style heroes in the Middle Ages. Such people would have been regarded as prideful sinners who disrupted society by denying their dependence on God and encouraging everyone to depend on them instead.

White follows Later Heidegger in spelling out the way the sequence of world styles that has given us our sense of what is intelligible and worth doing comes to pass. A new understanding of being must be both incomprehensible and yet somehow intelligible. To account for this possibility, Later Heidegger elaborates an idea already touched on in *Being and Time*,[17] that in a historical change a historical figure makes history by retrieving some practices from the past and giving them a new central role in the present.

As Later Heidegger puts it, world-disclosing is not the creation (*schaffen*) of a genius, but the drawing up (*schöpfen*) as from a well.[18] World-grounding takes place when a person or a work of art takes up and makes central some marginal practices already in the culture. A new style does not arise *ex nihilo*. Marginal practices of various sorts are always on the horizon. As Heidegger says: "In the destiny of being, there is never a mere sequence of things one after another... There is always a passing by and simultaneity of the early and the late."[19] For example, the printing press and Luther were already moving the culture in a new direction, which Descartes saw as a new individualism and freedom from authority. That idea became central in his attempt to take over his life and education from the ground up, and made possible Kant's definition of the Enlightenment as humanity reaching maturity, that is autonomy. Heidegger adds:

That which has the character of destiny moves, in itself, at any given time, toward a special moment of insight which sends it into another destiny, in which, however, it is not simply submerged and lost.[20]

Heidegger calls such a reconfiguration of the current background style a new grounding or an originating leap. But again he makes clear that this sort of ground is a non-ground. It does not guarantee that any given world will last

---

[17] Heidegger, *Being and Time*, Section 74.

[18] Heidegger, "The Origin of the Work of Art," 76.

[19] Martin Heidegger, "The Thing," in *Poetry, Language, Thought*, trans. Alfred Hofstadter (New York: Harper & Row, 1971), 184, 185.

[20] Martin Heidegger, "The Question Concerning Technology," in *The Question Concerning Technology and Other Essays*, trans. William Lovitt (New York: Harper Torchbooks, 1977), 37.

forever. All past cultural worlds and the institutions that sustained them have died. As he remarks:

When...we visit the temple in Paestum at its own site or the Bamberg cathedral on its own square—the world of the work that stands there has perished.[21]

Indeed, cultures, like the people and the things that focus their style, must die if new worlds are to be disclosed. Heidegger comments:

Where history is genuine it does not pass away by merely ceasing; it does not just stop living like the animals. History only dies *historically*.[22]

And White comments in turn:

In Western history, the rational animal died for Dasein to become the image of God; God's favorite creature died for Dasein to become the conscious subject.[23]

White sums up this view toward which Heidegger was groping in *Being and Time* as follows:

Dasein is rooted in the temporality of being. The changing revelation of being gives Dasein its possibilities: what it is able-to-be. The way being withholds itself imposes Dasein's impossibilities: what it is not able-to-be, at least not yet.[24]

And she adds:

Heidegger comments that his contemporaries do not wish to see this more profound sort of time because then "they would have to admit that the foundations on which they continue to build one form of metaphysics after another *are no foundations at all*".[25]

Death and Finitude

Focusing on the background practices as a non-ground and on the history of being as the birth and death of cultural styles enables White to give a new interpretation of Heidegger's account of death in *Being and Time*. Since her account, I will argue, is the most illuminating and convincing yet proposed, it is worth quoting at length the autobiographical passage in her Preface where she introduces it, before turning to the currently accepted accounts that her interpretation overthrows.

---

[21] Heidegger, "The Origin of the Work of Art," 40, 41.
[22] Heidegger, *Introduction to Metaphysics*, 189.   [23] White, *Time and Death*, 0.4.
[24] White, *Time and Death*, 0.3.
[25] White, *Time and Death*, 0.3, quoting Martin Heidegger, *Nietzsche*, vol. 4, trans. David Farrell Krell (San Francisco: Harper, 1982), 163/Martin Heidegger, *Nietzsche* II, *Gesamtausgabe* vol. 6.2 (Frankfurt am Main: Klostermann, 1997), 219.

[*Being and Time*] had always seemed to fall apart into two halves: If we describe the view expressed in it as "phenomenological existentialism," then the first half seemed to be the phenomenology and the second the existentialism. The turning point comes at the discussion of death. From a discussion of tool-use, familiarity, language, and other practices, we seemed to turn abruptly to a discussion of how the individual ought to face death...

A fresh and careful study of the text began to reveal quite a different issue than the one that the familiar accounts of the matter addressed. Absurdities dissolved, and trivialities disclosed what lay beneath their surface. The new meaning taking shape in the chapter on death began to reach out into the surrounding chapters, especially the ones on Dasein's experience of time. The ontological level of the whole discussion in the second half of *Being and Time* shifted from the personal and subjective to the cultural and historical. Soon it became clear that not only was the second half of the book a necessary extension of the first, but it tied directly into the works that followed throughout Heidegger's career.[26]

The usual accounts of death in *Being and Time* assume that in talking about death Heidegger must be referring to the event that comes at the end of a person's life when that person ceases to exist, and Heidegger does begin his chapter on death by talking about such an *antic* event, which he calls demise. But Heidegger also says that an *ontological* interpretation of death reveals that death is not demise and that thinking of death as a future happening that will someday befall one is the inauthentic denial of death.

White situates her book as an attempt to cut through the critical confusion on this subject:

My book is devoted to articulating the vision of Heidegger's work which grows out of a new understanding of what he was trying to address in his discussion of death. I acknowledge that the discussion of this issue in *Being and Time* is far from clear; its intentional false starts and dead ends easily mislead the reader. But a careful study of the distinctions Heidegger makes there show many common assumptions about his analysis to be problematic. Comments about death in his later works sharpen the issue and bring the discussion of *Being and Time* into sharper focus, perhaps even for Heidegger himself. The consistency that this new interpretation of death brings to that book in its internal structure and in its relation to subsequent works suggests that he was driving at this understanding from the beginning, even if initially that drive was more of a grope.[27]

White is clear that much of the confusion is Heidegger's fault, but not because he should not have started with demise. The phenomenologist has to begin by describing and working through the everyday cover-up to arrive at the phenomenon that is being concealed. What makes the chapter on death misleading

---

[26] White, *Time and Death*, "Preface."   [27] White, *Time and Death*, "Preface."

is that Heidegger fails to make clear where his analysis of the inauthentic misunderstanding of death ends and the authentic ontological understanding of finitude begins.[28]

Thus we get interpreters such as Sartre who, early on, took the account of death in the first sections of the death chapter to be Heidegger's own account and so ended up with an existentialist account of death as an event in the future at which point a human being ceases to exist[29]—an event one must hide to avoid facing the absurdity of life. Others, as White points out, "recognize that Heidegger calls death a 'way to be' (245) and that for him death is a matter of 'being-toward-death.'" But then, "at best they have taken death to be a matter of a person's attitude about or relationship to physical death, that is, a way of caring about one's demise."[30]

An example of such an approach can be found in the work of Michael Zimmerman, whose interpretation White singles out for telling criticism. Such interpreters assume that in writing about death, Heidegger must be talking about demise and think that, in the light of our mortality, we can gain a new seriousness and unity in how we live our lives. According to Charles Guignon, who holds a view similar to Zimmerman's, Heidegger thinks of an authentic human life as a narrative in which, by facing one's demise, one can gain a complete and coherent understanding of the whole of one's life history. As he puts it:

The inauthentic anyone-self . . . is dispersed, distracted, and fleeing in the face of its own death. To be authentic is to recognize the gravity of the task to which one is delivered over and to take full responsibility for one's life. Authentic Dasein lives resolutely, coherently, with "sober joy," expressing in each of its actions a sense of its being-toward-the-end.[31]

---

[28] White focuses on this basic misunderstanding in Paul Edwards's ridiculing of Heidegger's account of death (Paul Edwards, "Heidegger on Death: A Deflationary Critique," *The Monist* 59/2 (April, 1976), 161–8). She rightly dismisses all such interpretations in her article. As White says succinctly: "I want to argue that the problem which Heidegger is addressing has been fundamentally misconceived by both these authors as well as many others . . . To understand what Heidegger is saying we must make a radical distinction between the death of a person and the existential death of Dasein" (Carol J. White, "Dasein, Existence and Death," *Philosophy Today* 28 (Spring 1984), 53). But the mistake is still being made. For example, Taylor Carman does a careful and devastating job of showing that Herman Philipse's recent discussion of Heidegger on death in *Heidegger's Philosophy of Being: A Critical Interpretation* (Princeton, NJ: Princeton University Press, 1998) is an "astonishing misreading" of the text. See Taylor Carman, *Heidegger's Analytic: Interpretation, Discourse, and Authenticity in Being and Time* (Cambridge: Cambridge University Press, 2003), 278.

[29] Jean-Paul Sartre, *Being and Nothingness: A Phenomenological Essay on Ontology*, trans. Hazel E. Barnes (New York: Pocket Books, 1966).

[30] White, *Time and Death*, 2.5.

[31] Charles Guignon, *Heidegger and the Problem of Knowledge* (Indianapolis, IN: Hackett, 1983), 135, 136.

Taylor Carman's excellent book *Heidegger's Analytic: Interpretation, Discourse, and Authenticity in Being and Time* offers a profound critique of such moralizing views. Carman points out that according to this edifying interpretation,

[a] concept of death minimally appropriate to human beings as such must be a biographical notion, a notion of the conclusion or resolution of a human life understood as a series of actions, events, episodes, life experiences, and so on. Biographical dying is the ending of a life inasmuch as that life can be understood retrospectively as a whole, perhaps narrated in part as a story. Dying, biographically understood in this way, is what Heidegger calls "demise" (*Ableben*).   (291)[32]

Carman, in contrast, sees clearly that:

the very structure of being-in-the-world as my own . . . makes it impossible in principle for me to take up a merely observational or biographical point of view on myself and my existence. I am so directly involved in my life that I can't "understand my own existence as anything like a finite life span . . . organized by a beginning, a middle and an end."[33]

William Blattner takes seriously that demise cannot be the ontological death that Heidegger is trying to describe and tries to work out what Heidegger must have had in mind by death. He tells us:

[What Heidegger] is primarily interested in is not the being-at-its-end of human life, but a sense of end that is tied exclusively to the conceptual framework of Dasein's originary way of being, to existence and understanding. Human life stops; neither existence nor understanding can be said to stop as such, however.[34]

Blattner thus distinguishes between "*demise*, which is the stopping of Dasein's life, and *death*, which is the end of Dasein in some other sense."[35] He goes on to note that fear of demise is a cover-up of death, which Heidegger says is "the possibility of no-longer-being-able-to-be-there" (294), the possibility "of the utter impossibility of existence" (307).

Blattner sees that death has something to do with the collapse of an individual's world. He contends that the death we cover up by fearing demise is, in fact, an impending anxiety attack in which Dasein would lose its ability to cope with things and therefore lose its ability to be. To defend this original interpretation, Blattner gives a masterful account of what Heidegger means by anxiety that I can only touch on here. He tells us that:

---

[32] Carman, *Heidegger's Analytic*, 279.   [33] Carman, *Heidegger's Analytic*, 272.
[34] William Blattner, "The Concept of Death in *Being and Time*," *Man and World* 27 (1994), 49–70. Reprinted in Hubert Dreyfus and Mark Wrathall (eds.), *Heidegger Reexamined*, vol. 1: *Dasein, Authenticity, and Death* (London: Routledge, 2002), 323.
[35] Blattner, "The Concept of Death in *Being and Time*," 324 (my italics).

Dasein's being…is an ability-to-be. The end or limit of this ability is the inability-to-be. The condition Heidegger calls "death" is a limit-situation for that ability-to-be, one in which one confronts this limitation…This situation occurs when Dasein is beset by anxiety, in which none of its possibilities matters to it differentially, in which all are equally irrelevant to it.[36]

On this account, being toward death is being *ready* for an anxiety attack. As Blattner puts it:

Only through resoluteness—silently throwing oneself into the possibility of death, and being prepared for the attendant anxiety (343)—does one come face to face with what sort of entity one is, and hold on to that understanding.[37]

But, since an anxiety attack is sudden and unmotivated—"It is part of Dasein's being that death is always possible, that anxiety may strike it at any time"[38]—it is hard to see how one should live in order to be ready for it, and Blattner does not even try to explain what a life of readiness for an anxiety attack would be like. Perhaps, living like an epileptic, resigned to having breakdowns after which one has to collect one's wits and go on.

   Indeed, it's not clear that Heidegger holds that Dasein *can* be ready for the sort of anxiety attack that Blattner equates with death. The text Blattner cites is about how resolute Dasein is ready for the anxiety of *conscience*. It turns out that, rather than being ready for anxiety, the highest form of resoluteness, forerunning resoluteness,[39] is *constantly anxious* without its world falling apart. Heidegger brings forerunning, resoluteness, death, and anxiety together in the following summation:

[Forerunning] brings [Dasein] face to face with the possibility of…being itself in an impassioned freedom towards death—a freedom which has been released from the illusions of the "anyone," and which is factical, certain of itself, and *anxious*.[40]

If *authentic* Dasein is *constantly* anxious, that is, senses its finitude and lives appropriately, that would seem to suggest that authentic resolute forerunning, since it has already integrated its finitude into its life, need not be constantly ready for the sort of anxiety attack that "may strike…at any time" in which life is seen to have no intrinsic meaning, nothing matters, and Dasein is paralyzed.

---

[36] Blattner, "The Concept of Death in *Being and Time*," 325.

[37] Blattner, "The Concept of Death in *Being and Time*," 314.

[38] William Blattner, *Heidegger's Temporal Idealism* (Cambridge: Cambridge University Press, 1999), 88.

[39] For a discussion of Heidegger's distinction between resoluteness and forerunning resoluteness, see Chapter 2, this volume.

[40] Heidegger, *Being and Time*, 311 (Heidegger's italics removed; my italics added).

But Blattner is surely right that an anxiety attack as a complete breakdown of Dasein and its world bears a structural similarly to whatever Heidegger means by death as Dasein's no more being able to be there. Perhaps, Heidegger would want to say that an anxiety attack, for which one can never be ready, and which one therefore flees, is the nearest experience an inauthentic Dasein can have to death.

In any case, as we shall soon see when we return to Blattner after discussing John Haugeland's and White's views, the kind of sudden and unmotivated world collapse experienced in an anxiety attack is the wrong sort of phenomenon to count as the ontological breakdown Heidegger calls death.

Taylor Carman's account of death offers an answer to how one can be *constantly* dying, not just *ready* for death, but it runs into its own problems. Carman sees, like White before him, that, with his ontological/formal understanding of death, Heidegger wants to cover

not just persons but projects, loves, hopes, epochs, cultures, and worlds dying off. Loves, hopes, and worlds die, and not just in a secondary metaphorical sense transferred from a more basic literal concept of the perishing of organisms or the demise of persons.[41]

And Carman, therefore, suggests that death is "the constant closing down of possibilities, which is an essential structural feature of all projection into a future."[42] He adds:

[S]uch things die by dying to us, or rather by our dying to them as possibilities.[43]

Our possibilities are constantly dropping away into nullity, then, and this is what Heidegger means when he says—what might sound otherwise hyperbolic or simply false—that "Dasein is factically dying as long as it exists" (295). To say that we are always dying is to say that our possibilities are constantly closing down around us.[44]

This, however, is a very implausible view. Possibilities are also always opening up. Moreover, as a reader of Kierkegaard, Heidegger could not have had such a narrow understanding of possibilities. It would be like saying that by making a defining commitment such as marriage, you close down all the other possible marriages you might have had. But if your commitment is wholehearted, you sense it as closing down trivial possibilities to gain ones worth living for.

Besides, the constant closing of possibilities could not be the kind of ontological dying Heidegger has in view. Carman, like White, is right that the dying of a culture or a love, like the loss of one's identity, are ways in which a particular way of being can fail to make sense. As such, each is the total collapse of a current world and makes possible the arrival of another. But, for this very reason, Heidegger

[41] Carman, *Heidegger's Analytic*, 284.   [42] Carman, *Heidegger's Analytic*, 285.
[43] Carman, *Heidegger's Analytic*, 281.   [44] Carman, *Heidegger's Analytic*, 282.

could not accept Carman's assimilation of death to the constant loss of possibilities each time we make a choice. The gradual closing down of possibilities does not have the right ontological structure to deal with the death of one world and the birth of another. A change of worlds, according to Kierkegaard and Heidegger, happens in a kind of discontinuity or leap. Carman's loss of specific possibilities is something that happens on the background of a stable world. His interpretation can't account for Heidegger's claim that death is "the possibility of the impossibility of any existence at all" (307), since this suggests a closing down to the zero point, which the nullity of choice doesn't involve. As something that happens *in* the world, choice simply does not have the structure of ontological dying—the total collapse *of* the world that Heidegger has in mind.[45]

Carman may well have Heidegger's account of death wrong, but his criticism of my account of death is absolutely right. He says:

> [W]hereas Charles Guignon ascribes to Heidegger what seems to me an overly robust or metaphysically optimistic account of the ontological structure of the self, Hubert Dreyfus sees in the account of forerunning resoluteness what I think is an overly impoverished or pessimistic conception of authentic existence.[46]

What anxiety reveals, he suggests, is "that Dasein has no possibilities of its own and that it can never acquire any."[47]

Hence, "anxiety is the revelation of Dasein's basic groundlessness and meaninglessness."[48]

---

[45] As an explanation of Heidegger's view of existential dying, or death as a way of life, Carman's account faces not only phenomenological difficulties but exegetical ones as well. Heidegger does, indeed, mention the sort of nullifying of possibilities Carman describes. Carman quotes the crucial passage: "Having an ability-to-be [Dasein] always stands in one possibility or another: it constantly is *not* other possibilities, and it has waived these in its existentiell projection" (331). But though this loss of possibilities is described as a nullity of projection, it is not the null projection of death. Heidegger is not talking at this point in the text about the existential projection involved in death; rather he is referring to the nullifying effect of ordinary existentiell choice. He says, "the nullity we have in mind belongs to Dasein's being free for its existentiell possibilities. Freedom, however, *is* in the choice of *one* possibility, that is, in tolerating not having chosen the others, and one's not being able to choose them" (331). This loss of particular possibilities due to our freedom of choice cannot be "the possibility of the impossibility of any existence at all" (307).

That this nullity of choice has nothing to do with dying should also be clear from its place in Heidegger's exposition. The nullity of choice is mentioned only once and then only in the guilt chapter; never in the chapter on death. Recognizing this problem leads Carman to the implausible and unjustified assertion that death is a subcategory of guilt, something Heidegger never says. In fact it's clear from Heidegger's placement of this mention of freedom and choice in the chapter on guilt that the nullity of choice is a subspecies of guilt if it is to be subsumed under any other nullity. More likely, the nullity of choice is supposed to be a third nullity—the nullity of the present—as opposed to the nullity of guilt, which is the nullity of the past, and of death, which is the nullity of the future.

[46] Carman, *Heidegger's Analytic*, 271.

[47] Carman, *Heidegger's Analytic*, 286. See Hubert L. Dreyfus, *Being-in-the-World: A Commentary on Heidegger's Being and Time, Division I* (Cambridge, MA: MIT Press, 1991), 305.

[48] Carman, *Heidegger's Analytic*, 286, 310.

It's true that in my *Commentary* I avoid all reference to demise by claiming that death means that Dasein's identity can never be definitively settled. That is, that Dasein can never have an "eternal" identity in the sense proposed by Kierkegaard in *Fear and Trembling*, one that defines Dasein for its whole life,[49] and that alone rules out the Zimmerman and Guignon interpretation. In my *Commentary* I take this to be a serious structural lack in Dasein's way of being. Heidegger does, indeed, hold that one has to be constantly ready to give up one's defining commitment, but, as Carman sees, this vulnerability looks like a negative feature of Dasein's finitude only to those with a metaphysician's longing for absolute certainty.[50]

He also sees that somehow for Heidegger death is something positive, but he and I are, unfortunately, on the list of those who have failed to find the phenomenon that makes sense of this claim.

Julian Young makes a valiant attempt. First, like White, he notes an important shift in Heidegger's understanding of death from an individual to a cultural phenomenon:

In *Being and Time* Heidegger's primary (though not exclusive) focus is the individual—individual "Dasein". Authenticity, anxiety in the face of death, mortality itself, its key concepts, are all, in their primary application, individual attributes. During the 1930s and the first half of the 1940s, however, his focus shifts strongly away from individual and on to collective Dasein. What concerns him during this period is, above all, the health or otherwise of the culture as a whole.[51]

But, whereas White sees Heidegger as having always been concerned with cultural death and so retroactively reads early Heidegger's apparent concern with individual death as a sign of his confusion, Young claims that while Heidegger later changed his mind, death in *Being and Time* clearly denotes the individual Dasein's encounter with nothingness, that is with total meaningless destruction:

Being and Time is, I suggest, a work of "heroic nihilism". It is heroic because it advocates "living in the truth" about death, nihilistic because the "truth" it discovers is that beyond the intelligible world of entities, is the absolute nothing, "the abyss".   (194)[52]

---

[49] Søren Kierkegaard, *Fear and Trembling*, trans. Alastair Hanny (Harmondsworth: Penguin Books, 1986).

[50] Carman rightly notes that I made the same mistake in assuming that ontological guilt in *Being and Time* means that there is something wrong with Dasein, that is, that it can't get behind its thrownness; whereas it is precisely the metaphysical demand that we overcome our finitude and achieve total clarity about our taken for granted understanding of being that Heidegger rejects.

[51] Julian Young, *Heidegger's Philosophy of Art* (Cambridge: Cambridge University Press, 2001), 127.

[52] Young, *Heidegger's Philosophy of Art*, 131–2.

Young, then, goes on to claim that, after *Being and Time*, Heidegger totally changed his account of death. He tells us:

No longer is [death] to be thought of as the "abysmal", "empty" or "negative" nothing. Rather, it is to be understood "positively" as the nothing of "plenitude", the nothing that is to be sure "something completely and utterly Other (*Anderes*) than beings", but, for all that, undoubtedly "something (*etwas*)" (*Gesamtausgabe* 15, 363)...[A]s Schopenhauer succinctly put it, that the "Other" of entities is not an "absolute" but only a "relative" nothingness.

According to Young, this change has important implications not only for understanding the death of cultures, but for the attitude an individual should assume in the face of his or her inevitable demise.

Understanding one's (in Kantian language) "membership" [in] the mystical realm of "plenitude" abolishes anxiety, establishes one as ultimately secure in one's world because one understands, now, that that which surrounds the clearing is no longer abysmal but is, rather, the richness of all those concealed (and unintelligible) possibilities of disclosure which, in addition to one's ego, one is.[53]

But this is a view White would certainly not accept. Young's idea of plenitude reifies the worlds that may someday arrive as if they were already fully formed and waiting in the wings. It, thereby, misses the finitude that White so well shows to be essential to world-disclosing. Heidegger denies the metaphysical plenitude of other worlds waiting to be born, and offers, instead, a down-to-earth, finitist account of that plenitude:

[A]bsence is not nothing; rather it is precisely the presence, which must first be appropriated, of the hidden fullness and wealth of what has been and what, thus gathered, is presenting, of the divine in the world of the Greeks, in prophetic Judaism, in the preaching of Jesus.[54]

The plenitude turns out to be marginal practices still remaining from other cultural epochs. New worlds for Heidegger, then, are not present but hidden. They are not, as Young cites Rilke as saying, like "the other side of the moon." Rather new worlds arise by a leap that shifts marginal practices from the wings to center stage.[55]

---

[53] Young, *Heidegger's Philosophy of Art*, 132–3.   [54] Heidegger, "The Thing," 184.
[55] Michel Foucault, "Nietzsche, Genealogy and History," in *Foucault Reader*, ed. Paul Rabinow (New York: Pantheon Book, 1984), 84. Not *all* marginal practices, however, need come down to us from what Heidegger calls our heritage. As my mention of the printing press suggests, some new practices are introduced by technology; others might be introduced by cultural invasions, and so forth.

Like Schopenhauer's view of the "relative nothingness" of the Other that Young alludes to as the "Other of entities," Rilke's account of the plenitude that lies outside the current clearing is a view that Heidegger would certainly not accept. One must remember that Heidegger's recounting of Rilke's views cannot be assumed uncritically to be Heidegger's own views since Heidegger thinks that Rilke is, in the last analysis, still in the grip of metaphysics.[56]

Even more implausibly, Young, like Schopenhauer, wants to use this metaphysical conception of relative nothingness to ground a sort of immortality for Dasein. As he tells us:

One feels safe, that is dwells, in one's mortality because, knowing that one belongs also to the realm of immortality, one can, in the words of Rilke that Heidegger quotes, "face . . . death without negation". (*Poetry, Language, Thought*, 125)[57]

Just as the will, for Schopenhauer, is what is essential while the self is an illusion, so that the will survives the death of individuals precisely because it has nothing to do with selves, so Young claims that, for Heidegger, what is essential about each individual Dasein, that is, being a world-discloser, somehow survives the individual ego's death. He says:

Understanding one's transcendence transforms one's world into an unconditionally "safe" place because one knows that nothing that happens in it can annihilate one's essential self.[58]

But this talk of a substantive essential self is not at all Heideggerian. Being a world-discloser is, indeed, what is essential about Dasein but, since Dasein's openness or transcendence arises from the finite stand it takes on itself through its activity in the world—that is, its essence is its existence—it cannot suffer the

---

[56] As evidence that Rilke has not worked his way out of the metaphysics of the subject, Heidegger cites the very claim to deep inwardness that Young would like to think of as Heidegger's own view:

Heidegger quotes Rilke as suggesting that however vast the world of space and time may be: "it hardly bears comparison . . . with the dimensions of our inwardness, which does not even need the spaciousness of the universe to be within itself almost unfathomable."

(Young, *Heidegger's Philosophy of Art*, 146)

Another hint that Young mistakenly attributes Rilke's views to Heidegger is that, after quoting a passage on Rilke's angels, Heidegger says that the angel is "*metaphysically the same* as the figure of Nietzsche's Zarathustra" (Martin Heidegger, "What Are Poets For?," in *Poetry, Language, Thought*, trans. Alfred Hofstadter (New York: Harper & Row, 1971), 134, Heidegger's italics).

White anticipates Young's mistake when she rightly observes that "Some remarks that Rilke makes obviously strike a responsive chord in Heidegger, but I have resisted quoting them in the body of the paper since sorting out the difference between the two thinkers would require too much space" (White, "Dasein, Existence and Death," 65. Reprinted in Dreyfus and Wrathall, *Heidegger Reexamined*, vol. 1: *Dasein, Authenticity, and Death*, 343).

[57] Young, *Heidegger's Philosophy of Art*, 133.   [58] Young, *Heidegger's Philosophy of Art*, 133.

loss of its ability-to-be without total annihilation. Or, to put it another way, Heidegger never takes back his claim in *Being and Time* that Dasein's essential feature is its *mineness*.

The most illumining and convincing account in the critical literature on Heidegger on death outside of White's, and indeed an account very similar to hers, has been proposed independently by John Haugeland. He approaches the question of death in Heidegger by starting with Kuhn's account of scientific revolutions, which are after all the collapse of one world and the arrival of another.[59]

Haugeland has from the start pointed out that in Heidegger's thinking Dasein does not refer to an individual human being but to a way of life that could include science or a culture.[60] He, therefore, can use his parallel of death with a scientific revolution as a model to give a convincing account of how, in *Being and Time*, Heidegger understands the dying of Dasein. Haugeland's account of resolute being-toward-death is "living in a way that explicitly has everything at stake."[61] And this means that the resolute Dasein lives in a way that is always at risk. As Haugeland puts it, "authentic Dasein faces up to and takes over the ultimate *riskiness* of its life as a whole—it lives resolutely as and only as ultimately *vulnerable*."[62]

---

[59] John Haugeland, "Truth and Finitude: Heidegger's Transcendental Existentialism," in *Heidegger, Authenticity, and Modernity: Essays in Honor of Hubert L. Dreyfus*, vol. 1, ed. Mark Wrathall and Jeff Malpas (Cambridge, MA: MIT Press, 2000).

[60] See John Haugeland, "Heidegger on Being a Person," in *Heidegger Reexamined*, vol. 1: *Dasein, Authenticity, and Death* and "Truth and Finitude," footnote 6. Haugeland points out that Dasein is always a public way of life. According to Haugeland, then, Heidegger's essential point is not that death is the death of an individual, but that Dasein can take over its death in a way that individualizes it. A resolute individual therefore dies to the extent that his or her way of life does, but that's far from the whole story. For Haugeland, then, the Kuhnian account of scientific revolutions is more than an analogy; it is a correct description of the life and death of scientific Dasein as a way of life.

In this foreword, I've limited myself to one aspect of Haugeland's published account of death in *Being and Time*. (I've also left aside his promised account of historicity in *Being and Time* and the history of being in Later Heidegger.) I'm thus restricting and distorting his view in order to bring out an important opposition between an account of world collapse restricted to individualized being-in-the-world, on the one hand, and, on the other, White's claim that one can see in retrospect that Heidegger's account of the death of Dasein was never meant to be about individuals at all but was supposed to be exclusively aimed at describing the death of cultures.

[61] Haugeland, "Heidegger on Being a Person," 73. I would have preferred he said "lucidly" rather than "explicitly," since lucidly avoids making it seem that this way of life is conscious or reflective, and so it better captures Heidegger's Kierkegaardian notion of transparency, that is, letting one's unconditional commitment become apparent in every aspect of one's life.

[62] Haugeland, "Heidegger on Being a Person," 352, footnote 9. One might think that world collapse is an event in the future that, like any possibility, can turn into actuality. If so, it would suffer from what Carman criticizes as the assumption that death is some *possible* future event that could

This interpretation makes sense of Dasein's forerunning into death as a way of life that is constantly ready for radical transformation. It fits Heidegger's remark that

forerunning discloses to existence the uttermost possibility of giving itself up and thus shatters any rigidity in the existence reached at any time.   (308)

Haugeland explains:

[H]olding itself free for taking it back belongs just as essentially to existential responsibility as does sticking to it as long as one reasonably (responsibly) can. The existential *understanding* that belongs to resoluteness...just *is* perseverant being toward death.[63]

Thus, on Haugeland's account, "being-toward-death" in *Being and Time* means working steadfastly to preserve one's identity and world, while also being able to give them up. For example, I have to be open to the possible collapse of my identity should my marriage fail or should my project to change my culture be no longer relevant. As Haugeland once said: "Resolute Dasein sticks with its identity without getting stuck with it."

Haugeland's use of Kuhn supports the interpretation that resolute Dasein must be sensitive to anomalies in its life and, moreover, be ready for a possible crisis in which these anomalies reveal that its identity is no longer livable.[64] In the face of such a crisis, resolute Dasein must lucidly accept the collapse of its world, its "way of life," so as to be open to disclosing a new world in which these anomalies make sense and are central.

Haugeland has not yet published the obvious extension of his analysis of Dasein's death as world collapse to cultural epochs. In her book, White explicitly makes the move Haugeland is poised to make, and applies the Kuhnian model not just to individualized ways of life but also to cultural styles. She also takes an exegetical step beyond Haugeland in grounding the analysis they share in the relevant texts. She notes the following suggestive passage from an essay by Heidegger on Parmenides:

[T]he essence of mortals calls upon them to heed the call which beckons them toward death. As the outermost possibility of mortal Dasein, death is not the end of the possible but the highest shelter (the gathering sheltering) of the mystery of calling disclosure

---

become *actual*. But world collapse escapes this objection because the possibility of the annihilation of a world is the annihilation of *all* possibilities, not the actualization of any possibility in the world.

[63] Haugeland, "Heidegger on Being a Person," 74.

[64] For a more detailed account of the role of anomalies, see Charles Spinosa, Fernando Flores, and Hubert Dreyfus, *Disclosing New Worlds: Entrepreneurship, Democratic Action, and the Cultivation of Solidarity* (Cambridge, MA: MIT Press, 1997), especially footnote 25 on 193.

(Martin Heidegger, *Early Greek Thinking* (New York: Harper & Row, 1975), 101 / Martin Heidegger, *Vorträge und Aufsätze* (Frankfurt am Main: Klostermann, 2000), 248).[65]

Young would no doubt give this passage a metaphysical, quasi-Schopenhauerian, interpretation according to which the gathering sheltering that calls for disclosure would be other possible worlds, somehow waiting in the wings to be actualized. If one remembers, however, that gathering is for Heidegger the way the practices collect together to call to thinkers and artists to bring a new world into being,[66] one can understand the "gathering sheltering" calling for disclosure as the marginal practices themselves moving toward a new coordination and thus bringing forth a new style.

The marginal practices, in Haugeland's terms the anomalies, draw the current world toward collapse, as well as being the reserve that will form the basis of a new one. As White puts it, "It is being which 'calls' to mortals, to ourselves as Dasein, disclosing itself in new ways and calling Dasein to its proper being."[67] The new world with its new possibilities arises from the collapse of the old world, and someday it too will die. That is, it will make sense no longer, become impossible, unthinkable, and so give place to new forms of intelligibility.

As White points out, already in *Being and Time* we hear that human beings sense (anxiously) that they live in a finite, ungrounded, and vulnerable world so that it is always possible that their world will cease to make sense. Human beings as cultural preservers therefore feel called to work hard to preserve the intelligibility of their current world. Indeed, they cannot preserve what they would otherwise take as fixed. They could not actively preserve marriage, for instance, if they thought that it was divinely created and preserved in heaven. They could only honor it. Only by knowing that everything human, cultural, and so forth is vulnerable does preserving or transforming it make sense. Thus, only if there is the constant possibility of their world becoming impossible is there room for human begins to fulfill their essential nature as world-disclosers. In Later Heidegger, the cultural world is seen to be ungrounded and so constantly threatened. Thus everyone is called to understand his or her self as a world-preserver, which also

---

[65] White, *Time and Death*, 0.4.

[66] When Heidegger wants to emphasize this non-metaphysical sense of how new understandings of being arise, he calls the way practices gather into a new style to bring things out into their own "*Ereignis*," usually translated as "the event appropriation." Thus, in *Time and Being* he can say that the *Ereignis* sends being (Heidegger, *Time and Being*, 19).

[67] White, *Time and Death*, 0.4. Even in very late Heidegger when he is talking of things thinging, mortals are described as those who die, which presumably means those who, while contributing to the temporary world set up around a thing such as a celebratory meal, at the same time accept its ungroundedness and vulnerability. See Hubert Dreyfus and Charles Spinosa, "Highway Bridges and Feasts: Heidegger and Borgmann on How to Affirm Technology," this volume, Chapter 11.

means each one must be ready to accept the pain of the collapse of the shared world and to begin anew.

White cites a convincing text that comes close to, but at the same time casts doubt on, Young's account of Otherness while supporting her interpretation of the relation of death and world-disclosing:

> In lectures in 1943 Heidegger warns us of the "the suffering in which the essential otherness of what-is reveals itself in opposition to the tried and usual." He adds: "The highest form of suffering is the dying of death as a sacrifice for the preservation of the truth of being [i.e., being able to give up one's familiar world while being receptive to a strange new understanding of being—HLD]. This sacrifice is the purest experience of the voice of being."[68]

This passage also bears on Blattner's understanding of death as an anxiety attack. Readiness for anxiety would be readiness for a sudden and unmotivated breakdown of the world. It is hard to see what such readiness could be. How is it humanly possible to commit oneself to one's world (or identity) *and* at the same time envisage that at any moment it could stop making sense? It seems clear that, in the case of death, readiness for world collapse cannot mean imagining what it could be like and being ready to give up one's world, but, rather, being open to the vulnerability of one's world, and that means not building up defenses, that is, not resigning oneself to living in the world of the Anyone. So far, Blattner, Haugeland, and White could all agree.

The important difference between Blattner and Haugeland/White is that, for Blattner, death as an anxiety attack is an unmotivated and sudden collapse of all meaning, whereas for Haugeland and White death or world collapse is motivated by anomalies and takes place gradually, although, like any world transformation— like falling in love or grieving, for example—world transformation, like a gestalt switch, takes place in a special temporal way that Kierkegaard calls an Instant (*Augenblick*). One can't experience it in incremental steps. Such a transformation requires a willingness to let the old world go, to make a *sacrifice* as Later Heidegger says above, which is not like being hit out of the blue. Blattner's account is true to early Heidegger's description of the phenomenon of anxiety, but that precisely precludes it being an account of the phenomenon of the death of cultural worlds— a phenomenon that both Haugeland and White argue Heidegger is groping toward in *Being and Time*. According to White, this is the phenomenon that Heidegger

---

[68] White, *Time and Death*, 2.2, citing Martin Heidegger, *Parmenides*, trans. André Schuwer and Richard Rojcewicz (Bloomington, IN: Indiana University Press, 1998), 166f./*Parmenides* (Frankfurt am Main: Klostermann, 1992), 249f.

only finally succeeds in describing when he talks of the sacrifice involved in letting go of one's current cultural world to make way for another.

Thus, White goes beyond Haugeland's published account of death in *Being and Time* by seeing that comparing being-toward-death with revolutionary science is not just a way of getting a grip on what Heidegger means by Dasein's authentic being-toward-death as a way of life, as if being-toward-death were always someone's way of life. Rather, coming back to the death chapter in *Being and Time* from her reading of Later Heidegger, White sees both the parallel and the difference between individual being-toward-death as accepting the vulnerability of an *individual identity*, and world-preserving in the face of the vulnerability of a *whole cultural world*. She says:

[T]hroughout Heidegger's discussion of the inauthentic and authentic views of death he tacitly relies on an analogy or proportion between my demise as a person and my existential death as Dasein. I am to my death qua person as Dasein [being-in-the-world] is to its death qua Dasein [that is, world collapse]. In both respects I confront a "nothingness" impenetrable to my understanding, and death constitutes a sort of "other side" to what is . . . The tacit analogy, which lets him say similar things about both conceptions, actually hinders the distinction from being as clear as it should be.[69]

To make Heidegger clear, White reverses Haugeland's approach. She contends that, from Later Heidegger looking back, we can see that ontological death does not have to do with the finitude of individual human lives at all, but solely with the fact that there have been a series of understandings of being in our culture, a series of cultural worlds, and each has died, that is, become impossible and given way to another. Because Heidegger was unclear about this distinction, she claims, his death chapter in *Being and Time* is murky and misleading, but he gets clear about the distinction later. His ontological account of death is only fully worked out and consistent once he has discovered the history of being and so discovered what it means for the style of the culture to become unintelligible or impossible, and so for a cultural world to die.

What, then, for White is death as a cultural way to be? A culture is an ungrounded world. (1) Ungrounded worlds harbor the constant "possibility of the impossibility of any existence at all." (2) Thus cultures require world-preservers who make sacrifices to keep them alive. But (3) being-toward-death is a world-preserver's readiness to give up a culture and let the world go, when the culture no longer makes sense. (4) This is a prerequisite for receiving a new understanding of being.

---

[69] White, "Dasein, Existence and Death," 63, reprinted in Dreyfus and Wrathall, *Heidegger Reexamined*, vol. 1: *Dasein, Authenticity, and Death*, 341.

This might seem to make world-transforming by being receptive to a new understanding of being higher than world-preserving by being receptive to the current understanding of being. This may well be Nietzsche's view, but it is not Heidegger's. Being receptive to and acting on an understanding of being is as good as it gets for Heidegger. Sometimes for contingent reasons you can preserve; sometimes you've got to transform. These contingent reasons are the stuff of history.

According to White's retrospective reading of Heidegger's work, Heidegger, once he had discovered the history of being, sees that he should never have tried to present a phenomenological ontology of the death of individual human beings; rather, the proper subject of thought is the finite timeliness of shared human practices that make possible the birth and death of cultural worlds, which, in turn, gives rise to the temporality of history. As she puts it:

> Now we can see why Heidegger thinks that fundamental ontology must include consideration of "the problem of the finitude in man as the decisive element which makes the understanding of being possible" (Heidegger, *Kant and the Problem of Metaphysics*, 240/225). Our finitude is not just an incidental feature of our being. It is established in our relationship to being, more particularly in the relationship between Dasein's timeliness [the temporal structure of shared human practices] and the temporality of being [the history of understandings of being] and the role existential death [world collapse] plays at their intersection.

Summary

We have now examined eight different ways to interpret Heidegger on death and dying. To sum up, I'll group them by category in the order of their increasing plausibility.

1   Death is the inevitable event that ends a human life, an event that Heidegger calls demise.

   a) The simplest and most clearly mistaken way to understand Heidegger on death is to think of death as the *event* at the end of a human life when that life is annihilated, and to think of dying as the name for this process. (Sartre, Edwards, Philipse)

   b) More sophisticated, but still repudiated by the text, is the view that, while demise is the end of Dasein's possibilities, *dying* is a way of life that takes account of the certainty of that final event. Thus, dying, or being-toward-death, as a way of life gives life seriousness, and a narrative structure, and so makes possible a life that makes sense in terms of a beginning, middle, and end. (Zimmerman and Guignon)

2 Death is not demise at all.

    a) Death is the closing down of possibilities. Each choice I make makes some other courses of action impossible. (Carman)

    b) Dasein is essentially an ability-to-be and death is having an anxiety attack in which Dasein loses its ability to be. Dying would then be readiness for anxiety. (Blattner)

3 Heidegger is formalizing death and dying, and so treats death as a structural feature of all human lives.

    a) The negative version sees death as the structural condition that an individual's identity can always be lost. Dying is, then, the resigned, heroic acceptance of this condition. (Dreyfus)

    b) The positive version holds that what is essential about human beings— that they are world-disclosers—survives individual death. So identifying oneself with one's capacity as a world-discloser makes possible a "good death." (Young)

4 Death is equated with world collapse, and dying is understood as readiness for world collapse.

    a) Death is equated with the sort of world collapse that can befall individual human beings, and dying is staking all on one's current world, while sensing its vulnerability and being ready and able to give it up if it can't be made to work. (Haugeland)

    b) Death is equated with the sort of world collapse that can befall a cultural epoch, and dying is striving to preserve the culture's understanding of being while being ready to sacrifice it when confronted with anomalous practices that portend the arrival of a new cultural world. (White)

White sees the individual and the cultural accounts of death as opposed, and holds that Heidegger finally arrives at the latter view. "Authentic Dasein is in fact a harbinger of a new understanding of being,"[70] she contends, and she cites texts that clearly show that Later Heidegger thinks more and more about the death of cultures, and hardly at all about the death of particular human beings. Still, Haugeland is right that, while Heidegger in *Being and Time* is never concerned with the physical death of particular persons, he is, nonetheless, describing a possible way of life of individual human beings in the face of death.

To see how these two persuasive but opposed accounts of death can be related, it helps to spell out what White sees as the role of the individual in the

---

[70] White, "Dasein, Existence and Death," 64, reprinted in Dreyfus and Wrathall, *Heidegger Reexamined*, vol. 1: *Dasein, Authenticity, and Death*, 342.

"intersection" of cultural Dasein's timeliness and the temporality of being. It turns out that, according to White, authentic dying requires a special relation of the individual to the vulnerability of the cultural style:

For Heidegger dying is a particular way of existing. Dasein can die either authentically or inauthentically. As Dasein we always have to take up being-toward-the-end either by taking being for granted and thus simply moving within the possibilities of being that our culture has laid out, or by making an issue of it and thus determining where the limits of our cultural possibilities of being actually do lie.[71]

According to White, once we see how the dying of individuals relates to the death of cultures, we are in a position to grasp the understanding of death and dying Heidegger is groping for.

Standing with a foot on each of Haugeland's and White's shoulders, the reader, then, can see that they have each discovered a *general structure of finitude*, which has both an individual and a cultural instantiation. Haugeland, on the one hand, focusing on *Being and Time*, tells us how authentic individuals can integrate the vulnerability of their identity into their way of life. He thus convincingly spells out the existential side of *Being and Time* while treating the cultural parallels, in this case scientific and cultural revolutions, as analogs. White, on the other hand, argues, on the basis of her retroactive reading, that, from the start, Heidegger meant to restrict his account of death to the collapse of cultural understandings of being and, as we have just seen, she contends that authentic dying is the way individuals relate to the finitude and thus the vulnerability of their culture.

The way authentic *individuals* live their death, then, is by total commitment that stakes everything on their individual identity. They then show steadfastness in working to bring out that individual identity while accepting its vulnerability. That is, they live in anxiety and thereby remain open to anomalies that can show that their current way of life is untenable. If their current way of life breaks down, they are already building on the anomalies to form a new one.

On the cultural level, authentic *culture preservers* sense that their culture's finite understanding of what is meaningful and worthy is not grounded in reason or God but depends on them, so they devote themselves wholeheartedly to articulating the culture's current understanding of being. Moreover, since such authentic world-preservers sense the vulnerability of their current understanding of being, they keep the culture open to the anomalies that may eventually lead to its collapse, at the same time remaining receptive to the marginal practices that may become central and ground a new world.

---

[71] White, *Time and Death*, 2.7.

Once we appreciate the different phenomenon revealed by each interpretation, we can see that these phenomena are isomorphic so that one does not have to choose one interpretation at the expense of the other. Rather, we can abstract the structure of death and finitude from each interpretation and so see that, for each, death is world collapse, and authentic dying means both resisting world collapse by preserving and trying to make sense of anomalies, while at the same time remaining open to possible world collapse, thereby being able, should it happen, to accept it as making possible a new beginning. If we are authentic, we are always actively preserving or transforming. Indeed, preserving and transforming each imply the other. One can only preserve what is transformable. One can only transform what requires preserving.

Conclusion

So far, all contributors to the above discussion of Heidegger's understanding of death either identify death with demise, or else deny that death as a structure instantiated in individual or cultural world collapse has anything at all to do with the event at the end of a human life that Heidegger calls demise. But, if one is to do justice to the phenomenon and to the text, it is important to be clear that those who identify death with world collapse need not deny that the structure of world collapse can also be instantiated in a terminal condition coextensive with the event of demise—in which, as in all instances of world collapse, "Dasein is no longer able to be there" (294).

We must bear in mind that, when Heidegger says that death is "the possibility of the absolute impossibility of Dasein," he is not making the *biographical* point that Dasein's current world will some day collapse. Heidegger is clear that the *existential* possibility of death is a possibility that can never become *actual* in the way something understood as potential can finally be realized. Yet Dasein does finally cease to exist for good.

Thus, there seems to be an important difference between terminal death, so to speak, and all other forms of existential breakdown. Even if, as White so convincingly argues, by their very nature as disclosive, both an identity and a world must be vulnerable, still, an individual might be lucky enough *never to experience the failure of his or her identity*, and the members of culture need not experience culture collapse. And conversely, one can actually *experience* identity and world collapse only if the collapse in question is not the terminal one.

One can, of course, abstract from these differences and arrive at a "formal" existential-ontological conception of death that covers both the repeatable and the final versions. What makes death "possible," in a special sense of possible, then, is not that it can never become actual, but that, like all forms of existential-ontological vulnerability, it has to be taken up by Dasein and lived in a way that affects its life from beginning to end. Heidegger tells us that, "The authentic possibility of the being of death is grasped only when the relationship to this possibility is such that it is thereby understood as a certainty of my being."[72] Death, then, becomes, as White puts it, a way of life. In this sense, all forms of ultimate vulnerability are equally certain. Still, there is something special about the *final* collapse of being-in-the-world; terminal death, unlike other forms of world collapse, is *inevitable*.

Heidegger, true to the phenomena as usual, does not deny physical death's inevitability. Unlike all other forms of existential-ontological breakdown, Heidegger tells us, "Death is something *distinctively* impending" (294). And, indeed, when thinking of terminal death, Heidegger goes beyond speaking merely of certainty and says, "death as the end of Dasein, is…certain…and *not to be outstripped*" (303, some italics removed).[73]

Here death as *certain* and death as *inevitable* part ways. I can be certain of my *vulnerability* to identity or world collapse as a *possibility* without ever experiencing it, but the terminal death that is co-extensive with demise, while, indeed, an instance of vulnerability, is inevitable, not just *possibly* inevitable. Thus, the existential death co-extensive with demise must be lived with a paradoxical combination of putting everything at stake in living one's identity, while at the same time acting in a way that is open to its *inevitable* (not just possible) final collapse.

Thus, something like demise comes back, requiring some interpretation. Even when we are clear that death can't be a future event, we are left open to Sartre's and Camus's conviction that, however one describes the non-event that terminates our lives, it might well make all our previous commitments seem absurd. Just how is one supposed to live steadfastly putting one's identity at stake while at the

---

[72] Martin Heidegger, *History of the Concept of Time: Prolegomena*, trans. Theodore Kisiel (Bloomington, IN: Indiana University Press, 1985), 317.

[73] Piotr Hoffman, "Dasein and 'its' Time," in *A Companion to Heidegger*, ed. Hubert L. Dreyfus and Mark A. Wrathall (Oxford: Blackwell, 2005) points out that Heidegger says in *Being and Time* that "a 'time' has been allotted to Dasein" (463) and uses this quotation and others like it to support his claim that the sort of death Heidegger is analyzing in *Being and Time* must, like demise, be individual, inevitable, and terminal. But this notion of an allotted time alone does not distinguish individual death from cultural death. Cultures too have their allotted times and invariably die. But neither does the notion of an allotted time support the counterclaim that both the *inevitable* and final end of a human life and the *contingent* collapse of an identity or of a cultural world are instances of the same structure. Indeed, since Heidegger can't say that terminal death is *necessary* but only that it is *inevitable*, it is hard to see how to state the distinctive differences among the ways cultures *invariably* die, identities *possibly* die, and individual terminal death is inevitable.

same time being open to its *inevitable* utterly final collapse? This is where phenomenology seems to leave off and ontology or faith must take over.

In the end, Heidegger eschews faith and turns to formalized ontology. But, as we have now seen, there is a tension in his ontology. There is a way in which *terminal* collapse has the same ontological structure and the same existential role in an authentic Dasein's life as do all other forms of existential-ontological breakdown. But there is also a way in which my final end is unique. In non-terminal breakdown, Dasein as an ability-to-be does, indeed, collapse, but something remains aware of the collapse and survives to open a new world.[74] In terminal breakdown, as far as we can tell, awareness and world-disclosing are over for good.

The deep confusion in the death chapter in *Being and Time*—a confusion that White notes but that her single-minded focus on cultural world collapse doesn't allow her to see—is that sometimes Heidegger is proposing a formalized account of the essence of existential-ontological collapse *in general*,[75] and sometimes he is giving an account of the *distinctively final* character of terminal death, which, if *essential*, would prevent it from being merely another instance of existential-ontological breakdown. What White's approach does enable one to see, however, is that Heidegger may well have thought of distinctive, terminal, individual death as the essential or paradigm case, in *Being and Time*, but that Later Heidegger came to think of the death of cultural epochs as essential or paradigmatic.

Thus the complexity in the phenomenon itself leads Heidegger to lay out two existential-ontological accounts of how to live in the face of death that are in tension. The one White brilliantly works out and defends takes world collapse as essential and so gives an account of demise merely as an instance of existential-ontological breakdown, ignoring the distinctive character of physical death's inevitability and finality. In White's version of Heidegger's account of finitude,

---

[74] This raises the difficult question: just what survives world or identity collapse so as to be aware that collapse has occurred? Clearly, Dasein as being-in-the world is precisely no longer there. Heidegger would certainly resist the Cartesian claim that what survives is consciousness. What must survive, then, is what survives the breakdown of Dasein in an anxiety attack, the lack of a world, or what Heidegger calls naked thrownness or the that-it-is-and-has-to-be (174). Heidegger says all that is left in an anxiety attack is an "individualized" "*solus ipse*" (233), which we must presumably understand not as a self-sufficient Cartesian subject and not as part of some larger All, but as pure, isolated, world-needy mineness. But, here, even a master phenomenologist like Heidegger may have run up against the limits of phenomenology.

[75] Blattner claims, in effect, that we should treat anxiety attacks, although they are neither inevitable nor terminal, and are not a response to the anomalies in the current world, as another form of worldcollapse related to death. That seems to be a plausible proposal, but it makes Heidegger's job of finding a formal ontological level of description that covers the essential features of all ways that Dasein becomes impossible even more difficult.

one is called constantly to experience one's vulnerability with anxiety, but one also senses that this vulnerability is a necessary condition of the joy of being a world-discloser, so that, far from *fear* of my inevitable *demise*, Dasein's authentic attunement to the world while disclosing it is anxious joy. As Heidegger says: "Along with the sober anxiety which brings us face to face with our individualized ability-to-be, there goes an unshakable joy" (358).

But Heidegger is rightly unwilling to take a stand on whether there is an afterlife waiting for something like Dasein. He is clear that "if 'death' is defined as the 'end' of Dasein—that is to say being-in-the-world—this does not imply any ontical decision whether 'after death' still another being is possible" (292). Heidegger is therefore not going to give us advice as to how to live our lives in the face of the *inevitability* of the terminal collapse of our being-in-the-world. He can say that we are called to live the possibility of this final collapse, as we are called to live the possibility of all forms of world collapse, by breaking out of the inauthenticity of the Anyone that sees death as a future event that can be ignored for now. Thus, "the analytic makes forerunning resoluteness basic as an ability-to-be which, in an existentiell manner, is authentic" (360). But, in the end, Heidegger was enough of a phenomenologist to realize that there was nothing *positive* he could say about how to live a life, taking account every moment that it is bound to end in total annihilation. He does not claim that in this case existential-ontology can give us binding guidance. "Existential interpretation will never seek to take over any authoritarian pronouncement as to those things which, from an existentiell point of view, are possible or binding" (360).

Despite interpreters' attempts to find Heidegger's existentiell recommendation for how to live in the face of our inevitable final end, one finds not Sartrian denial, nor the traditional Christian belief in an afterlife, nor Kierkegaard's claim that, without belief in an afterlife, faith can still reconcile vulnerability and total commitment, nor secular heroic nihilism in the face of the absurd. One finds, instead, the suggestion that none of these responses to terminal death need undermine finite forerunning resoluteness with its joy in the possibility of either preserving vulnerable identities and cultural worlds, or letting them go and disclosing new ones. But, beyond that, it seems that each of us, without Heidegger's guidance, has to relate to the inevitability of finally no longer being able to be there in his or her own way. Carol White chose to spend twenty years laboriously writing a masterful meditation on finitude and death that will long outlive her.

PART II

Hermeneutic Realism

4

Defending the Difference

The Geistes/Naturwissenschaften
Distinction Revisited (1991)

The difference between the *Natur* and the *Geisteswissenschaften*, where the *Geisteswissenschaften* means the humanities, is obvious. What needs to be argued is that there is a basic methodological difference between the empirical disciplines that study nature and the empirical disciplines that study human comportment. In this case the *Geisteswissenschaften* means the social sciences. There are many ways to approach the question of the unity and differences between these two types of discipline. I want to talk about a difference in the *goals* of the social and the natural sciences. I will argue that the relation of a science's practices to the object the science studies is different in the natural and social sciences, and that this difference leads to different disciplinary goals—*explaining* in the natural sciences and *understanding* in the social ones.

The attempt to draw a principled distinction between the methods of the natural and social sciences has had a surprising history. For a century the pressure to unify the sciences came from the attraction of the hard natural sciences as models for the soft social sciences. Those who opposed unification did so by arguing that the human sciences dealt with meaningful events and so required an interpretive approach different in principle from the covering law model of the sciences of nature. Just when the difference between the theoretical and the hermeneutic disciplines was becoming accepted, however, the line of attack suddenly shifted and now it has become fashionable to push for the methodological unity of the sciences by arguing that *all* disciplines are interpretive and their objects are all social constructs. The hope of hammering all of the disciplines into one hard objective science has thus given way to the desire to dissolve them all into a soft hermeneutical hash.

This second approach to unity is furthered by the fact that among philosophers any attempt to defend an essential difference between the hard sciences as converging on the objective truth about nature and the soft sciences as dealing with historically changing human meanings has become suspect. On the one hand, Thomas Kuhn and others have shown that science has a history of radical paradigm shifts and have claimed that this undermines the argument that science is converging on the truth about nature. On the other hand, eliminative materialists, such as Paul Feyerabend, Richard Rorty, and their followers, have convincingly argued that there is no in-principle reason why a social science might not predict the behavior of human beings under some objective description that eliminates reference to everyday meaningful entities and events and to people as agents.

Since many philosophers are convinced that no argument for the *in-principle* distinction between the methods of the *Geistes* and the *Naturwissenschaften* can be defended, it has become increasingly unpopular among "post-modern" philosophers even to raise the issue. Still, there does seem to be an obvious difference in the current status of the two types of disciplines. Put crudely: the natural sciences progress while the human sciences do not. So, rather than attempting to distinguish these disciplines by looking for an *essential* difference in their objects that necessitates an *essential* difference in their methods, we should ask a more modest question: What is there about the practices of each type of discipline that accounts for the natural sciences' ability to formulate objective theoretical truths about nature, and the social sciences' failure to discover similar types of truths about human beings?

Anyone who wants thus to defend the *disunity* of the sciences must fight on two fronts. He needs to show that, even though physical science is a social practice subject to radical paradigm shifts, it can still reveal the way the world is independent of our theories and practices, *and* that, even though the human sciences deal with human beings who are, among other things, objects, they can never be objective. Since the task of arguing for a basic, if not essential, difference between the natural and human sciences is double, my paper will be in effect two mini-papers.

How Natural Science Can Discover Truths about Nature

The status of the entities supposedly discovered by natural science, and the correlated question of the special authority of science in our culture, has increasingly become an issue of debate. Literary theorists, social scientists, and feminists, each for their own reasons, have found themselves allied with antirealist philosophers of science in their attack on the special claim of the natural sciences to tell us the truth about objective reality. The literary theorists would like to one-up the sciences by showing that scientific theories are after all just texts and therefore fall into the domain of the humanities. Social scientists, by pointing out that scientific truth is a product of shared practices, seek to annex science to the domain of sociology and anthropology. Feminists would like to undermine the authority of the scientific establishment, which they rightly regard as a bastion of male domination. All these groups would like to believe that natural science is just one more interpretive practice that has somehow conned our culture into thinking that it alone has access to the real. The stakes are high. As Evelyn Fox Keller recently put it:

> The question of whether scientific knowledge is objective or relative is at least in part a question about the claim of scientists to absolute authority. If there is only one truth, and scientists are privy to it...then the authority of science is unassailable. But if truth is relative, if science is divorced from nature and married instead to culture, then the privileged status of that authority is fatally undermined.[1]

There is, indeed, something wrong with our culture's worship of natural science, as if what science tells us about the fundamental particles has fundamental importance for all aspects of life. The success of such books as Fritjof Capra's *The Tao of Physics*, which tells us that we can breathe easier because science is no longer atomist and materialist but is now holistic and works with energy fields, shows that many people believe that science does tell us the final truth about reality. But the attempt to limit the influence of natural science by denying that it discovers anything at all—as the title of a recent book, *Constructing Quarks*, implies—is clearly an overreaction. It is a non sequitur to claim that because the development of physical theories depends upon scientists' practices and that the authority of science is constituted by way of broader social practices, physics does not discover truths about nature and so has no legitimate authority. If one wants to undermine the illegitimate authority of natural science, especially physics, in our culture it would be sufficient to show that although scientific theory can tell us the truth about physical nature, it does not have a special access to the truth about ultimate reality.

Before I can argue for this claim I need to define what I mean by scientific theory. Theorizing is a special form of intellectual activity, discovered by Socrates and refined by the philosophical tradition. It has six essential characteristics, never fully achieved, but approached to varying degrees. The first three are introduced by Socrates. (1) *Explicitness*. A theory should not be based on intuition and

---

[1] Evelyn Fox Keller, "The Gender/Science System: or, Is Sex to Gender as Nature is to Science?" *Hypathia* 2 (1987), 45.

interpretation but should be spelled out so completely that it can be understood by any rational being. (2) *Universality*. A theory should hold true for all places and all times. (3) *Abstractedness*. A theory must not require reference to particular examples.

Descartes and Kant complete the Socratic account of theory by adding two further requirements: (4) *Discreteness*. A theory must be stated in terms of context-free elements—elements that make no reference to human interests, traditions, institutions, etc. (5) *Systematicity*. A theory must be a whole in which decontextualized elements (properties, attributes, features, factors, etc.) are related to each other by rules or laws.[2]

Plato clairvoyantly expressed all five characteristics of theory in the myth of the cave: the theorist must remove his object of knowledge from the everyday world in order to see the universal relations between the explicit and abstract elements, in this case the ideas. Freed from all context, the elements form a system of their own—all ideas are organized by the idea of the Good. Plato saw that while everyday understanding is implicit, concrete, local, and partial, theories, by contrast, are explicit, abstract, universal, and total.

In the *Republic* Plato put the natural sciences of his day on only the third level of his four-level divided line since they did not satisfy two further conditions: indubitability and rational grounding. Yet the theoretical explanation of nature developed by modern natural science, although still only on Plato's third level, is the most successful version ever obtained of the sort of theory Plato envisaged. Indeed, while relinquishing indubitable and grounded knowledge, the modern natural sciences have been able to add a sixth characteristic of ideal theory. It is this characteristic that is sought in vain by the social sciences. (6) *Closure and prediction*. The description of the domain investigated must be complete, i.e., it must specify all the influences that affect the elements in the domain and must specify their effects. Closure permits precise prediction.

For this discussion it is irrelevant whether natural *scientists* ever achieve the ideal of theoretical explanation or whether, as is now generally believed, shared interpretations, metaphors, specific examples, etc. play a crucial role in the activities of normal scientists and their understanding and acceptance of theories. All I need claim for my argument is that *theories* can become more and more explicit and complete, making less and less reference to shared background

---

[2] In asserting that theories range over decontextualized, uninterpreted facts I am not endorsing a positivist account of theories as based on brute data. The basic data are meter reading and computer print outs. These "uninterpreted facts" are cut off from our everyday world of equipment and purposes but they are, of course, recontextualized or theory laden, otherwise they could not fill in variables asking for mass, charge, etc.

interpretations, metaphors, examples, etc.—and that there is no *in-principle* limit to such refinement.

Many recent philosophers of science, however, hold that science cannot even approach the ideal of theory. They contend that scientific entities are social constructions essentially related to human purposes. Such antirealists, as Arthur Fine puts it, "accept the behaviorist idea that the working practices of conceptual exchange exhaust the meaning of the exchange, giving it its significance and providing it with its content."[3] Such thinkers conclude from the fact that background practices are necessary for *access* to theoretical entities, that these entities must be *defined in terms of* these access practices.

Fine, in response to both realists and antirealists, tries to remain true to the understanding of science already in scientific practice. Like Michael Polanyi and Nancy Cartwright, he starts with the observation that the scientist "believes in the existence of those entities to which his theories refer."[4] Fine calls this the Natural Ontological Attitude (NOA). In this attitude one "accepts the evidence of one's senses [with regard to the existence and features of everyday objects] and … accepts, *in the same way*, the confirmed results of science."[5] Fine tells us:

NOA helps us to see that realism differs from various antirealisms in this way: realism adds an *outer* direction to NOA, that is, the external world and the correspondence relation of approximate truth; antirealisms add an *inner* direction, that is, human-oriented reductions of truth, or concepts, or explanations. NOA suggests that the legitimate features of these additions are already contained in the presumed equal status of everyday truths with scientific ones, and in our accepting them both as *truths*. No other additions are legitimate, and none are required.[6]

Heidegger expounded a similar view. In his 1927 Kant lectures he gives us his conception of the goal of scientific discipline (*Wissenschaft*):

Scientific knowing presupposes that existing Dasein[7] takes as a freely chosen task the revealing of the entity it approaches for the sake of revealing it. … The struggle is solely directed to the entity itself and solely in order to free it from its hiddenness.[8]

---

[3] Arthur Fine, *The Shaky Game: Einstein, Realism and the Quantum Theory* (Chicago, IL: University of Chicago Press, 1986), 140. For an example of such a constructivist account see Joseph Rouse, *Knowledge and Power: Toward a Political Philosophy of Science*(Ithaca, NY: Cornell University Press, 1987).

[4] Fine, *The Shaky Game*, 130.   [5] Fine, *The Shaky Game*, 126ff.

[6] Fine, *The Shaky Game*, 133.

[7] The best way to understand what Heidegger means by Dasein is to think of our term "human being," which can refer to a way of being that is characteristic of all people, or it can refer to a specific person—a human being.

[8] Martin Heidegger, *Phänomenologische Interpretation von Kants Kritik der reinen Vernunft, Gesamtausgabe*, vol. 25 (Frankfurt: Vittorio Klostermann, 1977), 2.

As I would put it, scientists are "background realists," i.e., their practices take the independent existence of their domain of objects for granted. We might call these who explicate this understanding hermeneutic realists.

Hermeneutic realists hold that a science's background realism cannot be used to *justify* the claim that the objects of science exist independently of the activity of the scientists, nor can this understanding *dictate* what methods or operating assumptions a science must accept. Rather, the role of the hermeneutic philosopher of science is (1) to spell out what everyday scientific practice takes for granted—in the case of natural science, that there is a nature independent of us and that current science is giving us a better and better explanation of how that nature works, and (2) to show that the self-understanding of the science is both internally coherent and compatible with the ontological implications of our everyday practices.

According to the hermeneutic realist, natural science's background realism is compatible with neither metaphysical realism nor antirealism. Scientists work within social practices that neither they nor philosophers can transcend, so science cannot justify a metaphysical realism which claims to have an *argument* that there is nature in itself, that nature has the structure science finds, and that science is converging on the one true account of this independent reality. Yet scientists take for granted they *can* discover the truth about nature as it is independent of scientific practices, so metaphysical antirealism is also unacceptable.

This minimal hermeneutic realism is first found in *Being and Time*. There Heidegger argues as follows: Only human beings make sense of things. So the intelligibility of each kind of thing, including natural things, depends upon our practices. Still nature as *a* being, or as an ensemble of beings, need not depend on us, for one way we make sense of things—find them intelligible—is as merely occurrent (*vorhanden*), i.e., as not related to our practices.

Occurrent beings are revealed when we take a detached attitude toward things and decontextualize them. Then things show up as independent of human purposes and even as independent of human existence. Decontextualizing takes place in two stages. First we use skills and instruments to isolate things and their properties, which then appear as meaningless objects, colors, shapes, sounds, etc. Such data are independent of our purposes but not independent of our senses. We then invent theories in which the occurrent data are taken up as evidence for quasars and quarks and other entities we cannot directly experience. These theoretical entities need not conform at all to our everyday understanding of objects, space, time, and causality. Our current theory tells us that these entities belong to natural kinds—types of things in nature such as water, gold, iron, etc.—and if correct, the theory describes the causal powers of these natural kinds. There is no way to stand outside current science and give it metaphysical support by arguing that there must be natural kinds or that these are what our science must be about. All that philosophy can do is show the coherence of the natural scientist's background assumption that there is some way nature is in itself.

If we encountered things only in using them, never in detachedly reflecting on them, i.e., if availableness (*Zuhandenheit*) were the only way of being we knew, we would not be able to make the notion of entities in themselves intelligible. But since we understand occurrentness, we understand that occurrent entities can have existed even if human beings had never existed. Indeed, given our understanding of occurrentness, we *must* understand things this way. To take a Heideggerian example, what it is to be a hammer essentially depends upon Dasein and its cultural artifacts. It belongs to the being of a hammer that it is used to pound in nails for building houses, etc. In a culture that always tied things together, there could be no hammers. But there could, nonetheless, be pieces of wood with iron blobs on the end, since wood and iron are natural kinds and their being and causal powers make no essential reference to human purposes.

Joseph Rouse in defense of what he takes to be Heidegger's social constructivism argues convincingly that what counts as an electron and even what counts as a physical cause depends on current scientific instruments and practices. Heidegger would agree. He would of course further agree that once our practices define what counts as an "X" we must still determine whether there are any "X"s. Heidegger would even accept that if the "X"s in question are available like hammers, then when we find out that there are "X"s we find entities that exist only relative to our practices. He would point out, however, that if what counts as an "X" has occurrentness as its way of being, then when we find that there are "X"s we find at the same time that these "X"s exist independently of us and of our scientific instruments and practices. This is what Heidegger means when he says:

Intraworldliness does not belong to the essence of the occurrent things as such, but it is only the transcendental condition...for the possibility of occurrent things being able to emerge as they are.[9]

Heidegger's account is thus compatible with holding that science is converging on getting it right about such natural kinds as gold and water and their causal powers.[10] But even if physical science is progressing in its understanding of

---

[9] Martin Heidegger, *The Basic Problems of Phenomenology*, trans. Albert Hofstadter (Bloomington, IN: Indiana University Press, 1982), 194.

[10] If these kinds of things turn out not to have the properties predicted and the natural kind terms referring to them have to be dropped from the lexicon of science, as phlogiston was, then some other

physical nature, this cannot be used to argue that the current scientific approach to nature is the only right one. A theory of the causal powers of natural kinds tells us only what is *causally* real, so modern science need not be the only way of understanding nature. As Heidegger sees it, many different practices can reveal nature as it is in itself.

What is represented by physics is indeed nature itself, but undeniably it is only nature as the object-area, whose objectness is first defined and determined through the refining that is characteristic of physics and is expressly set forth in that refining. Nature, in its objectness for modern physical science, is only *one* way in which what presences— which from of old has been named *physis*—reveals itself.[11]

Heidegger thus denies that modern physics has found *the* right vocabulary for describing nature. This, I presume, is the meaning of his Kuhn-like remark back in 1938:

[We cannot] say that the Galilean doctrine of freely falling bodies is true and that Aristotle's teaching, that light bodies strive upward, is false; for the Greek understanding of the essence of body and place and of the relation between the two rests upon a different interpretation of entities and hence conditions a correspondingly different kind of seeing and questioning of natural events. No one would presume to maintain that Shakespeare's poetry is more advanced than that of Aeschylus. It is still more impossible to say that the modern understanding of whatever is, is more correct than that of the Greeks.[12]

Here Heidegger is obviously trying to counter the claim that Galileo has refuted Aristotle. He is doing so, not as Kuhn does in *The Structure of Scientific Revolutions*, by holding that neither theory is true of nature, but rather by holding that *both* are true. This could be the innocuous observation that both are "illuminating," but in the context of the remark just quoted that "what is represented by physics is indeed nature itself," it must be the stronger claim that different theories can reveal different aspects of nature. Of course, if one thinks of Aristotle's theory of natural place as an account of *physical* causality meant to explain, for example, why rocks fall, in the same sense that modern physics claims to explain the same phenomenon, this position is untenable. On that account modern physics, as far as we know, would be right and Aristotle would simply be wrong. It may well be, however, that Aristotle and Galileo were

system of natural kind terms might, in principle, still be found which do refer to the natural kinds there really are; although, of course, we could never know for certain we had the final account.

[11] Martin Heidegger, "Science and Reflection," in *The Question Concerning Technology and Other Essays* (New York: Harper & Row, 1977), 173–4.

[12] Martin Heidegger, "The Age of the World Picture," in *The Question Concerning Technology and Other Essays* (New York: Harper Torchbooks, 1977), 117.

asking *different kinds of questions*, and so each could be right about a different aspect of nature.

It follows from the above considerations that what counts as real for a culture depends upon the interpretation in its practices, but this does not make what is thus revealed any less real. We could call this position *plural realism.* For a plural realist there is no point of view from which one can ask and answer the metaphysical question concerning the one true nature of ultimate reality. Given the dependence of the intelligibility of all ways of being on our practices, and the dependence of what counts as elements of reality on our purposes, the question makes no sense. But since different practices reveal different realities or domains of intelligibility, and since no one way of revealing is exclusively true, accepting one does not commit us to rejecting the others. Donald Davidson holds a similar view: If we are right in our claims about reality under various descriptions, then what we are right about has whatever properties it has even if these descriptions are not reducible to a single description, and that physical reality has whatever properties it has whether we describers and our ways of describing things exist or not.

There are no clear limits as to what kinds of cultural entities can be encountered. In natural science, however, there seems to be one right answer as far as physical causality is concerned. Radically different theories than those proposed by modern science presumably would not reveal physical causal powers. As Heidegger once put it:

The spiritual...offers less resistance than in the field of natural science, where nature immediately takes its revenge on a wrongheaded approach.[13]

This suggests how one should respond to scientific relativists such as Richard Rorty who scoff at the idea of science learning nature's own language. Granted that we can never completely decontextualize our data, and that therefore our scientific theories are always to some extent parasitical upon our cultural practices and language, still once we discover that we have practices that can reveal meaningless occurrent data divorced from essential reference to our purposes, we can use recontextualization in theories to distance our science further and further from the everyday world. It is as if nature *is* teaching the natural scientist, not *nature's own language*, since only a Platonist thinks that representations exist independently of meaningful practices, but rather nature is leading natural scientists to improve *their* language for representing her under an objectified aspect.

---

[13] Martin Heidegger, *The History of the Concept of Time* (Bloomington, IN: Indiana University Press, 1985), 203.

It is helpful to compare Heidegger and Rorty here. Both argue that the real can show up differently given different practices (vocabularies, Rorty would say), and neither wants to allow that there is a privileged description that founds all the others. Anyone who claims to have a description of ultimate reality claims a point of view outside of all particular, finite interpretations, and both Heidegger and Rorty think, given their understanding of understanding, that the very idea of such an interpretation-free understanding of what ultimately is does not make sense. But Rorty thinks that this is an argument against accepting even a minimal hermeneutic realism where science is concerned, whereas Heidegger shows how one can reject the claim that there is *a* correct description of reality, and still hold that there can be *many* correct descriptions, including a correct causal description of objectified physical nature. Natural science can be getting it righter and righter about how things *work* even if there is no one right answer to how things are.

Why Current Human Sciences Must Be Hermeneutic

The phenonemon that leads one to expect a basic difference between the natural sciences and the disciplines that study human beings is clear. The natural sciences may not be as rational nor as cumulative as once believed, but they still show stability and progress. For extended periods such sciences as physics exhibit an agreed upon way of doing research. Occasionally disagreement arises as to how to account for anomalies. This then constitutes a crisis, which continues until the anomalies are removed by some new scheme which gains agreement, establishing a new normal science. But even when previously accepted theories are abandoned many results are conserved.

The human sciences, on the other hand, have been neither stable nor cumulative. These "dubious disciplines," to use Foucault's pejorative phrase, do not progress through revolutions like physical science, but merely go through episodes in which certain fads tend to dominate research until some competing fad lures most researchers onto its bandwagon. One style of research gives way to another not because the new research is based upon a theory that explains certain anomalies the old theory failed to explain, but simply because researchers have become bored and discouraged with the old approach. The new style, introducing new methods and problems, allows everyone to forget the old problems. Thus the human sciences are subject to frequent factionalism and reorganization, but this is not a crisis—a period of competing paradigms. It is a pre-paradigm state. The human sciences are not even generally stable nor are they even somewhat cumulative.

But disagreement arises as soon as one tries to interpret the above contrast. Rorty, for example, accepts the difference between normal and non-normal science but rejects the attempt to use it to draw a distinction between the natural and the human sciences.

The line... is not the line between the human and the non-human but between that portion of the field of inquiry where we feel rather uncertain that we have the right vocabulary at hand and that portion where we feel certain that we do. This *does*, at the moment, roughly coincide with the distinction between the fields of the *Geistes-* and the *Naturwissenschaften*. But this coincidence may be *mere* coincidence.[14]

Thus Rorty holds that while at present the human sciences are unable to find an agreed upon vocabulary, this fact has nothing to do with the essential nature of man or of science. It is simply an effect of the complexity of the domain and the immaturity of the human sciences.

But this way of dismissing the difference seems too simple. The argument that the human sciences are young is beginning to show its age. Looked at historically the social sciences make a quite different impression than sciences such as biology or meteorology that are struggling with a very complex domain. These latter sciences are making slow but steady progress in developing more and more complicated theories that take into account more and more factors, whereas the human sciences first seek to develop a general theory using one approach, then scrap that attempt *in toto* and take up some other equally simplistic research program.

To take a recent example. The behaviorists sought a complete description of human action in terms of elements of behavior and sought covering laws that predicted the occurrence of particular behavioral events. When this approach came up against hard problems such as linguistic behavior, however, it was quickly abandoned and cognitivism became popular. Cognitivists reject all of the behaviorists carefully compiled results and seek to explain human behavior by analyzing the rule-like relations holding between mental representations. Both approaches aim, in the ideal limit, at attaining the sort of complete explanatory account that allows one to predict precisely the effects of alterations in an object's internal and external environment, and each fails to achieve its goal. It looks more and more like there must be something about human activity, on the one hand, and the nature of theoretical explanation, on the other, which do not fit together.

Why does the sort of theoretical explanation that succeeds brilliantly in the natural sciences fail in the human sciences? The problem I believe lies in the attempt to apply theory to the everyday world. Just as physical science

---

[14] Richard Rorty, *Philosophy and the Mirror of Nature* (Princeton, NJ: Princeton University Press, 1979), 352.

predicts and explains everyday changes of place in terms of meaningless, context-independent properties such as mass and position, which can be abstracted from the everyday world, so a theoretical science of human beings seeks to emulate natural science by abstracting meaningless, context-free features from everyday, context-dependent, meaningful human activities, and then predict and explain these everyday activities in terms of formal relations between these elements. Insofar as these would-be sciences follow the ideal of physical theory, they must predict and explain *everyday activities*, using *decontextualized features*. But since the context in which human beings pick out the everyday objects and events whose regularities theory attempts to predict is left out in the decontextualization necessary for theory, the everyday objects and events human beings pick out do not always coincide with those elements over which the theory ranges. Therefore predictions, though often correct, are not reliable. Indeed, predictions will work only as long as the elements picked out and related by the theory happen to coincide with the objects and events picked out in their everyday activities by the human beings falling under the theory.

A striking example of what happens when one tries to study human beings as objects was given inadvertently by a Stanford psychologist who announced that his science had discovered that, although people classify some people as talkative and although there is general agreement among participants in the everyday world as to which people belong in this class, the concept of talkativeness is unfounded. If you count the number of words uttered by an individual in a day, the would-be theorist explained, you find that there is no significant difference in the quantity of words uttered by so-called normal and by so-called talkative people.

It never occurred to this objective psychologist that what makes a person count as talkative may be the meaning of what is said and the situation in which it is said. Talkative people presumably say little of importance and say it during other people's lectures, at funerals, etc. The general agreement among participants in the everyday world as to who is talkative is no illusion. Rather the sort of data collection appropriate to the natural sciences, where one studies objects and counts noises, is simply inappropriate to the study of human beings' understanding of themselves and other human beings. People making judgments such as who is talkative agree because they dwell in a shared background of meaningful practices. In general, in the human sciences, if one is to understand what is going on, one must share a general human background understanding with the person or group being studied. Shared agreement disappears as soon as the meaning of the situation is bracketed out in the attempt to attain the sort of objectivity appropriate to natural science.

This thesis can be further illustrated by the sort of difficulties that, according to Pierre Bourdieu, confront Levi-Strauss's structuralist theory of gift exchange. In *Outline of a Theory of Practice*, Bourdieu argues that Levi-Strauss's formal, reversible rules for the exchange of gifts—abstracted as they are from everyday gift-giving—cannot account for and predict actual exchanges. His point is not that theory leaves out the subjective, so-called phenomenological, qualities of gift exchange. That would not be a valid objection. The natural sciences legitimately abstract from subject-relative properties. Bourdieu's point is that Levi-Strauss's abstraction of the pure objects exchanged leaves out something essential. The tempo of the event actually *determines what counts as a gift.*

In every society it may be observed that, if it is not to constitute an insult, the counter-gift must be *deferred* and *different*, because the immediate return of an exactly identical object clearly amounts to a refusal.[15]

Predictions based only on formal principles fail in those cases in which what formally counts as a gift in the theory is rejected because it is reciprocated too soon or too late to count as a gift in everyday practice.

It is all a question of style, which means in this case timing and choice of occasion, for the *same act*—giving, giving in return, offering one's services, paying a visit, etc.—can have completely different meanings at different times.[16]

In general the meaning of the situation plays an essential role in determining what counts as an object or event; yet it is precisely this contextual meaning that theory must ignore. Thus imprecision in the human sciences as they are now constituted is inevitable because what counts as an everyday fact depends on a background of meanings and skills which is excluded by the decontextualization required by theory.

The question then arises: Can the human sciences provide a theoretical account of the social background practices? If the background skills could be captured in strict rules then we could still hope for an objective social science. I must therefore pause here to sketch the phenomenological considerations that lead me to conclude that there is no reason to think that there can be a *theory* of skills.

Skill acquisition usually begins with the student learning and applying rules for manipulating context-free elements. This is the element of truth in cognitivism. Thus a chess beginner must follow strict rules relating such features as center

---

[15] Pierre Bourdieu, *Outline of a Theory of Practice*, trans. Richard Nice (Cambridge: Cambridge University Press, 1977), 5 (my italics).
[16] Bourdieu, *Outline of a Theory of Practice*, 6.

control, material balance, etc. After one begins to understand a domain, however, one sees meaningful aspects, not context-free features. Thus a more experienced chess player sees context-dependent aspects such as unbalanced pawn structure or weakness on the king side. A further stage of proficiency is achieved when, after a great deal of experience, one is able to see a situation as having a certain significance tending toward a certain outcome, and certain aspects of the situation stand out as salient in relation to that end. Given a certain board position all masters conclude after a few seconds of examination that the issue is to attack or defend the king side.

Finally, after even more experience an expert simply sees immediately what must be done, presumably because the current situation is perceived as similar to another already experienced one. The chess master, for example, sees the issues in a position almost immediately, and the right move just pops into his head. There is no reason to suppose the beginner's features and rules, or any other features and rules, play any role in such expert performance.[17] Connectionist models of brain functioning, which make no use of the features and rules, might be able to capture such learning, but such nets do not yield a psychological theory.

The same holds for the shared social skills that make possible picking out objects and events. These skills can no more be understood theoretically, i.e., in terms of features and rules, than any other skills. But if what human beings pick out as specific sorts of objects depends on background skills, which are not rule-governed, then what counts as a certain sort of object is not rule-governed either. Predictive failure is a constant possibility in any area where facts such as being talkative or being a gift depend on background practices not integrated into the theory. Prediction will fail whenever an object that according to the theory has the defining features of a given type is nonetheless not counted by those in the culture as belonging to that type.

The natural way to cope with this problem is to abandon the attempt to find what one might call first-order interpretation-free features and to settle for second-order features such as the participants' *judgments*, e.g., judgments as to whether what was just exchanged counted as a gift. Such judgments, or scores on questionnaires, could be treated as context-free facts or features and then related by theory to explain and predict other objectively determined judgments or test scores. Economics attempts to be such a second-order science. It accepts the

---

[17] One can, of course, recall the rules one once used and act on them again, but then one's behavior will be halting and clumsy just as it was when one mastered the rules as an advanced beginner. For a more detailed account of the stages of skill acquisition and the implications of this account for cognitive science, cf. Hubert L. Dreyfus and Stuart Dreyfus, *Mind over Machine* (New York: Free Press, 1988).

current understanding of money, property, etc. and current desires to maximize possessions etc. It then seeks laws relating these socially defined elements. As long as the practices defining the objects and goals of a group remain constant, economic laws can in principle be as predictive as those of physics. But if background conditions determine, in a way which in principle falls outside a theory, what counts as the events over which the theory ranges, the theory is at the mercy of changes in these conditions, which at any moment can undermine the predictive power of the theory.

It might seem that if one could make explicit the theory's boundary conditions one could at least predict when the theory would fail. Thus ecological theories are explicitly understood as applying only as long as the temperature of the earth remains relatively constant. And, indeed, if the conditions that form the background of a human science such as economics could be made explicit, one could gain a kind of scientific closure by stating the limits within which a given economic theory was meant to be predictive. But in the human sciences the background conditions are not physical facts, nor are they psychological facts, such as what agents desire and what they believe is rational. They are not facts at all. As I have tried to show, the background conditions are patterns of skilled behavior, which embody an interpretation of what counts as facts, i.e., what counts as objects and events in various domains.

The problem for the social sciences is that these background conditions change, yet the social scientist cannot state precisely in advance what aspects of these patterns have to remain constant for his predictions to continue to be fulfilled. In general, since the boundary conditions of the human sciences are not facts but interpretations, social sciences such as economics, which build on second-order judgments that presuppose these interpretations, are not only incomplete and unstable in comparison with theoretical disciplines such as physics; they are incomplete and unstable even when compared to disciplines with changing background conditions such as ecology.

To sum up. Even the best predictive theories in the human sciences may at any moment encounter exceptions. Given the lack of any solid predictive successes, other approaches inevitably arise in the discipline, which offer competing types of systematic accounts. Such competing types of account do not agree on method, evidence, or even on what are the problems. We then have neither normal science nor even revolutionary science, but just the sort of pre-paradigmatic instability characteristic of the social sciences from their inception to the present.

It follows from the above considerations that the only vocabulary that could make the human sciences theoretical would be one that picked out entirely different features than those abstracted from our everyday activities—features that would remain invariant through changes in background practices. Eliminativists argue that if there were such features and we were able to find them by some sort of luck or divination, then the study of human beings could, in principle, be closed, predictive, and normal.

Entertaining such logical possibilities has little use, however, except to keep philosophers from claiming that, *in principle*, the study of human beings can never be normal. But from the fact that there is no in-principle argument against the possibility of an objective theory of human beings, one cannot conclude, as Rorty seems to do, that the instability of the social sciences is an historical accident. Since we have no reason to believe that the features a theory of human activity requires exist, and no way to find them if they do, the abstract possibility of eliminating reference to meaning should not prevent us from noticing and trying to account for the evident differences between the *Geistes* and *Naturwissenschaften*.

The argument I have presented enables us to see why the only kind of predictive human sciences anyone has tried to develop, indeed, the only kind we can concretely envisage, i.e., sciences based on features abstracted from everyday life, cannot succeed. Either current social sciences must, like economics, build on a background they cannot adequately describe and so whose changes they cannot predict, or else, like behaviorism and cognitivism, human sciences must use features obtained by abstracting from all practical contexts to predict events in practical contexts. But since the practical context determines what counts as the events one wants to predict, any attempt to obtain completeness in this way is bound to fail. This leads to an attempt to formalize the background practices themselves. But since the background practices are skills, they cannot be understood in terms of features and rules. Thus there can be no theory of the everyday world.

Conclusion

Nancy Cartwright has pointed out that scientists too must share background practices that enable them to pick out events in the everyday world that count as instances of the events and objects referred to in their theories, cases of force or of absorption, for example. So, what then is the difference between the natural and human sciences? The difference is that in the social world instances of a given type of object or event are *defined* by the practice of picking them out. A gift *is* whatever the natives take to be a gift. But in natural science the practices for picking out instances of the theory in the everyday world do not define these instances. What in everyday scientific practice counts as a force, for example, must be compatible with the way forces behave under ideal conditions such as weightlessness or in a vacuum. The natives cannot be wrong about what, in the everyday world, is a gift, but, since the everyday world can be transformed by degrees into an artificial world, the scientists can discover they have been wrong about what in the everyday world they have been picking out as an instance of some theoretical entity such as a force. In general, the answer I would give to Cartwright's objection is that in the natural sciences shared background skills are, indeed, necessary for decontextualizing features and for applying theories, but, unlike in the human sciences, these skills do not define what counts as the objects of the theory. Rather, the background skills function progressively to free the science's objects from dependence on *all* practices, including the practices that reveal them.

Thus, although *physics* is a social practice, *physical theory* has, in the course of its development, progressively left behind our shared everyday understanding of space, time, objects, and causality. There is no in-principle limit to how far this decontextualizing can go. This is why we can make sense of the idea of an ideal natural science getting a correct view of causal nature—a view a Martian could understand and accept. But there is no equivalent idea of an ideal social science converging on the interpretation-free truth about such a practice as gift-giving or such comportment as being talkative. On the contrary, in the human sciences, as we have seen, producing an account of meaningful human comportment requires concepts that are essentially dependent upon social meanings. Decontextualizing is thus impossible in the human sciences if the human sciences wish to predict comportment in our meaningful everyday world.

I have tried to give a sketch of the phenomenological arguments of a hermeneutic philosophy of science that could serve as a substitute for the old in-principle arguments of traditional philosophy of science. Even if philosophers cannot prove that nature has an objective structure that is revealed by science, hermeneutic phenomenology can show that there is no contradiction in the idea of natural science converging on the causal structure of nature itself. Likewise, even if philosophers cannot rule out the possibility of human beings being explained as objects, hermeneutic phenomenology can show why the attempt to explain the everyday world in terms of features and rules cannot work. Thus a description of the relation of theory to scientific and to everyday background practices, as well as an account of the background skills themselves, can show why the distinction between normal and pre-paradigm science parallels the distinction between the *Natur* and *Geisteswissenschaften*. It can thus show that the *disunity* of the sciences is no mere historical accident as Rorty claims. Indeed, we should expect a crucial difference between natural and human science to arise just where it has arisen and to remain as long as these disciplines exist.

5

Heidegger's Hermeneutic Realism (1991)

The status of the entities supposedly discovered by natural science, and the correlated question of the special authority of science in our culture—a question posed two decades ago by Thomas Kuhn's *Structure of Scientific Revolutions*—has recently become a central issue of debate. Literary theorists, social scientists, and feminists, each for their own reasons, have found themselves allied with Kuhn in their attack on the special claim of the natural sciences to tell us the truth about objective reality. The literary theorists would like to one-up the sciences by showing that scientific theories are after all just interpretive texts and therefore fall into the domain of the humanities. Similarly, social scientists, by pointing out that scientific truth is a product of shared practices, seek to annex science to the domain of sociology and anthropology. Feminists would like to undermine the authority of the scientific establishment, which they regard as a bastion of male domination. All these groups would like to believe that natural science is just one more interpretive practice that has somehow conned our culture into thinking that it alone has access to the real. The stakes are high. As Evelyn Fox Keller recently put it: "The question of whether scientific knowledge is objective or relative is at least in part a question about the claim of scientists to absolute authority. If there is only one truth, and scientists are privy to it...then the authority of science is unassailable. But if truth is relative, if science is divorced from nature and married instead to culture, then the privileged status of that authority is fatally undermined."[1]

There is, indeed, something wrong with our culture's worship of natural science, as if what science tells us about the fundamental particles has fundamental importance for all aspects of life. The success of such books as Fritjof

---

[1] Evelyn Fox Keller, "The Gender/Science System: or, Is Sex to Gender as Nature is to Science?" *Hypathia* 2 (1987), 45.

Capra's *Tao of Physics*, which tells us that we can breathe easier because science is no longer atomist and materialist but is now holist and works with energy fields, shows that many people believe that science tells us the final truth about reality. But the attempt to limit the influence of science by denying that it discovers anything at all—as the title of a recent book, *Constructing Quarks*,[2] implies—is clearly an overreaction. It is a non sequitur to claim that because the development of physical theories depends upon scientists' practices and the authority of science is constituted by way of broader social practices, physics does not discover truths about nature and so has no legitimate authority. If one wants to undermine the illegitimate authority of natural science, especially physics, in our culture, it would be sufficient to demonstrate that although natural science can tell us the truth about the causal powers of nature, it does not have special access to the truth about ultimate reality. This is exactly what Martin Heidegger attempts to show.

Many interpreters, however, understand Heidegger as holding the instrumentalist view that scientific entities are social constructions essentially related to human purposes, or else a form of operationalism equating scientific entities with their intraworldly effects or measurements. Such forms of antirealism, as Arthur Fine puts it, "accept the behaviorist idea that the working practices of conceptual exchange exhaust the meaning of the exchange, giving it its significance and providing it with its content."[3] But Heidegger never concluded from the fact that our practices are necessary for *access* to theoretical entities that these entities must be *defined in terms of* our access practices. I will seek to show that in *Being and Time* Heidegger is what one might call a minimal hermeneutic realist concerning nature and the objects of natural science, and that he remained such in his later work, even when he became severely critical of the understanding of being underlying scientific research and technology.

To begin with, Heidegger is not an instrumentalist. Unlike the pragmatists, Heidegger accepts the Greek view that human beings are capable of a mood of pure wonder in which they can form theories that do not have any necessary relation to their needs and purposes. In his course on Kant, contemporaneous

---

[2] Andrew Pickering, *Constructing Quarks* (Chicago, IL: University of Chicago Press, 1984).

[3] Arthur Fine, *The Shaky Game: Einstein, Realism and the Quantum Theory* (Chicago, IL: University of Chicago Press, 1986), 140. See Joseph Rouse, *Knowledge and Power: Toward a Political Philosophy of Science* (Ithaca, NY: Cornell University Press, 1987), and Mark Okrent, *Heidegger's Pragmatism: Understanding, Being, and the Critique of Metaphysics* (Ithaca, NY: Cornell University Press, 1988). Both these authors seem to think that Heidegger holds or should hold that the entities scientists discover are defined in terms of the practices that disclose them.

with the publication of *Being and Time*, Heidegger describes scientific discipline (*Wissenschaft*) as follows:

Scientific knowing presupposes that existing Dasein[4] takes as a freely chosen task the revealing of the entity it approaches *for the sake of revealing it....* Thereby are discontinued all behavioral goals which aim at the application of the uncovered and known; and all those boundaries fall away that confine the investigation within planned technical purposes—the struggle is solely directed to the entity itself and solely in order to free it from its hiddenness and precisely thereby to help it into what is proper to it, i.e., to let it be the entity that it is in itself.[5]

Heidegger remained an anti-instrumentalist in this sense all his life. In 1954 he wrote: "Even where, as in modern atomic physics, theory—for essential reasons—necessarily becomes the opposite of direct viewing, its aim is to make atoms exhibit themselves for sensory perception, even if this self-exhibiting of elementary particles happens only very indirectly and in a way that technically involves a multiplicity of intermediaries."[6]

To understand Heidegger's position, it helps to compare it to a view recently defended by Fine. Fine starts with the observation that the scientist "believes in the existence of those entities to which his theories refer."[7] He calls this the Natural Ontological Attitude (NOA). In this attitude, he tells us, one "accepts the evidence of one's senses [with regard to the existence and features of everyday objects] and ... accepts, *in the same way*, the confirmed results of science."[8] He then adds:

NOA helps us to see that realism differs from various antirealisms in this way: realism adds an *outer* direction to NOA, that is, the external world and the correspondence relation of approximate truth; antirealisms add an *inner* direction, that is, human-oriented reductions of truth, or concepts, or explanations. NOA suggests that the legitimate features of these additions are already contained in the presumed equal status of everyday truths with scientific ones, and in our accepting them both as *truths*. No other additions are legitimate, and none are required.[9]

Heidegger, like Fine, wants to remain true to the understanding in scientific background practices—whatever scientists take for granted in their scientific activity. Let us call this view hermeneutic realism. Hermeneutic realists hold

---

[4] *Dasein* in colloquial German can mean "everyday human existence." The best way to understand what Heidegger means by *Dasein* is to think of our term "human being," which can refer to a way of being that is characteristic of all people, or to a specific person—a human being.

[5] Martin Heidegger, *Phänomenologische Interpretation von Kants Kritik der reinen Vernunft*, *Gesamtausgabe*, vol. 25 (Frankfurt: Vittorio Klostermann, 1977), 2.

[6] Martin Heidegger, "Science and Reflection," in *The Question Concerning Technology and Other Essays* (New York: Harper & Row, 1977), 173.

[7] Fine, *The Shaky Game*, 130.   [8] Fine, *The Shaky Game*, 127.

[9] Fine, *The Shaky Game*, 133.

that scientists' background realism cannot be used to *justify* the claim that the objects of science exist independently of the activity of the scientists, nor can this understanding *dictate* what methods or operating assumptions a science must accept. Rather, the role of the hermeneutic philosopher of science is (1) to spell out what everyday scientific practice takes for granted—in the case of natural science, that there is a nature independent of us and that current science is giving us a better and better explanation of how that nature works, and (2) to show that the self-understanding of the science is both internally coherent and compatible with the ontological implications of our everyday practices.

According to the hermeneutic realist, the background realism of natural science is compatible with neither metaphysical realism nor antirealism. Scientists work within social practices that neither they nor philosophers can transcend, so science cannot justify a metaphysical realism that claims to have an *argument* that there is a nature in itself, and that science is converging on the one true account of this independent reality. Yet scientists take for granted they *can* discover the truth about nature as it is independent of scientific practices, so antirealism in the form of metaphysical idealism or of instrumentalism is also unacceptable.

In *The Basic Problems of Phenomenology* Heidegger makes an ontological place for the realistic view that besides the way nature shows up in our world there is a way nature is in itself whether or not *Dasein* exists.

An example of an intraworldly entity is nature. It is indifferent in this connection how far nature is or is not scientifically uncovered, indifferent whether we think this being in a theoretical, physico-chemical way or think of it in the sense in which we speak of "nature out there," hill, woods, meadow.... Nonetheless, intraworldliness does not belong to nature's being. Rather, in commerce with this being, nature in the broadest sense, we understand that this being *is* as something occurrent[10] ... which on its own part always already is. It is, even if we do not uncover it, without our encountering it within our world. Being within the world *devolves upon* this being, nature, solely when it is *uncovered as* a being.[11]

Heidegger's hermeneutic realism concerning natural entities such as trees and dinosaurs and presumably even quarks is also evident in *Being and Time*: "Entities *are*, quite independently of the experience by which they are disclosed,

---

[10] I have modified all translations. The terms *Zuhandenheit* and *Vorhandenheit* are standardly translated as "readiness-to-hand" and "presence-at-hand." These are the ways of being of equipment in use and of objects merely contemplated, respectively. "Availableness" and "occurrentness" convey a better sense of these two ways of being. The entities that have these ways of being are called "available" and "occurrent."

[11] Martin Heidegger, *The Basic Problems of Phenomenology* (Bloomington, IN: Indiana University Press, 1982), 168–9.

the acquaintance in which they are discovered, and the grasping in which their nature is ascertained."[12] But this passage continues: "being 'is' only in the understanding of those entities to whose being something like an understanding of being belongs" (228). It seems that although natural entities are independent of us, the being of nature depends upon us. "It must be stated that the entity as an entity is 'in itself' and independent of any apprehension of it; yet, the being of the entity is found only in encounter and can be explained, made understandable, only from the phenomenal exhibition and interpretation of the structure of encounter."[13] The basic point Heidegger wants to make—that nature *is* in itself and yet it is illegitimate to ask about "being" in itself—is summed up in two paradoxical propositions: "1) Beings are in themselves the kinds of entities they are, and in the way they are, even if... Dasein does not exist. 2) Being 'is' not, but there is being, insofar as Dasein exists."[14]

Getting this point sorted out requires getting clear about how Heidegger is using his terms. Only *Dasein* makes sense of things. So the intelligibility of each kind of thing, or the understanding of the way of being of each, including natural things, depends upon *Dasein*. But nature as a being, or as an ensemble of beings, need not depend on us, for one way *Dasein* can make sense of things—find them intelligible—is as occurrent, that is, as not related to our everyday practices. As Heidegger says succinctly: "The cosmos can be without human beings inhabiting the earth, and the cosmos was long before human beings ever existed."[15]

Occurrent beings are revealed when *Dasein* takes a detached attitude toward things and decontextualizes them—in Heidegger's terms, deworlds them. Then things show up as independent of human purposes and even as independent of human existence. Deworlding takes place in two stages. First, we use skills and instruments to decontextualize things and their properties, which then appear as meaningless objects, colors, shapes, sounds, and so forth. Such data are independent of our purposes but not independent of our senses. We then invent theories in which the occurrent data are taken up as evidence for quasars and quarks and other entities we cannot directly experience. These theoretical entities need not conform at all to our everyday understanding of objects, space, time, and causality. Yet our current theory tells us that these entities

---

[12] Martin Heidegger, *Being and Time*, trans. John Macquarrie and Edward Robinson (New York: Harper & Row, 1962), 228. Page references to *Being and Time* will appear in parentheses after the quotation.
[13] Martin Heidegger, *The History of the Concept of Time* (Bloomington, IN: Indiana University Press, 1985), 217.
[14] Heidegger, *The History of the Concept of Time*, 153.
[15] Martin Heidegger, *The Metaphysical Foundations of Logic* (Bloomington, IN: Indiana University Press, 1984), 169.

belong to natural kinds—types of things in nature such as water, gold, iron, and so forth—and if correct, the theory describes the causal powers of these natural kinds. There is no way to stand outside current science and give it metaphysical support by arguing that there must be natural kinds or that these are what our science must be about. All that hermeneutic phenomenology can do is show the coherence of the natural scientist's current practices for dealing with natural kinds as the way nature is in itself.

Of course, this understanding is achieved by human beings. If it were not for *Dasein* as a clearing in which entities could be encountered, the question of whether there could be entities independent of *Dasein* could not be asked, and more important, without *Dasein*'s giving meaning to the occurrent way of being, the question would not even make sense. However, since human beings do exist and have an understanding of occurrentness as a way of being, we can make sense of the questions, What was here before we started to exist? and even, What would be left of nature if *Dasein* ceased to exist or *had never existed*? Indeed, the counterfactuals licensed by scientific laws require us to take such questions as legitimate.

Still, we must ask our questions from within that understanding of being that alone gives sense to the questions. We cannot meaningfully ask, What would have been the case if *Dasein had never existed*? if by that we mean, if the above questions made no sense? That would be to treat being—intelligibility—as if it were in itself. When Heidegger considers this move, he warns: "Of course only as long as Dasein *is* (that is, only as long as an understanding of being is ontically possible) 'is there' being. When Dasein does not exist, 'independence' 'is' not either, nor 'is' the 'in-itself'" (255). There is no intelligibility in itself. We cannot ask whether things were intelligible before we were around, or if they would go on being intelligible if we ceased to exist. Intelligibility is not a property of things; it is relative to *Dasein*. When *Dasein* does not exist, things are neither intelligible nor unintelligible. If *Dasein* does not exist, entities are not revealed as anything, not even as occurrent. "*In such a case* it cannot be said that entities are, nor can it be said that they are not. But *now,* as long as there is an understanding of being and therefore an understanding of occurrentness, it can indeed be said that *in this case* entities will still continue to be [i.e., be occurrent]" (255; my gloss in brackets). Since we do exist and make sense of entities as occurrent, we can make sense of things as being independent of us, even though this mode of intelligibility, that is, this understanding of being, like any other depends on us. In short, making sense of reality as independent is something that we do, but what there independently is does not depend on us. "The fact that reality is ontologic-ally grounded in the being of Dasein does not signify that only when Dasein exists and as long as Dasein exists can the real be as that which in itself it is" (255).

If we encountered entities only in using them, never in detachedly reflecting on them, so that *availableness* was the only way of being we knew, we would not be able to make the notion of entities in themselves intelligible. But since we understand *occurrentness*, we can understand that occurrent entities would have been even if *Dasein* had never existed. Indeed, given our understanding of occurrentness, we *must* understand things this way. An example will help us to see the importance of the contrast between the available and the occurrent here. What it is to be a hammer essentially depends upon *Dasein* and its cultural artifacts. It belongs to the being of a hammer that it is used to pound in nails for building houses, and so forth. In a culture that always tied things together, there could be no hammers, because there would be nothing that it was to be a hammer. But there could, nonetheless, be pieces of wood with iron blobs on the end, since wood and iron are natural kinds, and their being and causal powers make no essential reference to human purposes.

Joseph Rouse, in defense of what he takes to be Heidegger's social constructivism, argues convincingly that what counts as an electron and even what counts as a physical cause depends on current scientific instruments and practices. Heidegger would agree. He would of course further agree that once our practices define what counts as an X, we must still determine whether there are any Xs. Heidegger would even accept that if the Xs in question are available, like hammers, then when we find out that there are Xs, we find entities that exist only relative to our practices. He would point out, however, that if what counts as an X has occurrentness as its way of being, then when we find that there are Xs, we find at the same time that these Xs exist independently of us and of our scientific instruments and practices. This is what Heidegger means when he says, "Intraworldliness does not belong to the essence of occurrent things as such, but it is only the transcendental condition...for the possibility of occurrent things being able to emerge as they are."[16]

In the years immediately following the publication of *Being and Time* Heidegger suggests that the "evidence" that there is a nature independent of us is provided not by science but by anxiety. Joseph Fell points out that in a footnote in *The Essence of Reasons* Heidegger claims that "nature is primordially manifest in Dasein because Dasein exists as attuned and affected in the midst of beings," and, in *What is Metaphysics*, he adds that anxiety "discloses beings in their full but heretofore concealed strangeness as the pure other."[17]

---

[16] Heidegger, *Basic Problems of Phenomenology*, 194.

[17] See Martin Heidegger, *The Essence of Reasons* (Evanston, IL: Northwestern University Press, 1969), 83, and "What Is Metaphysics?" in *Basic Writings* (New York: Harper & Row, 1977), 105,

Such pronouncements must have been taken to be reminiscent of Fichte, according to whom the ego *posits* nature as its pure other, for in his book on Schelling, Heidegger feels called upon to repudiate the idea that pure otherness is a meaning given by human beings.

> *Being & Time* has also among other things been equated with Fichte's basic position and interpreted by it, whereas if there is any possibility of comparison at all here, the most extreme opposition is dominant. But "opposition" is already false since the thinking in *Being & Time* is not just "realistic" in contrast to the unconditional "egoistic" idealism of Fichte.... According to Fichte the ego throws forth the world... according to *Being & Time*... *Dasein* is the thrown.[18]

Dasein is presumably thrown into nature, and the nature *Dasein* is thrown into need not be thought of as an unstructured, viscous being-in-itself, as in Sartre. Anxiety reveals nature as pure otherness, but this does not imply that nature has no ontic structure.

Still, there is a further problem that makes Heidegger seem to be, if not a Fichtian, at least a Kantian, idealist. Since time, understood as a sequence of nows, before and after some present now, depends upon *Dasein*'s temporality, it might seem to follow that nature cannot be in time. Heidegger seems to assert as much when he says, "There is no nature-time, since all time belongs essentially to Dasein."[19] And he repeats this claim as late as 1935: "Strictly speaking we cannot say: There was a time when man *was* not. At all *times* man was and is and will be, because time temporalizes itself only insofar as man is."[20] This, however, still leaves open the possibility that, just as in the case of spatiality, "the homogeneous space of nature shows itself only when the entities we encounter are discovered in such a way that the worldly character of the available gets specifically deprived of its worldliness" (147), so when temporality is detemporalized, a pure sequence of natural events would remain. In his discussion of space Heidegger adds: "The fact that space essentially shows itself in a world is not yet decisive for the kind of being that it possesses. It need not have the kind of being characteristic of something that is itself spatially available or occurrent" (147). Likewise, natural time need not even be occurrent; still, some sort of pure sequential ordering of events might well remain. This would allow us to make sense of what Heidegger

quoted by Joseph Fell in "The Familiar and the Strange: On the Limits of Praxis in the Early Heidegger," in *Heidegger: A Critical Reader*, ed. H. Dreyfus and H. Hall (Cambridge, MA: Basil Blackwell, 1991).

[18] Martin Heidegger, *Schelling's Treatise on the Essence of Human Freedom* (Athens, OH: Ohio University Press, 1985), 187–8.

[19] Heidegger, *Basic Problems of Phenomenology*, 262.

[20] Martin Heidegger, *Introduction to Metaphysics* (New York: Doubleday, 1961), 71.

calls the cosmos and of a nature in itself revealed by science. Perhaps these unresolved tensions were troubling Heidegger when, in a 1929 lecture, he admitted: "The question of the extent to which one might conceive the interpretation of Dasein as temporality in a universal-ontological way is a question which I myself am not able to decide—one which is still completely unclear to me."[21]

Whatever Heidegger's answer, it must not contradict his claim that natural entities do not depend for their structure upon the world or upon human temporality. As Heidegger says in *Basic Problems*: "Occurrent things are...the kinds of things they are, even if they do not become intraworldly, even if world-entry does not happen to them and there is no occasion for it at all."[22] After all, we do know substantive facts about nature. We know not only that dinosaurs existed, but that they were born, grew up, and died. That is why Heidegger calls nature "the cosmos" and not X or the thing in itself.

If it allows a sequence of natural events, Heidegger's account is compatible with holding that science is converging on getting it right about such natural kinds as gold and water and their causal powers.[23] But even though Heidegger presumably thinks that physical science is progressing in its understanding of physical nature, he does not think that this progress shows that the scientific approach to reality is the only right one, or even that physical science has the right approach to nature. In his lectures of 1928 he remarks: "Beings have stages of discoverability, diverse possibilities in which they manifest themselves in themselves.... One cannot say that, for example, physics has the genuine knowledge of the solar sphere, in contrast to our natural grasp of the sun."[24]

Thus even though Heidegger is a realist with respect to the entities discovered by natural science, he is not a physicalist, reductionist, or materialist. He argues at length in Sections 19, 20, and 21 of *Being and Time* that worldliness, and *Dasein*'s correlative ability to make ways of being intelligible and thus to disclose beings, cannot be understood in terms of the occurrent, and that therefore the occurrent, even recontextualized in a successful science of nature, cannot provide the fundamental building blocks of reality. A theory of the causal power of natural kinds tells us only what is *causally* real; it cannot account for *Dasein*'s ability to make intelligible various ways of being, thereby disclosing various beings,

---

[21] Heidegger, *The Metaphysical Foundations of Logic*, 210.

[22] Heidegger, *Basic Problems of Phenomenology*, 194.

[23] If these kinds of things turn out not to have the properties predicted and the natural kind terms referring to them have to be dropped from the lexicon of science, as phlogiston was, then some other system of natural kind terms might, in principle, still be found that do refer to the natural kinds there really are—although, of course, we would never know for certain we had the final account.

[24] Heidegger, *The Metaphysical Foundations of Logic*, 167.

including the entities described by physical science. Thus science cannot be a theory of *ultimate* reality. This is Heidegger's reason for rejecting all forms of *metaphysical* realism. "Realism tries to explain reality ontically by real connections of interaction between things that are real.... [But] being can never be explained by entities but is already that which is 'transcendental' for every entity" (251). Thus he can say:

If we consider the work of Descartes in relation to the constitution of the mathematical sciences of nature and to the elaboration of mathematical physics in particular, these considerations then naturally assume a fundamentally positive significance. But if they are regarded in the context of a general theory of the reality of the world, it then becomes apparent that from this point on the fateful constriction of the inquiry into reality sets in, which to the present day has not yet been overcome.[25]

Heidegger further holds that modern science is not even the only way of revealing nature. If, like Aristotle, one wants to relate a wide variety of phenomena rather than to predict and control them, one may find final causes rather than the sort of causal powers discovered by modern physics. Thus there may be only one right answer to the search for physical causes, but many different projections can reveal nature as it is in itself.

What is represented by physics is indeed nature itself, but undeniably it is only nature as the object-area, whose objectness is first defined and determined through the refining that is characteristic of physics and is expressly set forth in that refining. Nature, in its objectness for modern physical science, is only *one* way in which what presences— which from of old has been named *physis*—reveals itself.[26]

Heidegger would thus deny that modern physics has found *the* right vocabulary for describing nature so that its vocabulary could be used for a foundational ontology. This, I presume, is the meaning of his Kuhn-like remark in 1938:

[We cannot] say that the Galilean doctrine of freely falling bodies is true and that Aristotle's teaching, that light bodies strive upward, is false; for the Greek understanding of the essence of body and place and of the relation between the two rests upon a different

---

[25] Heidegger, *The History of the Concept of Time*, 184–5. Alexander Nehamas finds what I take to be Heidegger's view of science already in Nietzsche. "[Nietzsche] does not object to science itself...but rather to an interpretation which refuses to acknowledge that science itself is an interpretation in the sense that it provides a revisable description of a part of the world which is no more [ultimately] real than any other. The problem has been that the methods of science have been assumed to be better than any others, and its objects have been considered to be more real or ultimate than anything else. Nietzsche attacks only this privileging of the methods and objects of science and not its methods or objects themselves." Alexander Nehamas, *Nietzsche: Life as Literature* (Cambridge, MA: Harvard University Press, 1985), 65.
[26] Heidegger, "Science and Reflection," 173–4.

interpretation of entities and hence conditions a correspondingly different kind of seeing and questioning of natural events. No one would presume to maintain that Shakespeare's poetry is more advanced than that of Aeschylus. It is still more impossible to say that the modern understanding of whatever is, is more correct than that of the Greeks.[27]

Here Heidegger is obviously trying to counter the claim that Galileo has refuted Aristotle. He is doing so, not as Kuhn does, by holding that neither theory is true of nature, but rather by holding that *both* are true. This could be the innocuous observation that both are "illuminating," but in the context of the remark just quoted that "what is represented by physics is indeed nature itself," it must be the stronger claim that different theories can reveal different aspects of nature. Of course, if one thinks of Aristotle's theory of natural place as an account of *physical* causality meant to explain, for example, why rocks fall, in the same sense that modern physics claims to explain the same phenomenon, this position is untenable. As an account of physical causality, modern physics, as far as we know, is right and Aristotle is simply wrong. Heidegger, however, clearly holds that Aristotle and Galileo were asking *different kinds of questions*, and so the answer each gives could be right about a different aspect of nature.

If one is interested neither in physical causality nor in final causes but prefers to recontextualize the occurrent in a theory about the cosmic mind, that might be true, too. It would not give one control of nature nor a way of finding one's interests reflected in the cosmos, but it might give one an insight into enlightenment. Likewise, if one does not want to base one's account of ultimate reality on our ability to decontextualize, but, like the Navajo, one is able to see the everyday world as sacred or full of gods (as long as these are not thought of as having physical powers), that might well allow sacred beings to show up.[28] Physics does not show Buddhism or the Navajo to be wrong, nor does it contradict Christianity. It can have no view on the ultimate meaning of reality. The ultimate *physical* power might well reside in quarks, but the ultimate *saving* power, for example, might be the Christ. The physical properties of iron are essential for making effective hammers but are irrelevant when it comes to making powerful crucifixes.

---

[27] Martin Heidegger, "The Age of the World Picture," in *The Question Concerning Technology and Other Essays*, p. 117.

[28] The way of being of the sacred is neither the way of being of equipment defined by its place in an equipmental whole, nor is it the way of being of the occurrent defined by its nonrelation to cultural practices. Heidegger notes in *Being and Time* that "perhaps even availableness and equipment have nothing to contribute as ontological clues in interpreting the primitive world; and certainly the ontology of thinghood does even less" (113). Later, Heidegger develops this idea in his account of the ways of being of the sacred, of things, and of works of art. See, e.g., "The Origin of the Work of Art," in *Poetry, Language, Thought* (New York: Harper & Row, 1971).

What counts as real for a culture depends upon the interpretation in its practices, but this does not make what is thus understood any less real. Where ultimate reality is concerned, later Heidegger could be called a *plural realist.* For a plural realist there is no point of view from which one can ask and answer the metaphysical question concerning the one true nature of ultimate reality. Given the dependence of the intelligibility of all ways of being on *Dasein*'s being the question makes no sense. But does this not lead us back to antirealism? No. A plural realist looks like an idealist or a relativist only if one thinks that only one system of description could correspond to the way things really are. For Heidegger, however, as we have seen, different understandings of being reveal different realities or domains of intelligibility, and since no one way of revealing is exclusively true, accepting one does not commit us to rejecting the others. There is a deep similarity between Heidegger and Donald Davidson on this point. Both would agree that if we are right in our claims about reality under various descriptions, then what we are right about has whatever properties it has even if these descriptions are not reducible to a single description, and both would further agree that physical reality has whatever properties it has whether we describers and our ways of describing things exist or not.[29]

Just as different cultural practices free different aspects of nature, so they free different sorts of cultural entities. Such historical entities have their own ontological status. Their way of being is not the de-worlded being of the occurrent.

There are entities...to whose being intraworldliness belongs in a certain way. Such entities are all those we call *historical* entities...all the things that the human being, who is historical and exists historically in the strict and proper sense, creates, shapes, cultivates: all his culture and works. Beings of this kind *are* only or, more exactly, arise only and come into being only as intraworldly. Culture *is* not in the way that nature is.[30]

Of course, not just any cultural interpretation will disclose entities. If, instead of encountering heroes or saints, a culture begins to develop practices for encountering aliens that are round and give out beams of light, it may well be that nothing will show up at all. But there are no clear limits as to what kinds of cultural entities can be encountered. In physical science, however, there seems to be one right answer as far as physical causality is concerned. Radically different theories than those proposed by modern science presumably would not reveal physical causal powers. Heidegger notes this difference between a cultural and a scientific interpretation: "The spiritual...offers less resistance than in the field of

---

[29] See Donald Davidson, "Mental Events," in *Essays on Actions and Events* (New York: Oxford University Press, 1980).

[30] Heidegger, *Basic Problems of Phenomenology*, 169.

natural science, where nature immediately takes its revenge on a wrongheaded approach."[31] This sentence suggests how Heidegger would respond to such scientific relativists as Richard Rorty who scoff at the idea of science's learning nature's own language. Granted that we can never completely decontextualize our data and that therefore our scientific theories are always to some extent parasitical upon our cultural practices and language, still, once we discover that we have practices that can reveal meaningless occurrent data divorced from reference to our purposes, we can use recontextualization in theories to distance our scientific theories further and further from the everyday world. Our Newtonian theories seemed to reveal a universe similar to our everyday experience of occurrent space and time, but our interaction with nature has led us to replace these theories with relativistic and quantum indeterministic theories. It is as if nature *is* teaching the natural scientist, not *nature's own language*, since only a Platonist thinks that representations exist independently of meaningful practices, but, rather, nature is leading natural scientists to improve *their* language for representing her under an objectified aspect.

In any case, as we have noted, once we have established what counts as real, we must still find out what specific things there are. The Greeks stood in awe of the gods that their practices revealed, and we have to *discover* the elementary particles—we do not construct them. The understanding of being establishes what can count as a fact in whatever domain, but it does not determine what the facts are. As Heidegger says: "Being (not beings) is dependent upon the understanding of being; that is to say, reality (not the real) is dependent upon care [i.e., *Dasein*]" (255).

Heidegger thus holds a subtle and plausible position beyond metaphysical realism and antirealism. *Nature* is whatever it is and has whatever causal properties it has independently of us. Different questions, such as Aristotle's and Galileo's, reveal different natural kinds and different kinds of causal properties. Different cultural interpretations of reality reveal different aspects of the real, too. But there is no right answer to the question, What is the ultimate reality in terms of which everything else becomes intelligible? The only answer to this metaphysical question is that *Dasein*, because it is the source of sense and so of the understanding of being and of reality, is the being in terms of whose practices all aspects of the real show up.

Heidegger's emphasis on scientific practices is remarkably similar to Kuhn's in *The Structure of Scientific Revolutions*, but they draw opposed conclusions from their shared insights. For Kuhn, once one sees that the background practices

---

[31] Heidegger, *The History of the Concept of Time*, 203.

determine what counts as true, it looks as if truth must be relative to current scientific practices, so there can be no truth about how things are in themselves. Kuhn argues persuasively in his Sherman lectures[32] that a given scientific lexicon of natural kind terms determines what can count as true, so that for Aristotle, for example, it was true that the sun was a planet and that there could not be a void, whereas for us, Aristotle's assertions are neither true nor false because "planet" and "void" have different meanings in the lexicon of modern science. Kuhn concludes that in general the assertions picking out the sort of things taken to exist at each stage of a science can be true at that stage, but are neither true nor false at some other stage in some other system of terms. Thus assertions are never true of things as they are in themselves.

Heidegger would, I think, agree with Kuhn's elegant argument that true statements in science can be made only relative to a lexicon. But the strong relativistic claim that no lexicon can be true of physical reality does not follow from the fact of incommensurate lexicons. Nor does relativism follow from Heidegger's acknowledgment that our practices are a more primordial form of truth that makes truth as agreement possible. On the contrary, it follows from Heidegger's account that several incompatible lexicons can be true, that is to say, agree with how things are in themselves. In each case there is something the theory claims to be true of, and in each case the theory either points out its referent as it is in itself or it is false. As Heidegger notes, once we see that Newton's laws are true, we see that they were true at the time of Aristotle. Conversely, if Aristotle's terms successfully picked out natural kinds (relative to final causes), his account is still true today.

Why doesn't Kuhn share this conclusion? Perhaps because he implicitly accepts the traditional view that in principle only one lexicon can point out the kinds in nature, and, since he has discovered that relative to different lexicons incompatible theoretical assertions count as true, he concludes that none can correspond to how things are in themselves. For Heidegger, on the contrary, as finite beings capable of discovering truth, we work out many perspectives—many lexicons—and thus reveal many ways things are in themselves. And just because we can reveal things from many perspectives, no single perspective can be *the* right one.

We can conclude by comparing Heidegger and Rorty once again, since their views on metaphysical realism are strikingly similar. Both argue that the real can show up differently given different practices (vocabularies, Rorty would say), and neither wants to allow that there is a way that ultimate reality is in itself so that

---

[32] Thomas Kuhn, "Sherman Memorial Lectures," University College, London, November 23–5, 1987, unpublished.

there is a privileged description that founds all the others. Anyone who claims to have a description of ultimate reality claims a point of view outside of all particular, finite interpretations, and both Heidegger and Rorty think, given their understanding of understanding, that the very idea of such an interpretation-free understanding of what ultimately is does not make sense. But Rorty thinks that this is an argument against accepting even a minimal hermeneutic realism where natural science is concerned, whereas Heidegger shows how one can reject the claim that there is a correct description of reality and still hold that there can be many correct descriptions, including a correct causal description of objectified physical nature. Natural science can be getting it righter and righter about how things *work* even if there is no one right answer to how things *are*.

6

How Heidegger Defends the Possibility of a Correspondence Theory of Truth with Respect to the Entities of Natural Science (2001)

Science has long claimed to discover the relations among the natural kinds in the universe that exist independently of our minds and ways of coping.[1] Today, most philosophers adopt an antirealism that consists in rejecting this thesis. Contemporary antirealists argue that the independence thesis is not just false but *incoherent*. Thus, these antirealists say they are as realist as it makes sense to be. Such *deflationary realists*, as I shall call them, claim that the objects studied by science are just as real as the baseballs, stones, and trees we encounter with our everyday coping practices, and no more.[2] In contrast to deflationary realism, I shall defend a *robust realism* that argues that the independence claim makes sense, that science can in principle give us access to the functional components of

---

[1] I would like to thank the following people who helped me work out my position, in many cases by arguing against it and writing detailed criticisms: William Blattner, Taylor Carman, David Cerbone, Donald Davidson, Dagfinn Føllesdal, Sean Kelly, Lisa Lloyd, Jeff Malpas, Stephen Neale, Joe Rouse, Ted Schatzki, Mark Wrathall, and especially Charles Spinosa.

[2] Crucial essays for the deflationary realist position are: Donald Davidson, "Three Varieties of Knowledge," in A. P. Griffiths, ed., *A. J. Ayer: Memorial Essays*, Royal Institute of Philosophy, Supplement 30 (Cambridge: Cambridge University Press, 1991), 153–66, and "On the Very Idea of a Conceptual Scheme," in *Inquiries into Truth and Interpretation* (Oxford: Clarendon Press, 1984), 183–98. For an independently developed account of deflationary realism, see Arthur Fine's description of what he calls the Natural Ontological Attitude in *The Shaky Game: Einstein, Realism and the Quantum Theory* (Chicago, IL: University of Chicago Press, 1986). Jeff Malpas and Joseph Rouse have generalized Davidson's arguments concerning the relation of *beliefs* to things to cover the relation of *all coping practices* to things. Malpas and Rouse have also tried to show, contrary to my view, that Martin Heidegger is a deflationary realist. See Jeff Malpas, *Donald Davidson and the Mirror of Meaning* (Cambridge: Cambridge University Press, 1992) and Joseph Rouse, *Knowledge and Power: Toward a Political Philosophy of Science* (Ithaca, NY: Cornell University Press, 1987) and *Engaging Science: How to Understand its Practices Philosophically* (Ithaca, NY: Cornell University Press, 1996).

the universe as they are in themselves[3] in distinction from how they appear to us on the basis of our daily concerns, our sensory capacities, and even our way of making things intelligible.[4]

The deflationary and the robust realist positions are each part of the heritage that Heidegger has left us. Consequently, I shall, in my first section, present the deflationary realist's arguments against independence. Then, in the second section, I shall show that, although Heidegger pioneered the deflationary realist account of the everyday, he sought to establish a robust realist account of science. In the third and final section, I shall draw on Saul Kripke's account of direct reference to work out Heidegger's account of formal indication, and using this worked-out version of Heideggerian rigid designation, I will argue that we do, indeed, have practices for achieving access to things that are independent of all our practices.

The Argument for Deflationary Realism

The argument for deflationary realism turns on the rejection of the traditional Cartesian view of human beings as self-sufficient minds whose intentional content is directed toward the world. Both Heidegger and Donald Davidson, a leading antirealist, reject this view and substitute for it an account of human beings as inextricably involved with things and people. Heidegger holds that human beings have to take a stand on who they are by dealing with things and by assuming social roles. Davidson thinks of human beings as language users who, in order to have any mental content of their own, must take up the linguistic conventions of their community. I call Heidegger and Davidson practical holists because they both claim that meaning depends ultimately on the inseparability of practices, things, and mental contents. Heidegger captures this idea in his claim

---

[3] When I speak of "things in themselves," I am not referring to Kant's notion of things independent of any conceptual scheme and hence unknowable, but rather to the knowable functional components of the universe. Some have thought that a belief in natural kinds requires that the "lines" in the universe between one kind and another must be sharp. I, however, assume that one needs only to be able to distinguish sharply between paradigm cases of kinds in order to describe the universe as divided into natural kinds.

[4] The question—whether the idea of an essential structure of the universe independent of our practices for investigating it makes sense—can be taken up without regard to other important discussions of the natural sciences. I, therefore, do not take a stand on: (1) whether unobservable entities are real (the question of instrumentalism), (2) whether events in the universe are lawful throughout or exhibit a degree of randomness (the question of determinism), and (3) whether there are good arguments for metaphysical realism based solely on conceptual analysis. See, for instance, John Searle, *The Construction of Social Reality* (New York: Free Press, 1995), 149–97, where he argues for the conceptual necessity of brute facts that are discovered, not constituted.

that human beings are essentially being-in-the-world; Davidson makes the same point in his causal theory of meaning.

Both thinkers claim that their holism enables them to answer the Cartesian skeptic. Heidegger argues that, if human beings are essentially being-in-the-world, then the skeptical question of whether the world and others exist cannot sensibly be raised by human beings, and, as Heidegger asks, "Who else would raise it?"[5] Heidegger thus claims that any attempt to *answer* the skeptic is mistaken. The attempt to take the skeptic seriously and prove that we can know that there is an external world presupposes a separation of the mind from the world of things and other people which defies a phenomenological description of how human beings make sense of everyday things and of themselves. Davidson argues, on the basis of a logical reconstruction of the way people learn a language that, although people may differ concerning the truth of any particular belief, in order for a person to acquire a language at all that person must share most of the beliefs of those who speak the language and most of these shared beliefs must be true.

It follows that we cannot make sense of the question whether the *totality* of things could be independent of the *totality* of our practices or whether things are *essentially dependent* on our practices. To raise these questions meaningfully requires thinking that we can conceive of the totality of things and of the totality of practices with sufficient independence from each other to claim that one is logically prior. But it turns out that we can get no perspective on our practices that does not already include things and no perspective on things that does not already involve our practices. Thus, practical holism seems to make unintelligible all claims about both things in themselves apart from our practices and the totality of practices apart from things. It seems that, since true statements about objects cannot imply *either* the dependence *or* the independence of objects vis-à-vis our practices, these statements must be understood as describing objects as they are in the only sense of "are" that is left, which is the "are" of ordinary situations. Thus we arrive at a deflationary view that repudiates both metaphysical realism and transcendental idealism.

Once the deflationary realist has argued that one cannot make sense of transcendental idealism or of metaphysical realism, he is able to accept the results of science at face value so long as he makes neither the robust realist's claim that science gives us an account of the functional demarcations of the universe as it is in itself, on the one hand, nor the extreme constructivist's claim that nature must

---

[5] Martin Heidegger, *Being and Time*, trans. John Macquarrie and Edward Robinson (New York: Harper & Row, 1962), 246–7.

be a cultural creation, on the other. When asked whether it makes sense to claim that things existed in nature before human beings came along and that they would have existed even if human beings had never existed, the deflationary realist can sound like a scientist, saying, on the basis of empirical findings, that of course it makes sense to claim that some types of entities were there before us and would still be there if we had never existed and others would not. But the Davidsonian practical holist says this on a background of meaning that makes any talk about nature as it is in itself incoherent.

Heidegger's Attempt at Robust Realism

Like Davidson, Heidegger answers the skeptic by showing that our practices and the everyday world are inextricably intertwined. Indeed, he argues at length that "Dasein is the world existingly."[6] Moreover, Heidegger seems to agree with the deflationary realists that, while entities show up as independent of us, the being or intelligibility of entities depends on our practices. So any talk of things in themselves must be put in scare quotes. Thus, Heidegger says of natural entities:

It must be stated that entities as entities are "in themselves" and independent of any apprehension of them; yet, the being of entities is found only in encounter and can be explained, made understandable, only from the phenomenal exhibition and interpretation of the structure of encounter.[7]

And he seems even more deflationary when he adds:

Of course only as long as Dasein [human being] is (that is, only as long as an understanding of being is ontically possible), "is there" being. When Dasein does not exist, "independence" "is" not either, nor "is" the "in-itself."[8]

Joseph Rouse, in his book *Knowledge and Power* (1987), sees the parallel between Heidegger's and Davidson's holistic answer to the skeptic and wonders why I fail to see that Heidegger must therefore be a deflationary realist. But, as I will now

---

[6] Heidegger, *Being and Time*, 416. When Heidegger speaks of everyday practices or everydayness, he generally means instrumental coping practices or these practices and what we encounter through them. When I speak of everyday practices, I refer more broadly to our familiar ways of encountering things in general, including therefore our familiar perceptual way. The only practices that I deal with in this paper as *non-everyday* are encounters with what I call the strange and scientific practices. More broadly, for me institutional practices, including scientific, religious, and certain aesthetic practices whose intelligibility is founded on non-everyday experiences, count as non-everyday practices. When, however, I explicitly describe Heidegger's views, I shall use the term "everyday" as he uses it.

[7] Martin Heidegger, *The History of the Concept of Time* (Bloomington, IN: Indiana University Press, 1985), 217.

[8] Heidegger, *Being and Time*, 255.

seek to show, in *Being and Time* Heidegger describes phenomena that enable him to distinguish between the everyday world and the universe and so claim to be a robust realist about the entities discovered by natural science. Moreover, he has the conceptual resources to turn his description of these phenomena into a persuasive defense of robust realism.

The first two phenomena Heidegger calls to our attention are two different ways of being. He points out that normally we deal with things as equipment. Equipment gets its intelligibility from its relation to other equipment, human roles, and social goals. Heidegger calls the equipmental way of being *availability* (*Zuhandenheit*). But Heidegger also points to another equally important phenomenon: we sometimes experience entities as independent of our instrumental coping practices. This happens in cases of equipmental breakdown. Heidegger calls the mode of being of entities so encountered *occurrentness* (*Vorhandenheit*). Occurrent beings are not only revealed in breakdown but also revealed when we take a detached attitude toward things that decontextualizes or—in Heidegger's terms—deworlds them. In this detached attitude, we encounter occurrent entities as substances with properties.

This experience of the occurrent is still contextual and meaningful in a weak sense. Were it not for a world in which entities could be encountered, the question of whether there could be entities independent of our concerns could not be asked, and, more importantly, without our giving meaning to the occurrent way of being, the question of independence would not make sense. So Heidegger concludes that the being or intelligibility of even the occurrent mode of being depends on us: "[B]eing 'is' only in the understanding of those entities to whose being something like an understanding of being belongs."[9] But he still insists that "entities *are* independently of the experience by which they are disclosed, the acquaintance in which they are discovered, and the grasping in which their nature is ascertained."[10]

This amounts to the seemingly paradoxical claim that we *have practices for making sense of entities as independent of those very practices.* This intellectual Gestalt figure can flip one of two ways depending upon whether one emphasizes the *dependence* on the practices or the *independence* from those very practices. It has thus led to a three-way debate in the scholarly literature over whether Heidegger is a robust realist, a transcendental idealist, or a deflationary realist.[11]

---

[9] Heidegger, *Being and Time*, 228, with a minor translation correction.

[10] Heidegger, *Being and Time*, 228, with a minor translation correction.

[11] Heidegger himself seems to be conflicted on the subject. Eight years after his seemingly realist stand in *Being and Time*, he writes in *Introduction to Metaphysics*: "Strictly speaking we cannot say: There was a time when man *was* not. At all *times* man was and is and will be, in so far as time

I have argued, using the above quotation from *Being and Time* to back me up, that Heidegger is a would-be robust realist.[12] William Blattner has countered that Heidegger must be understood as a transcendental idealist and that, consequently, all the citations that seem to support robust realism should be read as supporting merely empirical realism.[13] David Cerbone has responded to Blattner with a reading in the spirit of Davidson in which Heidegger's account of the inextricable involvement of human beings and the world commits him to the view that neither robust realism nor transcendental idealism is intelligible.[14]

In order to see more clearly why I claim that Heidegger is a would-be robust realist, we must return to the phenomenon of deworlding. As I said, Heidegger points out that in situations of extreme instrumental breakdown, we encounter things as occurrent, as independent of the instrumental world—that is, as having no *essential* relation to our everyday coping practices—and as all along underlying our everyday equipment. "[W]hat cannot be used just lies there; it shows itself as an equipmental thing which looks so and so, and which, in its availableness, as looking that way, *has constantly been occurrent too.*"[15]

Nature is thus revealed as *having been there all along.* In such cases, Heidegger holds, "*The understanding of being* by which our concernful dealings with entities within-the-world have been guided *has changed over.*"[16] Our practices for coping with the available are significantly different from our practices for dealing with the occurrent. Thus, Heidegger understands this changeover from dealing

temporalizes itself only insofar as man is" (Martin Heidegger, *Introduction to Metaphysics* (New Haven, CT: Yale University Press, 1959), 71). This claim follows from the argument, already in *Being and Time*, that without Dasein there would be no before and after. But Heidegger also says in a lecture given in 1928 and published in 1978: "The question of the extent to which one might conceive the interpretation of Dasein as temporality in a universal-ontological way is a question which I am myself not able to decide—one which is still completely unclear to me" (Martin Heidegger, *The Metaphysical Foundations of Logic* (Bloomington, IN: Indiana University Press, 1984), 210). I think Heidegger should have realized that the occurrent time of nature escapes idealism since it can be understood not in terms of our everyday sense of a before and after but only as an asymmetrical ordering of states.

[12]   Hubert Dreyfus, *Being-in-the-World: A Commentary on Heidegger's Being and Time, Division I* (Cambridge, MA: MIT Press, 1991).

[13]   William D. Blattner, "Is Heidegger a Kantian Idealist?" *Inquiry* 37 (1994), 185–201.

[14]   David R. Cerbone, "World, World-Entry, and Realism in Early Heidegger," *Inquiry* 38 (1995), 401–21.

[15]   Heidegger, *Being and Time*, 102–3, my italics. In his later marginal notes, Heidegger adds that this revealing of the occurrent does not require either actual breakdown or an active disregard of the use aspects of equipment but can also be arrived at by training oneself to focus on properties of entities in a way that is not directly related to our coping activity. See Martin Heidegger, *Being and Time*, trans. Joan Stambaugh (Albany, NY: State University of New York Press, 1996), 57, note.

[16]   Heidegger, *Being and Time*, 412, Heidegger's emphasis. Rouse rightly thinks that "Heidegger is disturbingly vague about the changeover which is said to occur," Rouse, *Knowledge and Power*, 74–5.

with things as available to dealing with them as occurrent as discontinuous. This changeover is crucial for Heidegger's answer to deflationary realism.

The radicality of this discontinuity is often hidden by inadequate phenomenological descriptions of breakdowns. When a hammer is so heavy that the carpenter cannot use it, it is then experienced as too heavy. But since being-too-heavy is context-dependent, it still presupposes the equipmental nature of hammers. But breakdown can be so severe that all that is left in experience is a mere something—"just occurrent and no more"[17]—whose properties are not connected to its function in any intelligible way and are thus beyond everyday understanding. Heidegger claims that, among other experiences, anxiety gives us access to this unintelligible occurrent. "Anxiety," he writes, "discloses...beings in their full but heretofore concealed strangeness as what is radically other."[18]

Of course, the uninterpreted beings experienced as radically other are not theoretical entities. Heidegger knows that for us to have access to theoretical entities the beings revealed in total breakdown must be recontextualized or reinterpreted in theoretical terms. Heidegger is thus clear that the data used by science are theory-laden. He says, "The 'grounding' of 'factical science' was possible only because the researchers understood that in principle there are no 'bare facts.'"[19] He is, unfortunately, not clear how these theory-laden data are supposed to be related to the radically other that is revealed in extreme breakdown; that is, he is not clear about how theoretical recontextualization is supposed to work.[20] The important thing for him is that theoretical entities are taken to be elements of nature, that is, of a universe that is anterior to and independent of our everyday mode of making sense of things. In this important sense, science is, according to Heidegger, about the *incomprehensible*. He writes:

Nature is what is in principle explainable and to be explained because it is in principle incomprehensible. It is *the incomprehensible pure and simple.* And it is the incomprehensible because it is the *"unworlded"* world [i.e. the universe], insofar as we take nature in this extreme sense of the entity as it is discovered in physics.[21]

---

[17] Heidegger, *Being and Time*, 103.

[18] Martin Heidegger, "What Is Metaphysics?" in *Basic Writings*, trans. David Farrell Krell (New York: Harper, 1977), 105. Joseph P. Fell develops this point in his "The Familiar and the Strange: On the Limits of Praxis in the Early Heidegger," in *Heidegger: A Critical Reader*, ed. Hubert Dreyfus and Harrison Hall (Cambridge, MA: Basil Blackwell, 1991), 65–80.

[19] Heidegger, *Being and Time*, 414.

[20] Rouse is again right in demanding Heidegger be more specific on this point. One could ask, for example, by what skills do the scientists interpret their data and, if skills are required, how does the scientist have the right to claim that the theoretical objects confirmed by their data are independent of all human activity?

[21] Heidegger, *The History of the Concept of Time*, 217–18.

The point is *not* that the phenomenon of total breakdown, theoretical inspection, or anxiety gives us *sufficient grounds* for believing in the independent existence of natural things none of whose properties we understand. Although the quotation may suggest this, we shall see that the phenomenon of total breakdown cannot supply such grounds. What the phenomenon of total breakdown supports is the more minimal claim that nature can be experienced as independent of our coping practices and as underlying everyday things. If we had only the "available" mode of encountering entities, we could never encounter entities more independent of our coping practices than particular hammers are. But, if Heidegger is right, we can deworld such entities and be led to see them as occurrent components of the universe.[22]

Heidegger clearly wants to embrace robust realism, for he exceeds the limits of deflationary realism when he writes: "[T]he fact that reality is ontologically grounded in the being of Daseindoes not signify that only when Dasein exists, and as long as Dasein exists, can the real be as that which *in itself* it is."[23]

We are now in a position to see that, in defending a robust realism concerning scientific entities, Heidegger makes two significant moves, which, although they seem to be the right way to proceed, do not, as Heidegger presents them, fully succeed in supporting robust realism.

1 Heidegger points to two special attitudes (confronting equipmental break-down and anxiety) that, on the face of it, break out of our everyday, equipment-using practices. Since Heidegger bases his account of meaning on equipment-using practices, he concludes that such special attitudes, by "deworlding" entities, break out of our everyday meanings altogether and give us access to the "incomprehensible" as it is in itself. But, if one has a broader conception of everyday meaning that includes perceiving things outside of use-relations, such a "switchover" would not get one outside the everyday.[24]

---

[22] Though Heidegger is a realist with respect to natural entities, he is not a reductionist, or a naturalist. He argues at length in Sections 19, 20, and 21 of *Being and Time* that our practical ability to disclose ways of being, and thus to discover beings, cannot be understood in terms of the occurrent, and that therefore the occurrent, even recontextualized in a successful science of nature, could not provide the fundamental building blocks of reality. Natural science can tell us only what is *causally* real, it cannot account for our ability to make intelligible various ways of being, thereby disclosing various domains of being or realities, one of which includes the entities described by physical science. Thus science cannot be a theory of *ultimate* reality. This is Heidegger's reason for rejecting *reductive* realism. He says: "Realism tries to explain reality ontically by real connections of interaction between things that are real...[But] being can never be explained by entities but is already that which 'transcendental' for every entity" (*Being and Time*, 251).

[23] Heidegger, *Being and Time*, 255 (my italics).

[24] Thus, Rouse can reasonably object that: "It is not that such things, which Heidegger calls 'present-at-hand' [occurrent], exist independent of the behavioral responses of persons within a

2 Heidegger contends that the switchover he describes gives us beings that can be recontextualized in a theory that makes no reference to our everyday practices. But he has no account of how the meaningless beings revealed by breakdown can serve as data for science nor what sort of practices could be left after the switchover that would allow dealing with the incomprehensible while leaving it independent of all our practices. That is, in showing we can encounter things shorn of their everyday *functionality*, Heidegger has not shown that we can encounter them as independent of *all* our practices for making things intelligible. There are still the very peculiar practices of making them intelligible as unintelligible.

In addition, when Heidegger later investigates how scientific research as an institution works, he claims that research is based on what he calls the projection of a total ground plan.[25] Research, he claims, is a modern way of studying nature that proceeds by setting up a *total* theory of how nature works and then dealing with the anomalies that show up when the theory is assumed to cover all phenomena. Thus, normal science has, for Heidegger, the ongoing job of trying to account for anomalies, while revolutionary advances in science occur when resistant anomalies lead scientists to propose a new ground plan.[26]

What is essential for modern science as research, then, is its totalizing claim. Heidegger argues that this totalizing claim is the modern version of the series of totalizing claims about the beingness of beings that have characterized our metaphysical culture perhaps since Anaximander, certainly since Plato. Thus a pervasive cultural practice of just the sort that the deworlding and recontextualization of the incomprehensible were meant to exclude turns out to be fundamental to Heidegger's account of modern scientific research as an institution. This acknowledgment of the cultural practices of research would seem to undermine robust realism.[27]

---

configuration of practices and functional equipment. It is that the appropriate behavioral responses to them are carefully shorn of any functional reference" (Rouse, *Knowledge and Power*, 74).

[25] Martin Heidegger, "The Age of the World Picture," in *The Question Concerning Technology and Other Essays* (New York: Harper Torchbooks, 1977), 115–54.

[26] Heidegger in 1938, thus, anticipates Thomas Kuhn's account of normal science in *The Structure of Scientific Revolutions*. Heidegger also already recognized in *Being and Time* that science progresses by means of revolutions. "The real 'movement' of the sciences takes place when their basic concepts undergo a more or less radical revision" (*Being and Time*, 29).

[27] Indeed, Rouse holds that later Heidegger gave up the realism of the *Being and Time* period. He notes Heidegger's Kuhn-like remark back in 1938:

[We cannot] say that the Galilean doctrine of freely falling bodies is true and that Aristotle's teaching, that light bodies strive upward, is false; for the Greek understanding of the essence of body and place and of the relation between the two rests upon a different interpretation of entities and hence conditions a correspondingly different kind of seeing and questioning of natural events. No one would presume to maintain that Shakespeare's poetry is more advanced than that of

We shall soon see, however, that the practices of research could, nonetheless, constitute an institution that could intelligibly be said to get at the functional components of the universe as they are in themselves. To save his robust realism, Heidegger would have to argue that, although the practice-based structure of encounter that gives us access to entities depends on us *essentially*, what we encounter only *contingently* depends on this structure. Then both our everyday and our scientific practices, although ineliminable from an account of the entities revealed by science, could be understood, not as *constitutive* practices, but as *access* practices allowing "genuine theoretical discovering."[28]

To do this Heidegger would need, to begin with, to find a practical form of noncommittal reference that could refer to entities in a way that allowed both that they could have essential properties and that no property that *we* used in referring to them need, in fact, be essential. It turns out that Heidegger had discovered such a practice in facing a different problem. In the 1920s he realized he wanted to talk about important features of human being and yet he could not claim at the beginning of his investigation that these were *essential* ones. This methodological requirement put him in opposition to Husserl in two related ways: Husserl held that (1) general terms refer by way of the essential features of the types the terms referred to, and (2) that one could have an immediate eidetic intuition of essential structures. Since Heidegger saw that his hermeneutic method deprived Husserl's eidetic intuition of any possible ground, he needed some other way to approach the essential structures of human being. How could he refer to kinds without knowing their essential features?

To solve this problem Heidegger developed an account of "noncommittal" reference made possible by what he called formal indicators or designators

---

Aeschylus. It is still more impossible to say that the modern understanding of whatever is, is more correct than that of the Greeks.   (Heidegger, "The Age of the World Picture," 117)

Here Heidegger is obviously trying to counter the claim that Galileo has refuted Aristotle. But he is not doing so, as Kuhn does in *The Structure of Scientific Revolutions*, by holding that neither theory is true of nature, but rather by holding that *both* are true. This could be the innocuous observation that both are "illuminating," but in the context of another of Heidegger's remarks, namely, "that what is represented by physics is indeed nature itself, but undeniably it is only nature as the object-area, whose objectness is first defined and determined through the refining that is characteristic of physics" (Martin Heidegger, "Science and Reflection," in *The Question Concerning Technology and Other Essays* (New York: Harper & Row, 1977), 173–4), it must be the stronger claim that different theories can reveal different aspects of nature. Of course, if one thinks of Aristotle's theory of natural place as an account of *physical* causality meant to explain, for example, why rocks fall, in the same sense that modern physics claims to explain that phenomenon, his position is untenable. The law-like gravitational account given by modern physics, as far as we know, is right and Aristotle is simply wrong. It may well be, however, as Heidegger holds, that Aristotle and Galileo were *asking different kinds of questions*, and so each could be right about a different kind of causality.

[28] Heidegger, *Being and Time*, 412.

(*formalen Anzeige*). Noncommittal reference begins with contingent features and arrives at essential features, if there are any, only after an investigation.[29] Heidegger explains:

> The empty meaning structure [of the formal designator] gives a direction toward filling it in. Thus a unique binding character lies in the formal designator; I must follow in a *determinate direction* that, should it get to the essential, only gets there by fulfilling the designation by appreciating the non-essential.[30]

Thus, Heidegger held that reference need not commit one to any essential features; rather, it binds one to investigate, in whatever way is appropriate to the domain, which features, if any, of an object referred to by its inessential features are essential. Heidegger continues:

> [We must] make a leap and proceed resolutely from there! ... One lives in a non-essential having that takes its specific direction toward completion from the maturing of the development of this having...The *evidence* for the appropriateness of the original definition of the object is not essential and primordial; rather, the appropriateness is absolutely *questionable* and the definition must precisely be understood in this question-ableness and lack of evidence.[31]

Although he never used this idea of noncommittal reference to defend his realism, this methodological principle—that one can designate something by its contingent properties and then be bound by that designation to search for its essential properties—would have allowed Heidegger to use the switchover to the occurrent and its properties to show how access practices can break free of everyday meaning. One could consider the properties, revealed by theory-driven practices after the switchover, to be strictly *contingent* properties of the entities revealed—properties that could serve as a way of designating entities whose

---

[29] See, e.g., *Being and Time*, 152, where Heidegger speaks of "a noncommittal *formal indicator*, indicating something that may perhaps reveal itself as its 'opposite' in some particular phenomeno-logical context." Henceforth I will translate *Anzeige* as "designator" rather than "indicator."

[30] Martin Heidegger, *Phänomenologische Interpretationen zu Aristoteles, Gesamtausgabe*, vol. 61 (Frankfurt: Vittorio Klostermann, 1985), 33 (translation by Hubert L. Dreyfus with Hans Sluga).

[31] Heidegger, *Phänomenologische Interpretationen zu Aristoteles*, 34–5. What Heidegger presum-ably has in mind here when he says that the phenomenological given is absolutely questionable is the fact that any interpretive investigation has to begin with everyday experience, which is likely to be distorted both by individual fleeing and by the tradition. Yet the investigator has to begin where he is and can only hope gradually to work himself out of cover-ups and distortions. The recognition that it is necessary to start with the contingent and distorted if one wants to get to the essential explains Heidegger's enigmatic remark in *Being and Time* concerning the hermeneutic circle: "What is decisive is not to get out of the circle but to come into it in the right way" (Heidegger, *Being and Time*, 195).

essential properties, if any, would have to be discovered by further investigation. The practices of investigation too would be considered contingent rather than constitutive.

Thus, Heidegger has the basic resources to answer the objections that he can get outside neither everyday practices (in a broad sense) nor culturally determined practices. But he does not use these resources. To do so he would need to admit that our everyday skills survive the switchover and that, indeed, they are necessary for (1) identifying the occurrent entities that the detached attitude reveals, and (2) working data over in labs so that they can be taken as evidence for the essential properties of theoretical entities. He could then add that none of these practices, however, was essential to what was revealed in the laboratory. For, after the switchover, everyday practices, as well as the practices of the scientific institution, would be themselves experienced and deployed as questionable or contingent, and so the entities encountered could, in principle, be encountered as essentially independent of us. Heidegger seems to say just this in an interesting passage in *Basic Problems*: "Intraworldliness does not belong to the essence of the occurrent things as such, but it is only the transcendental condition... for the possibility of occurrent things being able to emerge as they are [in themselves]."[32]

A Final Phenomenological Argument for Robust Realism

For the most part, we encounter people, equipment, and even natural things as both perceptually and instrumentally familiar and inextricably bound up with our everyday practices. We can, however—though we do it rarely—encounter things and even people in an attitude of unfamiliarity. A trivial instance of encountering something in this attitude can be produced quite easily. If we say a familiar word over and over, we eventually hear the word switch over into a strange acoustic blast. Let us call this experience *defamiliarization* and the way of being it gives access to *the strange*.[33]

---

[32] Heidegger, *Basic Problems of Phenomenology*, 194.

[33] Of course, not all encounters with the strange are alike, and I am not describing the unfamiliar in all its forms. Aesthetic wonder, which gives us extraordinary things that are sublime, does not give us strange things of the sort I am concerned with here, nor does the religious awe that gives us an experience of a radically other being, nor philosophical wonder that takes us outside the ordinary so we can relate ourselves to the everyday as a whole.

Defamiliarization is the breakdown of everyday coping, and all that remains of intelligibility after defamiliarization are coping practices that enable us to *identify* things in a noncommittal, contingent, prima facie not fully adequate way. Access to entities independent of our practices for making them intelligible is thus secured by a radical switchover in the *role played by everyday practices* so that they become *contingent practices* for identifying objects. If we were to engage in the investigation of the relation between the strange thing and its everyday mode of being, we might be able to describe it in terms of sufficient features to reidentify it, but we cannot even be sure of that. Hence, our everyday practices are understood as inappropriate for defining what shows up. As Heidegger puts it, "the appropriateness is absolutely *questionable* and the definition must precisely be understood in this questionableness."[34]

Reference here works in the same way that Saul Kripke describes the working of *rigid designation*, particularly the rigid designation of samples of a natural kind.[35] So, to take two of Kripke's examples, I start by investigating some shiny golden-colored stuff and eventually find out that its essence is to have an atomic weight of 197. Or, I contingently identify lightning as a flash of light in the night sky and eventually find out that it is an electrical discharge. Thus something is designated by a description or by a pointing that is not taken to get at the thing's essence,[36] and such a pointing or description leaves open the possibility that investigation may discover the thing's essence. As we have seen, Heidegger calls this mode of reference "noncommittal formal designation" and says it is empty but binding.

The practice of rigid or formal designation, as I have described it, shows that we do, indeed, have practices that enable us to read the paradox of our having practices for gaining access to things independent of those very practices in a robust realist way. Moreover, we can make sense of the strange as possibly having some necessary unity underlying the contingent everyday properties

---

[34] Heidegger, *Phänomenologische Interpretationen zu Aristoteles*, 34–5.

[35] Saul Kripke, *Naming and Necessity* (Cambridge, MA: Harvard University Press, 1980).

[36] I do not believe that the necessity involved in making claims about essences requires claims about David Lewis's possible worlds. Dagfinn Føllesdal, for instance, argues for a form of rigid designation much like Kripke's only with an even more minimal ontology. For Føllesdal, considerations of "all possible worlds" are resolved into considerations about objects which our language enables us to keep track of although we have many false beliefs about the objects, do not know many of their properties, and do not know how their properties will change over time" (Dagfinn Føllesdal, "Essentialism and Reference," in *The Philosophy of W. V. O. Quine*, The Library of Living Philosophers, vol. 18 (La Salle, IL: Open Court, 1986), 97–113, esp. 107; Kripke, *Naming and Necessity*, 15–21).

by which it is identified.[37] This unity is enough to make intelligible the notion of a natural kind whose essence is independent of our ways of making things intelligible.[38]

---

[37] The claim that essentialism follows from rigid designation is argued by all who care about rigid designation. For the claim closest to mine, see Dagfinn Føllesdal, "Conceptual Change and Reference," in *Cognitio Humana: Dynamik des Wissens und der Werte*, Deutscher Kongreß für Philosophie, Leipzig, September 23–7, 1996, lectures and colloquiums, ed. Christoph Hubig (Leipzig: Universität Leipzig, 1996), 356–9.

[38] A realist science would have to make sure that it had practices for seeking the essences of objects in its domain that did not depend on everyday canons of what makes sense. Such a realist science could separate itself from the everyday by granting full autonomy to a discipline of puzzle-solving within the theoretical projection. Under such a regime, a solution that solves a puzzle, no matter how perceptually and intellectually counterintuitive, would have the power to force scientists to abandon even their current principles of intelligibility. Quantum physics is a case study of long-accepted principles of intelligibility being cast aside. That solutions to puzzles create more puzzles suggests that puzzle-solving is the activity of letting the nature of the universe guide conceptions of it away from human ways of conceiving toward a view from nowhere, appropriate to the universe as it is in itself.

PART III

Historical Worlds

7

Heidegger's Ontology of Art (2005)

Introduction: World, Being, and Style

Heidegger is not interested in works of art as expressions of the vision of a creator, nor is he interested in them as the source of aesthetic experiences in a viewer. He holds that "modern subjectivism...immediately misinterprets creation, taking it as the self-sovereign subject's performance of genius,"[1] and he also insists that aesthetic experience "is the element in which art dies" (66/79). Instead, for Heidegger, an artwork is a thing that, when it works, performs at least one of three ontological functions. It *manifests*, *articulates*, or *reconfigures* the style of a culture from within the world of that culture. It follows that, for Heidegger, most of what hang in museums, what are admired as great works of architecture, and what are published by poets were never works of art, a few were once artworks but are no longer working, and none is working now. To understand this counter-intuitive account of art, we have to begin by reviewing what Heidegger means by world and being.

World is the whole context of shared equipment, roles, and practices on the basis of which one can encounter entities and other people as intelligible. So, for example, one encounters a hammer as a hammer in the context of other equipment such as nails and wood, and in terms of social roles such as being a carpenter, a handyman, etc., and all such sub-worlds as carpentry, homemaking, etc., each with its appropriate equipment and practices, make sense on the basis of our familiar everyday world. Heidegger calls this background understanding

---

[1] Martin Heidegger, "Der Ursprung des Kunstwerkes," in *Holzwege, Gesamtausgabe*, vol. 5 (Frankfurt am Main: Klostermann, 1977), 63, translated as "The Origin of the Work of Art," in *Poetry, Language, Thought*, trans. Albert Hofstadter (New York: Harper & Row, 1971), 76. In this chapter, page references to this essay will appear in parentheses in the text—the first number will refer to the page number in the *Gesamtausgabe*, the second will refer to the page number in translation.

our understanding of being. As he puts it in *Being and Time*, "being is that on the basis of which beings are already understood."[2]

When he wrote *Being and Time*, Heidegger thought that he could give an ontological account of the universal structures of worldhood and thus ground a "science of being." He was, therefore, not interested in what he called ontic accounts of specific sub-worlds and various cultures. It was only in the early 1930s that he realized that, in our Western culture at least, the understanding of being has a history. Then, he saw that the specific way that beings are revealed— what he then calls the truth of being—determines how anything shows up *as* anything and certain actions show us *as worth doing*. For simplicity, we can call the truth of being of a particular culture or a specific epoch in our culture the *style* of that world.

Style is the way the everyday practices are coordinated. It serves as the basis upon which old practices are conserved and new practices are developed. A style opens a disclosive space and does so in a threefold manner: (a) by *coordinating* actions; (b) by determining how things and people *matter*; and (c) by being what is *transferred* from situation to situation. These three functions of style determine the way anything shows up and makes sense for us.

One can best see these three functions of style in another culture. Sociologists point out that mothers in different cultures handle their babies in different ways that inculcate the babies into different styles of coping with themselves, people, and things. For example, American mothers tend to put babies in their cribs on their stomachs, which encourages the babies to move around more effectively. Japanese mothers, contrariwise, put their babies on their backs so they will lie still, lulled by whatever they see. American mothers encourage passionate gesturing and vocalizing, while Japanese mothers are much more soothing and mollifying.

In general American mothers situate the infant's body and respond to the infant's actions in such a way as to promote an active and aggressive style of behavior. Japanese mothers, in contrast, promote a greater passivity and sensitivity to harmony in the actions of their babies. The babies, of course, take up the style of nurturing to which they are exposed. It may at first seem puzzling that the baby successfully picks out precisely the gestures that embody the style of its culture as the ones to imitate, but, of course, such success is inevitable. Since *all* our gestures embody the style of our culture, the baby will pick up that pervasive

---

[2] Martin Heidegger, *Being and Time*, trans. John Macquarrie and Edward Robinson (New York: Harper & Row, 1962), 7 (references to *Being and Time* use the page numbers of the original German edition, which are found in the margins of the English translation).

style no matter what it imitates. Starting with a style, various practices will make sense and become dominant and others will either become subordinate or will be ignored altogether.

The general cultural style determines how the baby encounters himself or herself, other people, and things. So, for example, no bare rattle is ever encountered. For an American baby a rattle-thing is encountered as an object to make lots of expressive noise with and to throw on the floor in a willful way in order to get a parent to pick it up. A Japanese baby may treat a rattle-thing this way more or less by accident, but generally we might suppose a rattle-thing is encountered as serving a soothing, pacifying function. What constitutes the American baby as an *American* baby is its style, and what constitutes the Japanese baby as a *Japanese* baby is its quite different style.

Once we see that a style governs how anything can show up *as* anything, we can see that the style of a culture does not govern only the babies. The adults in each culture are completely shaped by it. It determines what it makes sense to do, and what is worth doing. For example, it should come as no surprise, given the caricature I have just presented of Japanese and American culture, that Japanese adults seek contented, social integration, while American adults are still striving willfully to satisfy their individual desires. Likewise, the style of enterprises and of political organizations in Japan aims at producing and reinforcing cohesion, loyalty, and consensus, while what is admired by Americans in business and politics is the aggressive energy of a laissez-faire system in which everyone strives to express his or her own desires, and where the state, business, or other organizations function to maximize the number of desires that can be satisfied without destructive instability.

The case of child-rearing helps us to see that our cultural style is in our artifacts and our bodily skills. Since it is not something inner, but a disposition to act in certain ways in certain situations, it is misleading to think of our style as a belief system, scheme, or framework. It is invisible both because it is in our comportment, not in our minds, and because it is manifest in everything we see and do, and so too pervasive to notice. Like the illumination in a room, style normally functions best to let us see things when we don't see *it*. As Heidegger puts it, the mode of revealing has to *withdraw* in order to do its job of revealing things. Since it is invisible and global, our current understanding of being seems to have no contrast class. We can't help reading our own style back into previous epochs, the way the Christians understood the Greeks as pagans in despair, and the Moderns understood the Classical Greeks as already being rational subjects dealing with objects. So how can we ever notice our style or the style of another epoch in our culture?

The Work of Art as *Manifesting* a World

Heidegger answers this question in two stages. First, he shows that art is capable of revealing someone else's world. He shows this by describing a Van Gogh painting of a peasant woman's shoes. (Whether, as art critics debate, the shoes are really a pair of peasant shoes or Van Gogh's own shoes is irrelevant to how the picture works.) Heidegger claims that the shoes are not a symbol; they don't point beyond themselves to something else. Instead, Van Gogh's painting reveals to us the shoes themselves in their truth, which means that the shoes reveal the world of the peasant woman—a world that is so pervasive as to be invisible to the peasant woman herself, who, even when she deals with her shoes, "simply wears them...without noticing or reflecting" (23/34).

The Van Gogh painting, however, manifests the peasant's world to the viewer of the painting. Art, then, can be seen as manifesting a world *to those outside* it. But, of course, a culture's language, its artifacts, and its practices all reflect its style. This leaves open the question: If the style necessarily withdraws, *how can anyone ever come to see the style of his or her own epoch*? To answer this question, we need to look further into Heidegger's account of the special function of art.

The Work of Art as *Articulating* a Culture's Understanding of Being

Heidegger's basic insight is that the work of art not only *manifests* the style of the culture; it *articulates* it. For everyday practices to give us a shared world, and so give meaning to our lives, they must be focused and held up to the practitioners. Works of art, when performing this function, are not merely *representations* of a pre-existing state of affairs, but actually *produce* a shared understanding. Charles Taylor and Clifford Geertz have discussed this important phenomenon.

Taylor makes this point when he distinguishes shared meanings, which he calls *inter-subjective* meanings, from *common* meanings. As he puts it: "Common meanings are the basis of community. Inter-subjective meanings give a people a common language to talk about social reality and a common understanding of certain norms, but only with common meaning does this common reference world contain significant common actions, celebrations, and feelings."[3] Taylor calls the way common meanings work *articulation.*

---

[3] Charles Taylor, "Interpretation and the Sciences of Man," in P. Rabinow and W. Smith (eds.), *Interpretive Social Science* (Berkeley, CA: University of California Press, 1979), 51.

A year after Taylor's article, in his famous paper on the cockfight in Bali, Clifford Geertz introduces the notion of style and argues that works of art and rituals produce and preserve a style. "A people's ethos is the tone, character, and quality of their life, its moral and aesthetic *style....* Quartets, still lives, and cockfights are not merely reflections of a pre-existing sensibility analogically represented; they are positive agents in the creation and maintenance of such a sensibility."[4] We might say, then, that art doesn't merely *reflect* the style of a culture; it *glamorizes* it and so enables those in the culture to see it and to understand themselves and their shared world in its light.

To appreciate the way the phenomenon Taylor and Geertz have seen defines art's function, it helps to turn to Thomas Kuhn. In *The Structure of Scientific Revolutions*, Kuhn argues that scientists engaged in what he calls normal science operate in terms of an exemplar or paradigm—an outstanding example of a good piece of work. The paradigm for modern natural scientists was Newton's *Principia*. All agreed that Newton had seen exemplary problems, given exemplary solutions, and produced exemplary justifications for his claims. Thus, for over two centuries scientists knew that, insofar as their work resembled Newton's, they were doing good science.

The Newtonian paradigm was later replaced by the Einsteinian one. Such a paradigm shift constitutes a scientific revolution. After such a revolution, scientists see and do things differently. As Kuhn puts it, they work in a different world. They also believe and value different things, but this is less important. Kuhn is quite clear that it is the paradigm—the exemplar itself—that guides the scientists' practices and that the paradigm cannot be explained in terms of a set of beliefs or values and spelled out using criteria and rules. As Kuhn notes, "paradigms may be prior to, more binding, and more complete than any set of rules for research that could be unequivocally abstracted from them."[5] Kuhn explicitly describes the work of science as articulating its paradigm: "in a science,... like an accepted judicial decision in the common law, [a paradigm] is an object for further articulation and specification under new or more stringent conditions."[6]

It seems almost inevitable after Kuhn to see whatever articulates a style as a paradigm. And, indeed, Geertz says: "it is [the] bringing of assorted experiences of everyday life to focus that the cockfight...accomplishes, and so creates what, better than typical or universal, could be called a paradigmatic human event."[7]

---

[4] Clifford Geertz, *The Interpretation of Cultures* (New York: Basic Books, 1973), 451.
[5] Thomas Kuhn, *The Structure of Scientific Revolutions*, 2nd edn. (Chicago, IL: University of Chicago Press, 1970), 46.
[6] Kuhn, *The Structure of Scientific Revolutions*, 23.
[7] Geertz, *The Interpretation of Cultures*, 450.

To sum up and generalize what Taylor, Geertz, and Kuhn have taught us: a cultural paradigm collects the scattered practices of a group, unifies them into coherent possibilities for action, and holds the resulting style up to the people concerned, who then act and relate to each other in terms of it.

Heidegger was the first to give a satisfactory ontological account of this phenomenon. He takes as his example the Greek temple. To begin with, it is clear that the temple is not a representation of anything; moreover, it is not the work of an individual genius. Nonetheless, the temple opened a world for the Greeks by articulating their style. The Greeks' practices were gathered together and focused by the temple so that they saw nature and themselves in the light of the temple. Everything looked different once the style was articulated. As Heidegger puts it, "tree and grass, eagle and bull, snake and cricket first enter into their distinctive shapes and thus come to appear as what they are" (31/42).

The temple also held up to the Greeks what was worth doing by manifesting distinctions of worthiness: "it is the temple work that first fits together and at the same time gathers around itself the unity of those paths and relations in which birth and death, disaster and blessing, victory and disgrace, endurance and decline acquire the shape of destiny for human being" (31/42). The temple thus "gave things their look and men their outlook on themselves" (32/43). And, like every cultural paradigm, it illuminated *everything*. Thus, as Heidegger says, "the *all-governing* expanse of this open relational context is the *world* of this historical people" (31/42).

Heidegger is not the first to have seen the role of artistic articulation. Hegel, Nietzsche, and Wagner had already discussed the function of the artwork in giving a people a sense of their identity. But Heidegger is the first to have defined art in terms of its function of articulating the understanding of being in the practices and to have worked out the ontological implications. Thus, Heidegger could argue against Nietzsche and the Romantics that it was the *artwork*, not the experience of the *artist*, that had ontological significance. Likewise, he could deny Hegel's claim that philosophy was superior to art, since what art showed symbolically, philosophy could rationalize and so make explicit.

Kuhn saw that the fact that the paradigm cannot be "rationalized" but only imitated is crucial to the paradigm's function. He says: "the concrete scientific achievement, as a locus of professional commitment, [is] prior to the various concepts, laws, theories, and points of view that may be abstracted from it.... [It] cannot be fully reduced to logically atomic components that might function in its stead."[8] The fact that the paradigm cannot be rationalized makes it possible

---

[8] Kuhn, *The Structure of Scientific Revolutions*, 11.

for the scientists to agree without having to spell out their agreement. As Kuhn says, "the practice of normal science depends on the ability, acquired from exemplars, to group objects and situations into similarity sets that are primitive in the sense that the grouping is done without an answer to the question, 'Similar with respect to what?'"[9] At a time of a scientific revolution, however, Kuhn tells us, the paradigm becomes the focus of conflicting interpretations, each trying to rationalize and justify it.

Similarly, Heidegger holds that a working artwork is so important to a community that the people involved must try to make the work clear and coherent and codify what it stands for. But the artwork, like the scientific paradigm, resists rationalization. Any paradigm could be paraphrased and rationalized only if the concrete thing, which served as an exemplar, symbolized or represented an underlying system of beliefs or values that could be abstracted from the particular exemplar. But the whole point of needing an exemplar is that there is no such system, there are only shared practices. Therefore the style resists rationalization and can only be displayed. Heidegger calls the way the artwork solicits the culture to make the meaning of the artwork explicit, coherent, and all encompassing, the *world* aspect of the work. He calls the way the artwork and its associated practices resist such explication and totalization the *earth* aspect.

Heidegger sees that the earth's resistance is not a drawback but has an important positive function.

To the Open there belong a world and the earth. But the world is not simply the Open that corresponds to clearing, and the earth is not simply the Closed that corresponds to concealment. Rather, the world is the clearing of the paths of the essential guiding directions with which all decision complies. Every decision, however, bases itself on something not mastered, something concealed, confusing; else it would never be a decision. (43–4/55)

Heidegger understands that if actions were fully lucid, as Sartre would have them be, they would be arbitrary and freely revocable and so not serious.[10] Like disposedness (*Befindlichkeit*) in *Being and Time*, earth supplies mattering and thus grounds the seriousness of decisions.

In "The Origin of the Work of Art," however, earth is understood no longer as an aspect of human being but as a function of the tendency in the cultural practices themselves to open worlds: "The earth cannot dispense with the Open

---

[9] Kuhn, *The Structure of Scientific Revolutions*, 200.

[10] This argument is first made by Søren Kierkegaard in his account of the breakdown of the Kantian ethical, and filled in phenomenologically in the freedom chapter in Maurice Merleau-Ponty, *The Phenomenology of Perception*, trans. Colin Smith (New York: Routledge, 2002).

of the world if it itself is to appear as earth in the liberated surge of its self-seclusion. The world, again, cannot soar out of the earth's sight if, as the governing breadth and path of all essential destiny, it is to ground itself on a resolute foundation" (38/49). Thus, earth is not passive matter, but comes into being precisely as what resists any attempt to abstract and generalize the point of the paradigm.

> The earth appears openly cleared as itself only when it is perceived and preserved as that which is by nature undisclosable, that which shrinks from every disclosure and constantly keeps itself closed up.   (36/47)
>
> The opposition of world and earth is a strife. But we would surely all too easily falsify its nature if we were to confound strife with discord and destruction. In essential strife, rather, the opponents raise each other into the self-assertion of their natures.   (37/49)[11]

The temple draws the people who act in its light to clarify, unify, and extend the reach of its style, but being a material thing it resists rationalization. And since no interpretation can ever completely capture what the work means, the temple sets up a struggle between earth and world. The result is fruitful in that the conflict of interpretations that ensues generates a culture's history.[12]

Such resistance is manifest in the materiality of the artwork. A Greek tragedy requires the sound of the poetry to create a shared mood for the spectators and thus open up a shared world, so, like all literary works, tragedies resist translation. More generally, Heidegger tells us:

> the temple-work, in setting up a world, does not cause the material to disappear, but rather causes it to come forth for the very first time and to come into the Open of the work's world. The rock comes to bear and rest and so first becomes rock; metals come to glitter and shimmer, colors to glow, tones to sing, the word to speak. All this comes forth as the work sets itself back into the massiveness and heaviness of stone, into the firmness and pliancy of wood, into the hardness and luster of metal, into the lighting and darkening of color, into the clang of tone, and into the naming power of the word.   (35/46)[13]

---

[11] Translation corrected—*Streit* does not mean striving.

[12] It is interesting to note that rituals, unlike the temple, do not set up a struggle between earth and world, presumably because they do not try to unify the whole culture. (The Balinese cockfight Geertz analyses glamorizes the role only of the males.) Cultures that do not have artworks in Heidegger's view do not have a history, since, for him, history means the series of total worlds that result from a struggle of interpretations as to the meaning of being. But it seems there can be more local works of art. The US Constitution, like a work of art, has necessarily become the focus of attempts to make it explicit and consistent, and to make it apply to *all* situations. Such attempts are never fully successful but this is not a drawback. The resulting conflict of interpretations is an important aspect of the history of the republic.

[13] The last phrase is a surprise. One would have expected the *sound* of the word as its earthy component. The naming power seems to be what opens a world. This may be simply a mistake on Martin Heidegger's part. But it may not be, since he never corrected it in his marginal notes.

What is dark and hidden and what is out in the open differs from culture to culture. How the line between the two is drawn is an aspect of the unique way the style of each particular culture is elaborated.

World demands its decisiveness and its measure and lets beings attain to the Open of their paths. Earth, bearing and jutting, strives to keep itself closed and to entrust everything to its law. The conflict is not a rift (*Riss*), as a mere cleft is ripped open; rather, it is the intimacy with which opponents belong to each other. This rift carries the opponents into the source of their unity by virtue of their common ground. It is a basic design, an outline sketch that draws the basic features of the rise of the lighting of beings.   (51–2/63)

In each epoch, then, the struggle between world and earth and its rift design manifests a different style. The temple requires the stone out of which it is built in order to do its job of setting up the tension between structure and stone; a temple made out of steel would not work. The cathedral, in its different style, uses stone and glass to show the struggle between light and darkness and that light is winning out. We now construct debased works of art such as the national highway system, which imposes such an efficient order on nature that earth is no longer able to resist.

The answers to our earlier questions should now be clear: the special function of art is precisely to let each group of historical people see the style of their own culture by showing it in a glamorized exemplar. Moreover, we can now add that such a function is an ontological necessity. As Heidegger puts it, "there must always be some being in [the] open, something that is, in which the openness takes its stand and attains its constancy" (49/61).

It follows that appreciating artworks when they are working, to talk like Heidegger, is the furthest thing from having private aesthetic experiences (55–6/68). Yet art is somehow connected with beauty. Heidegger describes art as "the shining of truth" (52/64), and describes beauty as the way artworks shine: "this shining . . . is the beautiful," he says (44/56).

But how does the temple shine? It is white, of course, and dazzling in the Greek sun, but what about other artworks such as somber cathedrals or dark tragedies. Do they shine too? Not literally, but remember that thanks to artworks some aspects of things and practices become salient and others marginal and that makes some ways of acting show up as worth doing, and others not show up at all. Thus the Greeks saw life and the cosmos *in the light of* their artworks. This is presumably the metaphorical sort of light Heidegger has in mind.

The way in which art thoroughly spans the being-in-the-world of human beings as historical, the way in which it illuminates the world for them and indeed illuminates human beings themselves, putting in place the way in which art is art—all this receives its law and structural articulation from the manner in which the world as a whole is opened up to human beings in general.[14]

To sum up: the work of art doesn't *reflect* the style of the culture or create it; it *illuminates* it.

Normally the illumination in the room must withdraw to do its work. But sometimes we can see the light bulb and also see everything in its light. In this way the artwork, like the sun in Plato's Allegory of the Cave, makes everything in the world intelligible, yet we can gaze upon it; but with the important difference that Plato thought the ground of the intelligibility of the world had to be outside the world, whereas Heidegger holds that it has to be something within the world. That means that, rather than being eternal like the Good, works of art can cease to work or, as Heidegger puts it, works of art can die.

> The Aegina sculptures in the Munich collection, Sophocles' *Antigone* in the best critical edition, are, as the works they are, torn out of their own native sphere.... [E]ven when we make an effort to cancel or avoid such displacement of works—when, for instance, we visit the temple in Paestum at its own site or the Bamberg cathedral on its own square— the world of the work that stands there has perished.   (29–30/40–1)

Another way to express the artwork's fragility is to note that, unlike Plato's idea of the Good, the work of art shows itself to be created. "[A] work is always a work, which means that it is something worked out, brought about, effected. If there is anything that distinguishes the work as work, it is that the work has been created" (45/56). But this does not mean that Heidegger follows Nietzsche in emphasizing the creator of the work. In fact, Heidegger claims that "art is the origin of the artwork and of the artist" (46/57). But Heidegger adds that "the impulse toward such a thing as a work lies in the nature of truth" (45/57; translation modified). Truth for Heidegger means disclosing. So, for Heidegger, opening a world is a way truth sets itself to work. We can now understand this to mean that a culture's practices tend to gather so as to open and illuminate a world, and they use the artwork to do so. Indeed, in his marginal comments to "The Origin of the Work of Art," Heidegger repeatedly notes that what he is referring to here is what he later calls the event of appropriation (*das Ereignis*). That is, what ultimately makes truth and art possible is the way cultural practices tend toward making sense, the way they gather together to bring things out in their ownmost, to let things and people appear in a rich rather than in a banal way.

---

[14] Martin Heidegger, *Hölderlins Hymne "Der Ister," Gesamtausgabe*, vol. 53 (Frankfurt am Main: Vittorio Klostermann, 1984), 23.

Thus far Heidegger has pointed out that the function of the artwork (like the accepted scientific paradigm) is to articulate the understanding implicit in the current practices. Paradigms thus reveal the current style to those who share it. But having devoted most of his essay to a description of the temple as the focus of the struggle of earth and world that fixes a culture's style and holds it up to the people, Heidegger has not yet arrived at the origin of the work of art—the way artworks work when they are functioning at their best—nor has he described how the practices come together to create new artworks that disclose new worlds. He turns to these issues at the end of his essay.

Heidegger: Artworks as *Reconfiguring* a Culture's Understanding of Being

Only when he realized that being itself had a history was Heidegger able to describe what he calls the *origin* (*Ur-sprung*) of the work of art. In setting the stage for this further move, he says:

in the West for the first time in Greece . . . [w]hat was in the future to be called being was set into work, setting the standard. The realm of beings thus opened up was then transformed into a being in the sense of God's creation. This happened in the Middle Ages. This kind of being was again transformed at the beginning and in the course of the modern age. Beings became objects that could be controlled and seen through by calculation. At each time a new and essential world arose.   (63–4/76–7)

Such changes are cultural revolutions and, as in scientific revolutions, they are made possible by the establishment of a new paradigm. As Heidegger says: "at each time the openness of what is had to be established in beings themselves, by the fixing in place of truth in figure" (64/77). That is, in each such case the being that shines in the clearing not only *configured* the style of the culture; it *reconfigured* it.[15] It follows that each time a culture gets a new artwork, the understanding of being changes and human beings and things show up differently. For the Greeks, what showed up were heroes and slaves; for the Christians, they were saints and sinners. There could not have been saints in ancient Greece; at best there could only have been weak people who let others walk all over them. Likewise, there could not have

---

[15] Heidegger also says: "whenever art happens—that is, whenever there is a beginning—a thrust enters history, history either begins or starts over again" (64/77). Heidegger seems to be confused about whether the Greek temple articulated or reconfigured because, in fact, it does neither. As the beginning of the history of being, the Greeks do not yet have a unified understanding of being to renew or to reconfigure. The temple and the pre-Socratic thinkers had to take the style that was already in the language and, for the first time, focus it and hold it up to the people. According to Heidegger, this is the origin (*Ur-sprung*) of our Western culture.

been Greek-style heroes in the Middle Ages. Such people would have been regarded as prideful sinners who disrupted society by denying their dependence on God and encouraging everyone to depend on them instead.

Once Heidegger describes the function of artworks when they are functioning as *revolutionary paradigms*, he can generalize the notion of a cultural paradigm from a work of art working to anything in the world that not only focuses, or refocuses, the current cultural style, but establishes a new one. Thus, he says:

> one essential way in which truth establishes itself in the beings it has opened up is truth setting itself into work. [The temple as articulating the Greek culture.] Another way in which truth occurs is the act that founds a political state. [Pericles, and, perhaps, Hitler.] Still another way in which truth comes to shine forth is the nearness of that which is not simply a being, but the being that is most of all. [God's Covenant with the Hebrews?] Still another way in which truth grounds itself is the essential sacrifice. [The Crucifixion?] Still another way in which truth becomes is the thinker's questioning, which, as the thinking of being, names being in its question-worthiness. [Philosophers do this by introducing a new vocabulary, such as "subject/object," and "autonomy." In this sense, for Heidegger, revolutionary scientists such as Galileo and Einstein are thinkers too.]   (49/61–2)[16]

In Heidegger's terms, articulating works of art *establish* a style; now Heidegger tells us, *founding* works reconfigure it. But just how does this founding work? After giving examples of such articulators as the Greek temple, the Bamberg Cathedral, and the tragedies of Sophocles, Heidegger suddenly, toward the end of "The Origin of the Work of Art," without examples, offers a few hasty remarks on the function of the artwork he calls founding: "We understanding founding here in a triple sense: founding as bestowing, founding as grounding, and founding as beginning. . . . We can do no more now than to present this structure of the nature of art in a few strokes" (63/75). Heidegger's three modes of founding correspond to the past, present, and future. First is *bestowing*, the role of the past. A new understanding of being must be incomprehensible yet somehow intelligible. To account for this possibility, Heidegger returns to an idea already touched on in *Being and Time* (see §74). In a historical change, some practices that were marginal become central, and some central practices become marginal. Reconfiguration is thus not the creation (*schaffen*) of a genius, but the drawing up (*schöpfen*) of the reserve of marginal practices bestowed by the culture as from a well (63/76). What ultimately bestows the material for the new style is the style of a people's language. Art takes place in a clearing, "which has already happened unnoticed in language" (62/74).

---

[16] In this connection it is interesting to note that Heidegger, who is infamous for saying that great philosophy can only be done in Greek or German, in GA 54 says that Descartes is a greater thinker than Kant, even though Descartes wrote in Latin and French, and never wrote a word in Greek or German.

So Heidegger now generalizes language to any form of "poetic projection": "projective saying...brings the unsayable as such into a world" (61–2/74). "Genuinely poetic projection is the opening up or disclosure of that into which human being as historical is already cast....Founding is an overflow, an endowing, a bestowal" (63/75–6).

In *grounding*, the present has to take up the marginal practices already in the culture into a new style that makes them central. Given the current understanding, the new style will, of course, seem weird and barely intelligible. "The setting-into-work of truth thrusts up the unfamiliar and extraordinary and at the same time thrusts down the ordinary" (63/75).

This makes possible a *new beginning* by opening a new future. Of course, a new style does not arise *ex nihilo*. Marginal practices of various sorts are always on the horizon. For example, the printing press and Luther were already moving people toward the individualism and freedom from authority that became central in Descartes's attempt to take over his life and education from the ground up. Thus, when speaking of the new beginning, Heidegger adds that while the new beginning is "a leap," "what is thus cast forth is...never an arbitrary demand" (63/75). He explains: "the peculiarity of a leap out of the unmediable does not exclude but rather includes the fact that the beginning prepares itself the longest time and wholly inconspicuously" (64/76).

The new beginning sets up a new future, by calling the people in the culture to be preservers.

Preserving the work does not reduce people to their private experiences, but brings them into affiliation with the truth happening in the work. Thus it grounds being for and with one another as the historical standing-out of human existence in reference to unconcealedness....The proper way to preserve the work is cocreated and prescribed only and exclusively by the work.   (55/68)

Heidegger admits he gives no example of reconfiguration. Such examples, Heidegger admits, are only "initial hints" (55/68). Indeed, the examples he uses are all Greek—the temples, the tragedies, the classical philosophers—and, as such, are powerful articulations of an already existing cultural style. There may well be good reasons for his not being able to find any examples of reconfiguration in Greece. As Kierkegaard remarks in his discussion of the Christian notion of the fullness of time, and Heidegger repeats in his appropriation of Kierkegaard's notion of the *Augenblick*, the experience of radical transformation of self and world is what differentiates the Christian world from antiquity.[17] After all, the

---

[17] Heidegger, *Being and Time*, 338, note.

Greeks believed in endless cycles of the same, not in radical creation. The most striking example of such a radical cultural transformation of a new beginning is the transformation of the Hebrew world into the Christian world.

So let us take a simplified account of this transformation as an illustration of the three aspects of founding. We are told that the Jews followed the Law so that one was guilty for one's overt acts, and that Jesus changed all this when, in the Sermon on the Mount, he said that anyone who looks at a woman lustfully has already committed adultery with her in his heart.

Jesus thrusts down or marginalizes the ordinary—the Law and the overt acts it condemns—when he practices healing even on the Sabbath, and he introduces the extraordinary new idea that what really matters is that one is responsible for one's desires. Purity, not rightness of action, is what is essential, and, in that case, one can save oneself not by willpower, but only by throwing oneself on the mercy of a savior and being reborn.

One might reasonably object that this emphasis on desire can't be such a radical change from Judaism after all, since the eighth commandment already enjoins one not to covet anything that is one's neighbor's, and coveting is surely a case of desire, not overt action. But Heidegger would surely be the first to point out that, if Jesus had not had some basis in the previous practices—something bestowed by the past—no one would have had a clue as to what he was talking about, so it was essential that, in his grounding of a new world, he take up and make central a marginal practice already bestowed by the culture. In the unique case of the Ten Commandments, it seems that the amount of marginal practice bestowed by the tradition can be quantified; it is reflected in one out of ten commandments.

But, of course, this is only the beginning. A world transformer such as Jesus can show a new style and so can be followed, as Jesus was followed by his disciples even though they could hardly understand what they were doing. But he will not be fully intelligible to the members of the culture until the preservers become attuned to his extraordinary new way of coordinating the practices—his new beginning—and articulate it in a new language and in new symbols and institutions.

Thus, although Heidegger never says so, it seems there must always be two stages in each cultural revolution: reconfiguration that thrusts down the ordinary and introduces the extraordinary, followed by an articulation that focuses and stabilizes the new style. Thus Jesus is interpreted in terms of *caritas* by St. Paul, Galileo is interpreted in terms of *gravitas* by Newton, and the implications of Descartes's new idea that we are subjects in a world of objects is worked out in terms of *autonomy* by Kant. It is because Kant is merely an articulator that, for Heidegger, Descartes, as a reconfigurer, is a more primordial thinker than Kant.

Conclusion: Can an Artwork Work for Us Now?

Heidegger thinks that our current understanding of being levels all meaningful differences and hides the earth so now there are only negative exemplars of our style—Heidegger takes as an example the power station on the Rhine, and another example might be our walk on the moon. So far the West has not produced any reconfiguring work of art that sets forth the earth and restarts history with a new struggle between earth and world. The question then arises for Heidegger whether our flexible style that turns everything, even ourselves, into resources could ever be reconfigured.

Of course, one cannot legislate a new beginning. But perhaps our marginal practices could gather into a new style, one, for example, in which marginal practices and attunements, such as awe in the face of nature, from our pre-Socratic past would begin to coalesce with the nature worship of the Romantics to affirm what is sometimes referred to as the Gaia Principle, i.e., that nature is god. Perhaps then some new paradigm would make those marginal practices central and marginalize our current practices, which, as Heidegger once put it, "are turning the earth into a gigantic filling station." Preservers might then see nature in the light of the new god, put solar panels on their homes, and stop buying SUVs.

It is too early to see how such a work of art manifesting this new understanding of being might begin to work, but a hint of how a different sort of new paradigm almost worked can be found in the music and style of the 1960s. Bob Dylan, the Beatles, and other rock groups became for many the focus of a new understanding of what really mattered. This new style coalesced in the Woodstock music festival of 1969, where people actually lived for a few days in an understanding of being in which mainline contemporary concerns with order, sobriety, willful activity, and flexible, efficient control were made marginal and subservient to pagan practices, such as openness, enjoyment of nature, dancing, and Dionysian ecstasy, along with neglected Christian concerns with peace, tolerance, and non-exclusive love of one's neighbor. Technology was not smashed or denigrated; instead, all the power of electronic communications was put at the service of the music that articulated the above concerns.

If enough people had recognized in Woodstock what they most cared about and recognized that many others shared this recognition, a new style of life might have been focused and stabilized. Of course, in retrospect it seems to us who are still in the grip of the technological understanding of being that the concerns of the Woodstock generation were not organized and encompassing enough to resist being taken over by the very practices it was trying to marginalize. Still we are left with a hint of how a new cultural paradigm might work. This helps us to understand why Heidegger holds that we must foster human receptivity and preserve the endangered species of pre-technological practices that remain in our culture so that one day they may come together in a new work of art, rich enough and resistant enough to reconfigure our world.

8

Between Technê and Technology

The Ambiguous Place of Equipment in *Being and Time* (1984)

Introduction

Heidegger's occasional retrospective remarks on *Being and Time* are mostly limited to pointing out the way *Being and Time* is already on the way to overcoming metaphysics by reawakening concern with Being,[1] or to acknowledging *Being and Time*'s transcendental neglect of the history of Being.[2] But one looks in vain through Heidegger's occasional references to his most celebrated work for an indication of how we are to fit *Being and Time* into the history of Being that later Heidegger elaborated. To what extent is *Being and Time* itself metaphysical? To what extent is it nihilistic? As a step toward answering these difficult questions, one might well begin by asking a more manageable question: To what extent is the account of the being of equipment in *Being and Time* a critique of the ontology of technology and to what extent is it a contribution to the development of a technological understanding of Being?

In his reflections on Nietzsche, Heidegger singles out the subject/object distinction as the philosophical development that makes possible modern technology:

In this revolutionary objectifying of everything that is, the earth, that which first of all must be put at the disposal of representing and setting forth, moves into the midst of human positing and analyzing. The earth itself can show itself only as the object of assault, an assault that, in human willing, establishes itself as unconditional objectification. Nature

---

[1] See Martin Heidegger, "Letter on Humanism," in *Basic Writings*, ed. David Farrell Krell (New York: Harper & Row, 1977).

[2] Martin Heidegger, *Nietzsche* II (Pfullingen: Gunther Neske, 1961), where Heidegger speaks of the questions of *Being and Time* as "hermeneutisch-transcendentale Fragen noch nicht seins-geschichtlich gedacht," 45.

appears everywhere—because willed from out of the essence of Being—as the object of technology.[3]

Insofar, then, as the analysis of Dasein as Being-in-the-world offers a phenomenological critique of the subject/object relation, *Being and Time* would seem to stand in direct opposition to the technological understanding of Being.

Likewise, the central theme of Division I of *Being and Time*, that ready-to-hand equipment is ontologically more fundamental than present-at-hand objects, in that present-at-hand objects can be made intelligible as privative (i.e., decontextualized) modes of equipment, whereas equipmental relations can never be built up by adding value predicates to present-at-hand objects, is directly opposed to the implicit ontology of objective thought. Calculating, logistic intelligibility is criticized by showing its dependence upon the non-formalizable everyday intelligibility of the primordial way human beings encounter entities within the world.[4]

The phenomenological description of our primordial way of encountering entities purports to light up a way of being that has not changed since the beginning of our history. In his lectures from the period of *Being and Time*, Heidegger does not hesitate to read this everyday understanding of beings as equipment back into the meaning of *ousia*.

That which first of all constantly lies-before in the closest circle of human activity and accordingly is constantly disposable is the whole of all *things of use* with which we constantly have to do, the whole of all those existent things which are themselves meant to be used on one another, *the implement that is employed* and constantly used products of nature: house and yard, forest and field, sun, light, and heat. What is thus tangibly present for dealing with is reckoned by everyday experience as that which *is*, a being, in the primary sense... [T]he pre-philosophical proper meaning of *ousia*... Accordingly *a being* is synonymous with an at-hand disposable.[5]

It is precisely the loss of the everyday understanding of the priority of things of use, reflected in Descartes's subject/object metaphysics, that provides the conditions for the rise of modern science:

---

[3] Martin Heidegger, "The Word of Nietzsche: 'God is Dead'," in *The Question Concerning Technology and Other Essays*, trans. William Lovitt (New York: Harper & Row, 1977), 100.

[4] For an elaboration and application of Heidegger's argument, see Hubert Dreyfus, *What Computers Can't Do* (New York: Harper & Row, 1979).

[5] Martin Heidegger, *Die Grundprobleme der Phänomenologie, Gesamtausgabe*, vol. 24 (Frankfurt am Main: Vittorio Klostermann, 1975), 152, 153. Heidegger would, however, be reluctant to read our everyday understanding of equipment back into prehistory. As he notes in *Being and Time*, trans. John Macquarrie and Edward Robinson (New York: Harper & Row, 1962), 113: "Perhaps even readiness-to-hand and equipment have nothing to contribute as ontological clues in interpreting the primitive world..."

We first arrive at science as research when and only when truth has been transformed into the certainty of representation.

What it is to be is for the first time defined as the objectiveness of representing, and truth is first defined as the certainty of representing, in the metaphysics of Descartes.[6]

Being and Time, then, sets out to rescue beings from objectivity and representation by returning to a pre-philosophical, a-historical understanding of equipment.

So it might have seemed in 1927, but Heidegger's later understanding of the history of Western thought reveals that things may not be so simple. Indeed, there are hints scattered throughout Heidegger's later works that in opposing the subject/object ontology by an appeal to the primacy of equipment, *Being and Time* was itself a formulation of the penultimate stage of technology.

As early as *The Origin of the Work of Art*—the only sustained treatment of equipmentality after *Being and Time*—Heidegger notes "the possibility...that differences relating to the history of Being may also be present in the way equipment *is*."[7] This immediately casts suspicion on the a-historical transcendental priority given to equipment in *Being and Time*. And, indeed, at this same point in the text Heidegger cautions against "making thing and work prematurely into subspecies of equipment."[8]

Heidegger, however, never works out a history of the being of equipment, so we will have to construct it from hints. The most important of these hints are Heidegger's discussion of the Greek notion of *technê* at the beginning of our history and his remark in "Science and Reflection" that, in the technological understanding of the being, subject and object no longer stand in a relation of representation but are both absorbed into a total systematic ordering ("Both subject and object are sucked up as standing-reserve").[9] It follows that opposing the Cartesian subject/object distinction in terms of an account of Dasein as a user of equipment becomes an ambiguous form of opposition, for it is no longer clear whether such an analysis offers a critique of technology in the form of a transcendental account of the pre-technological everyday understanding of equipment, or whether, under the guise of a transcendental account of everyday activity, such an analysis reflects a transition in the history of the way equipment *is* which prepares the way for technology. In other words, it is not clear whether *Being and Time* opposes technology or promotes it.

---

[6] Martin Heidegger, "The Age of the World Picture," in *The Question Concerning Technology and Other Essays*, trans. William Lovitt (New York: Harper & Row, 1977), 127.

[7] Martin Heidegger, "The Origin of the Work of Art," in *Poetry, Language, Thought*, trans. Albert Hofstadter (New York: Harper & Row, 1971), 32.

[8] Heidegger, "The Origin of the Work of Art," 32.

[9] Heidegger, "Science and Reflection," 173.

The answer to this question can only be found in a detailed analysis of the phenomenology of equipment and worldhood offered in *Being and Time*. As we turn to *Being and Time* our *Vorgriff* will be the hypothesis that the analysis of equipment in *Being and Time* is neither pre-technological nor fully technological, but rather, that *Being and Time* plays a transitional role in the history of the being of equipment. That, far from resisting the modern tendency to transform everything into standing-reserve, the understanding of the being of the ready-to-hand in *Being and Time* leaves equipment available for the assault of technology, the way the Cartesian understanding of the being of the present-at-hand made nature available for the assault of scientific research. Thus, early Heidegger might be said to have a privileged place in the transition from *technê* to technology, which corresponds to Descartes's privileged place in the transition from *theorea* to modern science.

Sketch of a History of the Being of Equipment

The way equipment *is* no doubt goes through as many stages as there are epochs in the history of Being. For our purposes, however, it will suffice to distinguish three stages. Sociologically we might equate these three periods with craftsmanship, industrialization, and cybernetic control, which find expression, respectively, in the Greek notion of *technê*, pragmatism, and systems theory as the basis of global planning.

Distinguishing three stages in the history of the being of equipment enables us to avoid two simple interpretations of the place of equipment in *Being and Time* which at first seem attractive. One reading notes the similarity between Heidegger's remark in *Being and Time* that "the wood is a forest of timber,the mountain a quarry of rock, the river is water-power,"[10] and his later observations that in the clearing opened up by technology, "the river is a . . . water-power supplier" [11] and "nature becomes a gigantic gasoline station."[12] This interpretation concludes that the identification of Nature in *Being and Time* as "an entity within-the-world which is proximally ready-to-hand"[13] shows that the understanding of equipment in *Being and Time* is already fully technological. The opposite interpretation, on the other hand, sees no step-wise history of the being of equipment but only a total opposition between the pre-technological and the technological. Since, according to Heidegger, "calculated being makes beings into what can be mastered by modern, mathematically structured technology, which is something

---

[10] Heidegger, *Being and Time*, 100.
[11] Heidegger, "The Question Concerning Technology," 16.
[12] Martin Heidegger, *Discourse on Thinking*, trans. by John Anderson and E. Hans Freund (New York: Harper & Row, 1959), 50.
[13] Heidegger, *Being and Time*, 128.

essentially different from every other hitherto known use of tools,"[14] and since *Being and Time* explicitly denies the possibility of a "mathematical functionalization"[15] of the ready-to-hand, this interpretation concludes that *Being and Time* presents an account of man's perennial tool-using stance that is radically opposed to the technological understanding of equipment.

The very possibility of these two simplistic readings suggests that *Being and Time* offers an understanding of the being of equipment that hovers ambiguously between that of craftsmanship and technology and so tempts readers to identify *Being and Time* with one or the other, while at the same time resisting either assimilation. We will now attempt to bring the intermediate position of *Being and Time* into focus by comparing what later Heidegger says about the Greek and the technological understanding of use, equipment, and nature with the account of these phenomena in *Being and Time*. Only then will we be in a position to move from these ontic considerations to an ontological account of the difference between the world of the craftsman, worldhood in *Being and Time*, and the way of revealing of technology.

The essential characteristic of equipment at any period is that it is used, but usefulness itself turns out to have a history. In *What Is Called Thinking?*, Heidegger attempts to recover Parmenides' understanding of *chrê* by discussing the early Greek understanding of "the useful":

"To use" means, first, to let a thing be what it is and how it is. To let it be this way requires that the used thing be cared for in its essential nature—we do so by responding to the demands which the used thing makes manifest in the given instance.[16]

"Using" does not mean the mere utilizing, using up, exploiting. Utilization is only the degenerate and debauched form of use. When we handle a thing, for example, our hand must fit itself to the thing. Use implies fitting response.[17]

The degenerate form of use—exploiting—clearly corresponds to the technological attitude in which equipment *is* only insofar as it is at our disposal—otherwise it is to be ignored or disposed of. To describe this "debauched" form Heidegger paraphrases Rilke on the *Ersatz*:

[O]bjects are produced to be used up. The more quickly they are used up, the greater becomes the necessity to replace them even more quickly and more readily...What is constant in things produced as objects merely for consumption is: the substitute—*Ersatz*.[18]

---

[14] Martin Heidegger, *An Introduction to Metaphysics*, trans. Ralph Manheim (Garden City, NY: Anchor Books, 1969), 162.

[15] Heidegger, *Being and Time*, 122.

[16] Martin Heidegger, *What Is Called Thinking?*, trans. Fred D. Wieck and J. Glenn Gray (New York: Harper & Row, 1968), 191.

[17] Heidegger, *What Is Called Thinking?*, 187.

[18] Martin Heidegger, "What Are Poets For?," in *Poetry, Language, Thought*, 130.

Equipment in *Being and Time* is not assimilable to either of these extremes. It is characterized by disposability: "Equipment... is manipulable in the broadest sense and at our disposal."[19] A hammer, for example, is defined in *Being and Time* in terms of its function—how it is *utilized*—its in-order-to. On this view it makes no sense to speak of equipment's essential nature, and, in spite of the manual implications of *Zuhandenheit*, in all the discussions of hammering there is no mention of hands. There is, in fact, no place for a "fitting response." Yet the hammer is not something standing by to be used up and disposed of like a styrofoam cup, a ball-point pen, or the latest type of fever thermometer. Rather, there is still talk of taking care of equipment—not the way the craftsman takes care of his personal tools, but the way the foreman takes care of industrial equipment. Thus, when manipulation ceases, care "can take on a more precise kind of circumspection, such as 'inspecting', checking up on what has been attained, or looking over the 'operations.'"[20] This seems to suggest a three-stage progression, or better a degeneration, in the history of equipment from use, to utility as fulfilling a function, to using up as exploitation.

The above decline from craftsmanship to industrial production to technology can be seen even more clearly if we turn from the equipment the craftsman uses to the equipment he produces. The craftsman, Heidegger tells us, must be understood as responding to his materials:

[A] true cabinetmaker...makes himself answer and respond above all to the different kinds of wood and to the shapes slumbering within wood—to wood as it enters into man's dwelling with all the hidden riches of its nature. In fact, this relatedness to wood is what maintains the whole craft.

Without that relatedness, the craft will never be anything but empty busywork, any occupation with it will be determined exclusively by business concerns.[21]

Indeed, without concern for the nature of its materials, craftsmanship turns into industrial production:

[W]hat maintains and sustains even this handicraft is not the mere manipulation of tools, but the relatedness to wood. But where in the manipulations of the industrial worker is there any relatedness to such things as the shapes slumbering within wood?[22]

In *Being and Time* we find no place for the resistance and the reliability of equipment—only its ongoing functioning or its breakdown. There is no mention of "the hidden riches of nature." In the language of the later Heidegger, *Being and*

---

[19] Heidegger, *Being and Time*, 98.   [20] Heidegger, *Being and Time*, 409.
[21] Heidegger, *What Is Called Thinking?*, 21, 22.
[22] Heidegger, *What Is Called Thinking?*, 23.

Time has no place for the withdrawal and resistance of the Earth. As Heidegger remarks in discussing Van Gogh's painting of the peasant's shoes, as if he were repudiating the simple pragmatism of *Being and Time*:

> The equipmental quality of the equipment consists indeed in its usefulness. But this usefulness itself rests in the abundance of an essential being of the equipment. We call it reliability. By virtue of this reliability the peasant woman is made privy to the silent call of the earth ...
>   The usefulness of equipment is ... the essential consequence of reliability.[23]

If equipmentality is equated merely with usefulness as utility without resistance or reliability, the stage is set for technology. Everything becomes available for cost/benefit analysis.

> [T]he setting-upon that challenges forth the energies of nature is an expediting... [E]xpediting is always itself directed from the beginning toward furthering something else, i.e., toward driving on to the maximum yield at the minimum expense.[24]

Having no nature of its own, industrialized equipment is ready to be absorbed into the constant restructuring that is the final form of technological organization—beyond objectification, and even beyond the fixed functions of the ready-to-hand.

> Everywhere everything is ordered to stand by, to be immediately at hand, indeed to stand there just so that it may be on call for a further ordering. Whatever is ordered about in this way has its own standing. We call it the standing-reserve [*Bestand*] ... Whatever stands by in the sense of standing-reserve no longer stands over against us as object.[25]

Heidegger's notion of *Bestand* enables us to distinguish three ways that nature can be understood. For the first thinkers, according to Heidegger, nature was self-contained:

> For the Greeks, *physis* is the first and the essential name for beings themselves and as a whole. For them the being is what flourishes on its own, in no way compelled, what rises and comes forward, and what goes back into itself and passes away.[26]

In *Being and Time* nature is encountered as a source of raw material:

> In the environment certain entities become accessible which are always ready-to-hand, but which, in themselves, do not need to be produced. Hammer, tongs, and needle, refer

---

23 Heidegger, "The Origin of the Work of Art," 34–5.
24 Heidegger, "The Question Concerning Technology," 15.
25 Heidegger, *What Is Called Thinking?*, 17.
26 Martin Heidegger, *Nietzsche*, vol. 1 (New York: Harper & Row, 1979), 81.

in themselves to steel, iron, metal, mineral, wood, in that they consist of these. In equipment that is used, "Nature" is discovered along with it by that use.[27]

In advanced technology, nature is attacked and transformed to insure that it will always be available for use and further development:

[A] tract of land is challenged into the putting out of coal and ore. The earth now reveals itself as a coal mining district, the soil as a mineral deposit.[28]

Challenging forth into revealing...concerns nature, above all, as the chief storehouse of the standing energy reserve.[29]

With respect to the being of nature, then, *Being and Time* shows itself to be again transitional. When *Being and Time* describes the river as water-power, there is no suggestion that this power is a gift, but neither is there talk of a hydroelectric power station, which dams up the river in order to convert it into a pure energy reservoir. But to understand fully the significance of *Being and Time*'s transitional position we must ask: Does *Being and Time* contend that the river is, *among other things*, a source of energy, or does it hold that the use of the river as water-power is *the primordial way* the river is encountered?

Here *Being and Time* reveals its profound ambiguity. At first it seems that approaching nature in terms of its utility—what one might call the pragmatism of *Being and Time*—is only one ontic way of encountering it. Indeed, according to a puzzling passage early in *Being and Time*, there are at least three ways of encountering nature. Nature can be encountered as ready-to-hand, present-at-hand, or as the nature that "stirs and strives":

As the "environment" is discovered, the "Nature" thus discovered is encountered too. If its kind of Being as ready-to-hand is disregarded, this "Nature" itself can be discovered and defined simply in its pure presence-at-hand. But when this happens, the Nature which "stirs and strives", which assails us and enthralls us as landscape, remains hidden.[30]

Yet, the rest of *Being and Time* concentrates on showing that nature as present-at-hand must be a privative mode of the ready-to-hand: "The entity which Descartes is trying to grasp ontologically and in principle with his '*extensio*', is rather such as to become discoverable first of all by going through an entity

---

[27] Heidegger, *Being and Time*, 100.
[28] Heidegger, "The Question Concerning Technology," 14.
[29] Heidegger, "The Question Concerning Technology," 21.
[30] Heidegger, *Being and Time*, 100.

within-the-world which is proximally ready-to-hand—Nature."[31] The nature that stirs and strives is never mentioned again.

These hesitations and contradictions regarding the place of nature must finally be settled on the level of ontology. Thus Heidegger's pragmatic view of nature only becomes clear in the discussion of reality at the end of Division I:

The "Nature" by which we are "surrounded" is, of course, an entity within-the-world; but the kind of Being which it shows belongs neither to the ready-to-hand nor to what is present-at-hand as "Things of Nature": No matter how this Being of "Nature" may be Interpreted, *all* the modes of Being of entities within-the-world are founded ontologically upon the worldhood of the world, and accordingly upon the phenomenon of Being-in-the-world.[32]

Nature is neither present-at-hand nor ready-to-hand, yet the being of nature must be understood as founded upon worldhood. To understand worldhood, however, Heidegger tells us, we must begin with an account of equipment. Now the primary point that distinguishes equipment from "mere things" is its thoroughgoing interrelatedness:

To the being of any equipment there always belongs a totality of equipment, in which it can be this equipment that it is.[33]

What it is to be a hammer is just to be related in appropriate ways to nails, carpenters, furniture, houses, families, and so on. In other words, what an item of equipment *is* is entirely dependent on how it is incorporated into a total equipment context. Thus:

As the Being of something ready-to-hand, an involvement is itself discovered only on the basis of the prior discovery of a totality of involvements. So in any involvement that has been discovered (that is, in anything ready-to-hand which we encounter), what we have called the "worldly character" of the ready-to-hand has been discovered beforehand.[34]

At this point, in a move whose full implications only become apparent later, Heidegger passes from speaking of *a* referential totality to talking of *the* referential totality.

The "for-the-sake-of-which" signifies an "in-order-to"; this in turn, a "towards-this"; the latter, an "in-which" of letting something be involved; and that in turn, the "with-which" of an involvement. These relationships are bound up with one another as a primordial totality...The relational totality of this signifying we call "*significance*". This is what makes up the structure of the world.[35]

---

[31] Heidegger, *Being and Time*, 128.   [32] Heidegger, *Being and Time*, 254.
[33] Heidegger, *Being and Time*, 97.   [34] Heidegger, *Being and Time*, 118.
[35] Heidegger, *Being and Time*, 120.

Thus, in spite of Heidegger's acknowledgment that nature is not ready-to-hand, it follows that *all* beings including those of nature are founded ontologically upon the structure of the equipmental totality, and, indeed: *"Readiness-to-hand is the way in which entities as they are 'in themselves' are defined ontologico-categorially."*[36]

Heidegger clearly wished to resist this conclusion. In a torturous footnote discussing nature in *The Essence of Reasons*, he protests that "a study of the ontological structure of 'environmental' being (insofar as it is discovered as tool)" is a *"preliminary characterization* of the phenomenon of world." Such an account, Heidegger assures us, only "prepares the way for the transcendental problem of world."[37] Yet in *Being and Time*, Division II, Chapter 4, when the temporal schema is introduced in its transcendental role as "the existential-temporal condition for the possibility of the world,"[38] the "present" dimension of the horizontal schema is still the in-order-to and Heidegger repeats on this transcendental level the claim of Division I that "significance-relationships... determine the structure of the world."[39] Thus, even on the transcendental level, the world is equated with the referential totality, and all entities, including nature, can only be encountered as they show up in the equipmental world.

In spite of Heidegger's published disclaimers, the dangerous consequences of the ontological priority given to Dasein's practical activity are everywhere evident in *Being and Time*. Even language is ontologically grounded in the totality of equipment:

> [I]n significance... there lies the ontological condition which makes it possible for Dasein, as something which understands and interprets, to disclose such things as "significations"; upon these, in turn, is founded the Being of words and of language.[40]

Here the pragmatic implications are so unacceptable that, rather than try to retroactively reinterpret *Being and Time*, Heidegger is obliged to repudiate the priority of the equipmental context. In his own copy of *Being and Time* he wrote at this point: "Unwahr. Sprache ist nicht aufgestockt, sondern *ist* ursrpüngliche Wesen der Wahrheit als Da."[41]

The full technological tendency implied in the ontological priority granted to the structure of the referential totality as the structure of the world only becomes apparent, however, when we investigate in slow motion Heidegger's sleight of hand with the notion of totality. As we have seen, when introducing the notion of

[36] Heidegger, *Being and Time*, 101.
[37] Martin Heidegger, *The Essence of Reasons*, trans. Terrence Malick (Evanston, IL: Northwestern University Press, 1969), 81.
[38] Heidegger, *Being and Time*, 416.   [39] Heidegger, *Being and Time*, 417.
[40] Heidegger, *Being and Time*, 121.
[41] Martin Heidegger, *Sein und Zeit* (Tübingen: Niemeyer Verlag, 1977), 442.

equipment, Heidegger tells us that a condition of the possibility of equipment is that it functions within a relatively autonomous local context (the workshop, the room, etc.) In *Being and Time* Heidegger calls these contexts "regions."

Something like a region must first be discovered if there is to be any possibility of allotting or coming across places for a totality of equipment that is circumspectively at one's disposal.[42]

But, to complete the ontological project of *Being and Time*, Heidegger must show "how the aroundness of the environment, the specific spatiality of entities encountered within the environment, is founded upon the worldhood of the world."[43] He thus expands the local context to a single overarching totality. He recognizes that this tendency to totalize is a specifically modern phenomenon whose full meaning he realizes has not yet been revealed:

In Dasein there lies an essential tendency towards closeness. All the ways in which we speed things up, as we are more or less compelled to do today, push us on towards the conquest of remoteness. With the "radio", for example, Dasein has so expanded its everyday environment that it has accomplished a de-severance of the "world"—a de-severance which, in its meaning for Dasein, cannot yet be visualized.[44]

It is as if *in Being and Time* Dasein is already uprooted from the dwelling in nearness, which is illustrated by Heidegger in his description of "the bridge which *gathers* the earth as landscape around the stream."[45] Indeed, the totality of equipment more closely resembles "the highway bridge...tied into the network of long-distance traffic,"[46] for equipment in *Being and Time* is finally taken to be dependent on one total network in which it is a node. This is a complete reversal of the ancient understanding evoked by Heidegger, in which the thing is not a slot in a global totality, but rather that which organizes a local region around itself:

---

[42] Heidegger, *Being and Time*, 136.   [43] Heidegger, *Being and Time*, 135.

[44] Heidegger, *Being and Time*, 140. From the point of view of the account of falling in *Being and Time*, it might seem that this tendency to bring everything close is the result of curiosity (Heidegger, *Being and Time*, 216), and so would be overcome by authentic resoluteness, as described in Division II. Indeed, we are told in Division II that resolute Dasein is plunged into its own concrete, local situation ("Resoluteness brings the Being of the 'there' into the existence of its Situation," Heidegger, *Being and Time*, 347), But it is also clear in Division II that this characteristic of resolute Dasein does not change the fact that the only clearing for encountering entities conceivable within the framework of *Being and Time* remains the public referential totality laid out by the Anyone ("The Anyone itself articulates the referential context of significance," Heidegger, *Being and Time*, 167.) In Division II, Heidegger states explicitly: "As phenomena which are examples of Being among, we have chosen the using, manipulation, and producing of the ready-to-hand...In this kind of concern Dasein's authentic existence too maintains itself, even when for such existence this concern is 'a matter of indifference'" (Heidegger, *Being and Time*, 403).

[45] Martin Heidegger, "Building, Dwelling, Thinking," in *Poetry, Language, Thought*, 152.

[46] Heidegger, "Building, Dwelling, Thinking," 152.

[T]he bridge does not first come to a location to stand in it; rather, a location comes into existence only by virtue of the bridge... *Accordingly, spaces receive their being from locations and not from "space."*[47]

The failure to realize "the origin of space in the properties peculiar to site,"[48] plus the ontologizing of the pragmatic structure of temporality, enables Heidegger in *Being and Time* to treat spatiality as a mode of temporality—a form of metaphysical violence he later retracts ("The attempt in *Being and Time*, Section 70, to derive human spatiality from temporality is untenable").[49]

The idea that in the technological world equipment more and more comes to fit together in one single totality is already a step from the relatively autonomous and autochthonous workshop of the craftsman toward the uprooted interconnectedness of industrial mass production. Its final achievement would be a world system under the feedback control of cybernetics. Heidegger makes a similar point in *The Question Concerning Technology*, when he criticizes Hegel's definition of the machine as an autonomous tool and contrasts the autonomous tools of the craftsman with the total ordering characteristic of the technological machine.

When applied to the tools of the craftsman, [Hegel's] characterization is correct. Characterized in this way, however, the machine is not thought at all from out of the essence of technology within which it belongs. Seen in terms of the standing-reserve, the machine is completely unautonomous, for it has its standing only from the ordering of the orderable.[50]

In *The Question Concerning Technology* the total system of ordering in which all beings are caught up, stored, and endlessly switched around is called the *Gestell*. This technological kind of revealing or clearing is contrasted with the worlding of the world of the craftsman. In fact, according to later Heidegger the technological totality is no world at all:

[I]n the ordering of the standing-reserve, the truth of Being remains denied as world.[51]

Heidegger's identification of the "phenomenon of world" (with its structure, worldhood) with a single referential totality in *Being and Time* can thus be seen as a transitional stage. By highlighting the interrelationship between all items of equipment and by defining equipment by its position in this referential

[47] Heidegger, "Building, Dwelling, Thinking," 154.
[48] Martin Heidegger, *On Time and Being*, trans. Joan Stambaugh (New York: Harper & Row, 1972), 23.
[49] Heidegger, *On Time and Being*, 23.
[50] Heidegger, "The Question Concerning Technology," 17.
[51] Heidegger, "The Question Concerning Technology," 48.

totality, *Being and Time* denies localness, thus removing the last barrier to global totalization, and preparing the way for the "total mobilization of all beings" that, according to later Heidegger, makes up the essence of technology.[52]

Conclusion

Seen in the light of the relation of nature and technology revealed by later Heidegger, *Being and Time* appears in the history of the being of equipment not just as a transition but as *the* decisive step toward technology. (A step later Heidegger tries, unconvincingly, to read back into Nietzsche.) As later Heidegger sees it, at the beginning of our history *technê* was subordinated to nature or *physis*:

If man tries to win a foothold and establish himself among the beings (*physis*) to which he is exposed, if he proceeds to master beings in this way or that way, then his advance against beings is borne and guided by a knowledge of them. Such knowledge is called *technê*.[53]

[T]he bringing forth of artworks as well as utensils is an irruption by the man who knows and who goes forward in the midst of *physis* and upon its basis.[54]

In *Being and Time*, however, the relation between *physis* and *technê* is transposed: Nature can be encountered only as it fits, or fails to fit, into the referential totality. This is a crucial reversal of the Greek understanding, for the "going-forward" of *technê* "thought in Greek fashion, is no kind of attack; it lets what is already coming to presence arrive."[55] In *Being and Time* there is no outright attack but no openness to arrival either. But it is precisely this lack of receptivity to "the nature that stirs and strives" that leaves open, indeed, encourages, the kind of attack and reordering of nature that encounters natural objects as *Bestand*.

---

[52] Martin Heidegger, *The Question of Being*, trans. Jean T. Wilde and William Kluback (New Haven, CT: College & University Press, 1958).

[53] Heidegger, *Nietzsche*, vol. 1, 81.   [54] Heidegger, *Nietzsche*, vol. 1, 82.

[55] Heidegger, *Nietzsche*, vol. 1, 82. That this is, indeed, a reversal of the traditional ontological view inherited from the Greeks is clear in Heidegger's lectures from the Summer Semester of 1925, *Prolegomena zur Geschichte des Zeitsbegriffs*, ed. Petra Jaeger, *Gesamtausgabe*, vol. 20 (Frankfurt am Main: Vittorio Klostermann, 1979), 270–1: "One will perhaps say that precisely this *Vorhandene*— the environing Nature—is the most real, the authentic reality of the world...Without this most real—viz., nature, earth, ground—everything earthly cannot be, perhaps not even Dasein itself. The workworld bears references to beings in themselves, a fact which, in the end, makes clear that it—the workworld, the world of concern—is absolutely not the primary being...This consequence, it appears, is unavoidable. But what then does it mean: the world of nature is in the sense of the analysis of most real?...The environing references in which nature is primarily present in a worldly way signifies just the opposite: that *the reality of nature is to be understood only as Worldhood*. The ontical dependence relations of worldly beings among themselves do not coincide with the fundamental ontological relationships. Tentatively, this is to say that even the being present-at-hand of nature as environment...first and foremost is revealed and there according to its meaning, from and in the world of concern."

This can be seen even more clearly if we look at the role assigned to care by the early Greeks, *Being and Time*, and technology. According to later Heidegger we must "conceive of the innermost essence of *technê*...as...care."[56] For the Greeks "such carefulness is more than practiced diligence; it is the mastery of a composed resolute openness to beings."[57] This sounds at first exactly like the characterization of *Sorge* in *Being and Time*. But Heidegger hastens to add: "The unity of *melete* and *technê*...characterizes the basic posture of the forward-reaching disclosure of Dasein, which seeks to ground beings *on their own terms*."[58] This qualification shows again that in *Being and Time* the relationship between Dasein and beings is reversed. Beings are discovered in terms of Dasein's concerns. The care structure is definitive of Dasein, the being whose being is an issue for it, and beings are disclosed in terms of Dasein's possibilities. The interconnection between significance, the totality of involvements, worldhood, and Dasein's possibilities as conditions for encountering beings is laid out in Division II.

Any discovering of a totality of involvements goes back to a "for-the-sake-of-which"; and on the understanding of such a "for-the-sake-of-which" is based in turn the understanding of signification as the disclosedness of the current world. In seeking shelter, sustenance, livelihood, we do so "for-the-sake-of" constant possibilities of Dasein which are very close to it; upon these the entity for which its own Being is an issue, has already projected itself.[59]

To be sure, Dasein is not a subject and the for-the-sake-of-which is not a goal. But this only shows that as far as the referential totality is concerned, Heidegger is already beyond the willful understanding of care as individual self-assertion, which gradually becomes explicit in the development of objectivity from Descartes to Nietzsche, and finds expression in early industrialization. For Rilke, Heidegger tells us, modern "'caring'" has the character of purposeful self-assertion by the ways and means of unconditional production."[60] Such willful self-assertion still resists impersonal, global technology. The account of worldhood in *Being and Time*, however, removes every vestige of resistance—that of *physis*, as well as that of will and subjectivity—to the technological tendency to treat all beings (even man) as resources. Nothing stands in the way of the final possibility that for Dasein the only issue left becomes ordering for the sake of order itself. This is the understanding of Being definitive of technological nihilism, an understanding prepared but not consummated by the account of equipment in *Being and Time*.

---

[56] Heidegger, *Nietzsche*, vol. 1, 164.   [57] Heidegger, *Nietzsche*, vol. 1, 164.
[58] Heidegger, *Nietzsche*, vol. 1, 165.   [59] Heidegger, *Being and Time*, 344.
[60] Heidegger, "What Are Poets For?," 120.

9

On the Ordering of Things

Being and Power in Heidegger and Foucault (1989)

The most central and obscure notion in Heidegger's writings is Being, and the same could be said of the notion of Power in the works of Foucault. For both thinkers these are not traditional stable entities. Heidegger offers a history of Being (*Seinsgeschichte*) in order to help us understand and overcome our current technological understanding of Being; and Foucault analyses several regimes of power in the course of his genealogy of the biopower that, he claims, dominates modern life.

These rough parallels suggest that it might be illuminating to see how far the comparison of Heidegger's "Being" with Foucault's "Power" can be pushed. Do these terms designate equivalent functions? To what extent do Heidegger's epochs of the history of Being match Foucault's regimes in the history of Power? To what extent do these two histories lead us to see our current cultural condition in similar ways? How does each envisage resistance?

Lest the striking difference in Heidegger's and Foucault's politics and lifestyles make this project seem hopeless from the start, we must remember Foucault's comment on Heidegger in his last interview:

For me Heidegger has always been the essential philosopher.... My entire philosophical development was determined by my reading of Heidegger.[1]

The other major influence was, of course, Nietzsche. Foucault tells us in the same interview: "I am simply Nietzschean, and I try to see, on a number of points, and to the extent that it is possible, with the aid of Nietzsche's texts...what can be done in this or that domain."[2] But it was through Heidegger that Foucault came

---

[1] Michel Foucault, "Final Interview," *Raritan* (Summer 1985), 8. Interview conducted by Gilles Barbedette and published in *Les Nouvelles* (28 June 1984).

[2] Foucault, "Final Interview," 9.

to appreciate Nietzsche. "It is possible that if I had not read Heidegger, I would not have read Nietzsche. I had tried to read Nietzsche in the fifties but Nietzsche alone did not appeal to me—whereas Nietzsche and Heidegger, that was a philosophical shock!"[3]

The Functioning of Being and Power

It is important to realize from the start that for Heidegger Being is not a substance or a process. Being, in the sense relevant here, is short for the understanding of Being, the truth of Being, or the meaning of Being.[4] For Heidegger all these terms call attention to the context in which people and things show up and can encounter each other. In *Being and Time* he shows that all human activity presupposes such a context in which objects and actions make sense—a context that both opens up and limits the kinds of objects that can be dealt with and the possible ways of dealing with them.

Heidegger is interested only in the most general characteristics of our under-standing of Being. He notes, however, that this understanding is embodied in the tools, language, and institutions of a society and in each person growing up in that society. These shared practices into which we are socialized provide a background understanding of what counts as objects, what counts as human beings, and ultimately what counts as real, on the basis of which we can direct our actions toward particular things and people. Thus the understanding of Being creates what Heidegger calls a clearing (*Lichtung*). Heidegger calls the unnoticed way that the clearing both limits and opens up what can show up and what can be done its "unobtrusive governance" (*Waltens*).[5]

Many of Foucault's difficult remarks concerning power make sense if we take him to be getting at a similar social clearing with an emphasis on the way embodied, everyday practices produce, perpetuate, and delimit what people can think and do. And since Foucault is not interested in how *things* show up but exclusively in *people's actions*, "Power," which is normally used to describe the way governments govern people's actions, seems an appropriate, if perhaps misleading, name for this selective aspect of the clearing. Foucault attempts to ward off any misunderstanding:

---

[3] Foucault, "Final Interview," 9.

[4] Later Heidegger distinguishes the understanding of Being from Being that "sends" various understandings. In his middle period he speaks of Being in a way that covers both meanings. "Being...is not God and not a cosmic ground. It is furthest from all beings and yet nearer to man than any being" (Martin Heidegger, "Letter on Humanism," in *Basic Writings*, ed. David Farrell Krell (New York: Harper & Row, 1977), 210).

[5] Heidegger, "Letter on Humanism," 212.

By power, I do not mean "Power" as a group of institutions and mechanisms that ensure the subservience of the citizens of a given state. By power, I do not mean, either, a mode of subjugation which, in contrast to violence has the form of the rule. Finally, I do not have in mind a general system of domination exerted by one group over another.... The analysis, made in terms of power, must not assume that the sovereignty of the State, the form of the law, or the overall unity of a domination are given at the outset; rather, these are only the terminal forms power takes.[6]

Each age has its distinctive form of power:

[T]o live in society is to live in such a way that it is possible to act on each other's actions. A society without power relations can only be an abstraction.[7]

For Foucault, as for Heidegger on Being, power is neither a fixed entity nor an institution:

One needs to be nominalistic, no doubt; power is not an institution, and not a structure; neither is it a certain strength we are endowed with; it is the name that one attributes to a complex strategical situation in a particular society.[8]

It is sometimes difficult to separate Foucault's discussion of those characteristics that belong to power *as such* from those that belong to the stage of power in which we now live. The best general description of power is found in Foucault's essay "Le sujet et le pouvoir." There, he clearly thinks of power not as a substance or process or force but as a clearing which, by opening up a finite field of possibilities, governs actions while none the less leaving them free.

[S]omething called Power, with or without a capital letter, which is assumed to exist universally in a concentrated or diffused form, does not exist. Power exists only when it is put into action.... It is a total structure of actions brought to bear upon possible actions...

Power is exercised only over free subjects, and only in so far as they are free. By this we mean individual or collective subjects who are faced with a field of possibilities in which several ways of behaving, several reactions and diverse comportments may be realized. [T]o "conduct" is at the same time to "lead" others...and a way of behaving within a more or less open field of possibilities. The exercise of power consists in guiding the possibility of conduct and putting in order the possible outcome. Basically power is less a confrontation between two adversaries or the linking of one to the other

---

[6] Michel Foucault, *L'Histoire de la* sexualité, vol. 1: *La Volonté de savoir* (Paris: Gallimard, 1976), 121, translated as *The History of Sexuality*, vol. 1: *An Introduction* (New York: Vintage, 1980), 92.

[7] Michel Foucault, "The Subject and Power," afterword in Hubert L. Dreyfus and Paul Rabinow, *Michel Foucault: Beyond Structuralism and Hermeneutics*, 2nd edn. (Chicago, IL: University of Chicago Press, 1983), 221–2.

[8] Foucault, "The Subject and Power," 93.

than a question of government.... To govern, in this sense, is to structure the possible field of action of others.[9]

We should not be surprised that in Volume 2 of *Histoire de la sexualité*, Foucault speaks in Heideggerian terms of his later work analyzing power. He first reminds us that "the proper task of a history of thought, as against a history of behaviors or representations, [is] to define the conditions in which human beings 'problematize' what they are, what they do, and the world in which they live."[10] He then puts this in later Heideggerian terms as a receptivity to being:

[It was a matter of] analyzing, not behaviors or ideas, nor societies and their "ideologies", but the *problematizations* through which *being offers itself as having to be thought*—and the *practices* on the basis of which these problematizations are formed.[11]

Seinsgeschichte and Genealogy

The space that governs human activity by determining what counts as a thing, what counts as true/false and what it makes sense to do, is not static, nor does it have abrupt discontinuities, but it does fall into a distinguishable, if overlapping, series of epochs.

Both Heidegger and Foucault, no doubt influenced by Nietzsche, begin with a prehistory in pre-Socratic Greece. Heidegger devotes many pages to showing that although pre-Socratic thought did not encompass the clearing (*Lichtung*), it did not deny it either. Their sense that what showed up as present depended upon what was not itself present is preserved in their understanding of the truth of Being as *aletheia* or unconcealment. But this understanding was lost when Socrates and Plato took Being to be the ground of the phenomena, and truth to be the correspondence of propositions to an independent reality.

[T]here has historically been a withdrawal of Being itself; there has been an abandonment by Being of beings as such.... Consequently, and from that time on, Being itself has remained unthought.[12]

Foucault's references to this first stage of our culture are much sketchier than Heidegger's, but he too points to the emergence of theoretical knowing among the Greeks as the great turning point in our history. The pragmatic and poetic

---

[9] Foucault, "The Subject and Power," 219–21.

[10] Michel Foucault, *L'Usage des plaisirs* (Paris: Gallimard, 1984), 16, translated as *The History of Sexuality*, vol. 2: *The Use of Pleasure* (New York: Vintage, 1986), 10.

[11] Foucault, *L'Usage des plaisirs*, 17, *History of Sexuality*, vol. 2, 11 (emphasis added).

[12] Martin Heidegger, *Nietzsche*, vol. 4 (New York: Harper & Row, 1982), 215.

discourse of early Greek civilization was destroyed by the rise of theory: "The Sophists were routed... [from] the time of the great Platonic division onwards, the [Platonic] will to truth has had its own history."[13] This change presumably altered all aspects of Greek life. For example, Foucault tells us that "When Hippocrates had reduced medicine to a system, observation was abandoned and philosophy introduced into medicine"[14] or "the West has managed... to annex sex to a field of rationality... we are accustomed to such 'conquests' since the Greeks."[15]

Heidegger, in keeping with his concerns as a philosopher, has an elaborate account of the epochs of Being associated with the words *physis*, *idea*, and *energeia*, and of the radical break between pre-Socratic *physis* and all later names for Being. He stresses the difference between the pre-Socratic understanding of Being and our own. For the pre-Socratics:

[t]hat which is, is that which arises and opens itself, which, as what presences, comes upon man as the one who presences, i.e., comes upon the one who himself opens himself to what presences in that he apprehends it.... To be beheld by what is, to be included and maintained within its openness and in that way to be borne along by it—to be driven about by its oppositions and marked by its discord—that is the essence of man in the great age of the [pre-Socratic] Greeks.[16]

In his published works Heidegger has much less to say about the Platonic and Aristotelian epochs and relatively little to add about the Romans, except that the translation of Greek terms into a philosophy expressing Roman practices lost the original sense of words such as *theoria*, which once focused the Platonic Greek understanding of Being.

By medieval times the clearing (*Lichtung*) had been completely forgotten and Being was equated with substances grounded in a supreme Being:

For the Middle Ages... to be in being means to belong within a specific rank of the order of what has been created—a rank appointed from the beginning—and as thus caused, to correspond to the cause of creation.[17]

Foucault, too, has little to say about Greek philosophy. He does, it is true, briefly describe hierarchical, monarchical power at the beginning of *Surveiller et punir*.

---

[13] Michel Foucault, *L'Ordre du discours* (Paris: Gallimard, 1971), 18–19.

[14] Michel Foucault, *Naissance de la clinique* (Paris: PUF, 1963), 55, translated as *The Birth of the Clinic* (New York: Vintage, 1975), 56.

[15] Foucault, *La Volonté de savoir*, 102–3/*The History of Sexuality*, vol. 1, 78.

[16] Martin Heidegger, "The Age of the World Picture," in *The Question Concerning Technology and Other Essays* (New York: Harper, 1977), 131.

[17] Heidegger, "The Age of the World Picture," 130.

What interests us is, in any case, how Heidegger's and Foucault's concerns converge upon the transformation that issues in the modern world and our current understanding of human beings.

Heidegger begins by telling us that "Metaphysics grounds an age, in that, through a specific interpretation of what is, and through a specific comprehension of truth, it gives to that age the basis upon which it is essentially formed."[18] Foucault says, more narrowly: "In any given culture and at any given moment, there is only one *episteme* that defines the conditions of possibility of all knowledge whether expressed in a theory or silently invested in a practice."[19]

Both view the account of representation in the classical age as the crucial but unstable beginning of modernity—a starting point that is not yet clear about its radically new understanding of Being—a new understanding that finally becomes explicit in Kant's interpretation of *man*.

At this point the parallel between the two thinkers comes into sharp focus, as can be seen when we compare Heidegger's account of the origin of man in "The Age of the World Picture" and Foucault's account in *Les Mots et les choses*. Heidegger tells us of a radical transformation in our understanding of being that took place in the seventeenth century: "What it is to be is for the first time defined as the objectiveness of representing, and truth is first defined as the certainty of representation in the metaphysics of Descartes."[20] The age of representation differs in fundamental ways from all other ages:

What is, in its entirety, is now taken in such a way that it only is in being to the extent that it is set up by man, who represents and sets forth. The being of whatever is, is sought and found in the representedness of the latter—the fact that the world becomes picture is what distinguishes the essence of the modern age.[21]

Foucault, always more concrete, brilliantly analyzes a representative picture, *Las Meninas*, where representation in its various forms is literally pictured. In *Las Meninas* the aspects of representation—the subject matter of the painting—have been dispersed into three separate figures. Their representations are spread out in the picture itself. These aspects are the producing of the representation (the painter), the object represented (the models and their gaze), and the viewing of the representation (the spectator). Each of these separate functions can be and has been represented by Velázquez. This dispersion of representation is necessary

[18] Heidegger, "The Age of the World Picture," 115.
[19] Michel Foucault, *Les Mots et les choses* (Paris: Gallimard, 1966), 179, translated as *The Order of Things* (New York: Vintage, 1973), 168.
[20] Heidegger, "The Age of the World Picture," 127.
[21] Heidegger, "The Age of the World Picture," 127–30.

so that all these functions can be laid out in an organized table. The price paid for this success is that the activity of representation, the unified temporal unfolding of the functions of representation, cannot be represented on the table. And it is this tension that produces the instability in the painting and in the *episteme*. The central paradox of the painting turns on the impossibility of representing the act of representing.

The answer to this paradox is that man does not only copy the order; he produces it. Heidegger explains:

To represent means to bring what is present at hand before oneself as something standing over against, to relate it to oneself, to the one representing it, and to force it back into this relationship to oneself as the normative realm.... What is decisive is that man himself expressly takes up this position as one constituted by himself and that he makes it secure as the footing for a possible development of humanity.[22]

As Foucault puts it:

Man appears in his ambiguous position as an object of knowledge and as subject that knows: enslaved sovereign, observed spectator, he appears in the place belonging to the King, which was assigned to him in advance by *Las Meninas*.[23]

With Kant, man becomes both the source of the meaning of objects and an object in the world, and philosophy becomes anthropology. In Heidegger's terms:

[O]bservation of and teaching about the world change into a doctrine of man, into anthropology.... The name "anthropology" as used here does not mean just some investigation of man by a natural science.... It designates that philosophical interpretation of man which explains and evaluates whatever is, in its entirety, from the standpoint of man and in relation to man.[24]

Anthropology is that interpretation of man that already knows fundamentally what man is and hence can never ask who he may be.[25]

Philosophy, according to Kant, awakens from its dogmatic slumber, only to fall, according to Foucault, into an anthropological sleep. Heidegger and Foucault thus both reach rhetorical heights as they look forward to the end of humanism. Heidegger:

Man cannot, of himself, abandon this destining of his modern essence or abolish it by fiat. But man can, as he thinks ahead, ponder this: Being subject as humanity has not always been the sole possibility belonging to the essence of historical man,... nor will it

---

[22] Heidegger, "The Age of the World Picture," 132.
[23] Foucault, *Les Mots et les choses*, 323/*The Order of Things*, 312.
[24] Heidegger, "The Age of the World Picture," 132.
[25] Heidegger, "The Age of the World Picture," 153.

always be. A fleeting cloud shadow over a concealed land, such is the darkening which that truth as the certainty of subjectivity... lays over a disclosing event that it remains denied to subjectivity itself to experience.[26]

Or Foucault:

As the archaeology of our thought easily shows, man is an invention of recent date. And one perhaps nearing its end.

   If those arrangements were to disappear as they appeared, if some event... were to cause them to crumble, as the ground of Classical thought did, at the end of the eighteenth century, then one can certainly wager that man would be erased, like a face drawn in sand at the edge of the sea.[27]

In the last stage of their thinking, both Heidegger and Foucault realize that man is, indeed, being wiped out, but this only reveals a long-term process, which is by no means encouraging. Heidegger and Foucault see us as caught in especially dangerous practices, which, both suggest, produced man only finally to eliminate him, as they more and more nakedly reveal a tendency toward the total ordering of all beings—a tendency that became possible as soon as the Greeks forgot the truth of being and substituted the will to truth. Heidegger calls this current understanding of Being technological, and he is concerned to show how it distorts our understanding of *things*; Foucault calls it disciplinary biopower and focuses primarily on how it distorts the social order and our relation to other *human beings*. Both hold that it distorts our understanding of ourselves and leads to a pervasive sense of distress.

   Heidegger, for a time, like many current critics of the modern age, was under the illusion that the danger was that man was dominating everything and exploiting all beings for his own satisfaction[28]—as if man were a subject in control, and the objectification of everything were the problem. As Foucault points out in *Les Mots et les choses*, with the help of Heideggerian hindsight, in *Being and Time* and even after his "turning," Heidegger himself was still caught up in the Kantian doubles. Indeed, as late as 1940 Heidegger still held that from the beginning of modernity up to the present, man has been in control:

Western history has now begun to enter into the completion of that period we call the *modern* and which is defined by the fact that man becomes the measure and the center of beings. Man is what lies at the bottom of all beings: that is, in modern terms, at the bottom of all objectification and representability.[29]

   [26] Heidegger, "The Age of the World Picture," 153.
   [27] Foucault, *Les Mots et les choses*, 398/*The Order of Things*, 387.
   [28] Heidegger himself was caught up in the subjectivist understanding of the human condition in *Being and Time*.
   [29] Heidegger, *Nietzsche*, vol. 4, 28.

But by 1946 Heidegger clearly distances himself from this view. He interprets Rilke, for example, as criticizing the objectification of all beings:

It is by the positioning that belongs to representation that Nature is brought before man. Man places before himself the world as the whole of everything objective, and he places himself before the world.

Where Nature is not satisfactory to man's representation, he reframes or redisposes it.

The whole objective inventory in terms of which the world appears is given over to, commended to, and thus subjected to the command of self-assertive production.

Modern science and the total state, as necessary consequences of the nature of technology, are also its attendants. The same holds true of the means and forms that are set up for the organization of public opinion and of men's everyday ideas.... At the bottom, the essence of life is supposed to yield itself to technical production.[30]

But Heidegger himself is clear that all this exploitation and control is not man's doing, and man never was anything but an effect of other forces.

Even this, that man becomes the subject and the world the object, is a consequence of technology's nature establishing itself, and not the other way around.[31]

Thus, in his final analysis of technology, Heidegger is critical of those who, still caught in the subject/object picture, think that technology is dangerous because it embodies instrumental reason.

The current conception of technology, according to which it is a means and a human activity, can ... be called the instrumental and anthropological definition of technology.[32]

Modern technology is "something completely different and therefore new."[33] The essence of modern technology is ordering for its own sake:

Everywhere everything is ordered to stand by, to be immediately at hand, indeed to stand there just so that it may be on call for a further ordering. Whatever is ordered about in this way has its own standing. We call it the standing-reserve [*Bestand*].... Whatever stands by in the sense of standing-reserve no longer stands over against us as object.[34]

The goal of technology, Heidegger tells us, is more and more flexibility and efficiency simply for its own sake: "[E]xpediting is always itself directed from the beginning toward furthering something else, i.e., toward driving on to the

---

[30] Martin Heidegger, "What are Poets For?" in *Poetry, Language, Thought* (New York: Harper & Row, 1971), 110–12.

[31] Heidegger, "What are Poets For?," 112.

[32] Martin Heidegger, "The Question Concerning Technology," in *The Question Concerning Technology and Other Essays* (New York: Harper, 1977), 5.

[33] Heidegger, "The Question Concerning Technology," 5.

[34] Heidegger, "The Question Concerning Technology," 17.

maximum yield at the minimum expense."[35] Heidegger sees this modern understanding as gradually absorbing both subjects and objects:

The subject–object relation thus reaches, for the first time, its pure "relational", i.e., ordering, character in which both the subject and the object are sucked up as standing-reserves. That does not mean that the subject–object relation vanishes, but rather the opposite: it now attains to its most extreme dominance.... It becomes a standing-reserve to be commanded and set in order.[36]

If man is challenged, ordered, to [optimize everything], then does not man himself belong even more originally than nature within the standing-reserve? The current talk about human resources, about the supply of patients for a clinic, gives evidence of this.[37]

In spite of Heidegger's self-critique, and his correction of his early view that domination by man was the problem, Foucault too, in the social realm, went through a stage where he thought the problem was that some men or classes dominated and excluded others, and only later saw that exclusion, calling for the liberation of the repressed, was not the problem. Power is not an instrument for exclusion that has fallen into the wrong hands, but a pressure toward ever-greater optimization. Sex, for example, becomes "a thing to be not simply condemned or tolerated but managed, inserted into systems of utility, regulated for the greater good of all, made to function according to an optimum."[38] Thus Foucault's auto-critique:

We must cease once and for all to describe the effects of power in negative terms: it "excludes," it "represses," it "censors," it "abstracts," it "masks," it "conceals." In fact, power produces; it produces reality; it produces domains of objects and rituals of truth. The individual and the knowledge that may be gained of him belong to this production.[39]

At bottom, despite the differences in epochs and objectives, the representation of power has remained under the spell of monarchy. In political thought and analysis, we still have not cut off the head of the king. Hence the importance that the theory of power gives to the problem of right and violence, law and illegality, freedom and will, and especially the state and sovereignty.... To conceive of power on the basis of these problems is to conceive of it in terms of a historical form that is characteristic of our societies: the juridical monarchy. Characteristic yet transitory.[40]

The theory of sovereignty... does not allow for a calculation of power in terms of the minimum expenditure for the maximum return.[41]

---

[35] Heidegger, "The Question Concerning Technology," 15.
[36] Martin Heidegger, "Science and Reflection," in *The Question Concerning Technology*, 173.
[37] Heidegger, "The Question Concerning Technology," 18.
[38] Foucault, *La Volonté de savoir*, 34–5/*The History of Sexuality*, vol. 1, 24.
[39] Michel Foucault, *Surveiller et punir* (Paris: Gallimard, 1975), 196, translated as *Discipline and Punish* (New York: Pantheon, 1977), 194.
[40] Foucault, *La Volonté de savoir*, 117/*The History of Sexuality*, vol. 1, 88–9.
[41] Michel Foucault, "Two Lectures," in *Power/Knowledge* (New York: Pantheon, 1980), 105.

Our Contemporary Understanding of Being/Power

In their final analysis of our current situation, both Heidegger and Foucault contend that, in spite of the appearance that we have passed through several epochs, since the classical age our modern Western practices exhibit an underlying, continuous directionality, a "destining" (Heidegger), a "strategy without a strategist" (Foucault). Heidegger and Foucault agree that this directionality of our practices has reached a final phase in this century. In the way it now regulates our most important practices, its underlying direction has become clear. Our culture is facing the greatest danger in its history, for, while previous clearings (*Lichtung*) were static and partial, leaving a certain leeway for the way things and human beings could show up and be encountered, our current understanding is progressively taking over *every* aspect of the natural and social world.

Unlike the hierarchical, top-down order of the medieval understanding of Being and of monarchical power, which was centralized but not extended to all details of the world, the modern understanding of Being/Power is bottom-up, leveling and totalizing. Heidegger emphasizes the totalization in his phrase "total mobilization," while Foucault includes both totalizing and leveling in referring to "normalization."

Normalization is more than socialization into norms. Such socialization is the way the understanding of Being or Power governs the actions of the members of any society. Normalization, however, is uniquely modern. "A normalizing society is the historical outcome of a technology of power centered on life."[42] In this understanding, which has emerged more and more clearly since the classical age, norms are progressively brought to bear on *all* aspects of life.

To understand how normalization works we have to bring Foucault's insight into the way the human sciences serve to extend social norms, together with Heidegger's account of the technological understanding of Being underlying modern science. To begin with, for Heidegger science is a form of technology. According to Heidegger this can be seen in the modern understanding of theory: "[T]he 'theory' that modern science shows itself to be is something essentially different from the Greek *theoria*."[43] What is original in modern theory is the totalizing. Since Galileo, scientific research has been based on the idea that there must be *one system* into which all of physical reality must be made to fit:

[E]very procedure...requires an open sphere in which it moves. And it is precisely the opening up of such a sphere that is the fundamental event in research. This is

---

[42] Foucault, *La Volonté de savoir*, 190/*The History of Sexuality*, vol. 1, 144.
[43] Heidegger, "Science and Reflection," 166.

accomplished through the projection within some realm of what is—in nature, for example—of a fixed ground plan of natural events. The projection sketches out in advance the manner in which the knowing procedure must bind itself and adhere to the sphere opened up. This binding adherence is the rigor of research.[44]

This is what Heidegger means when, in speaking of Descartes, he describes representing as "forcing things into our normative realm."

Heidegger's understanding of modern science is exactly like Thomas Kuhn's in *The Nature of Scientific Revolutions*. What Heidegger calls research, Kuhn calls normal science. Normal science operates by setting up a *total* interpretation of some region of reality and then attempts to show that the anomalies that emerge can be fitted into the general account. Normal science assumes beforehand that the general plan is correct, and thus that the anomalies have no truth to tell—that in the end, all anomalies must be brought under the law. Normal science progresses precisely by causing and overcoming anomalies. Foucault sees that modern norms supposedly grounded in science likewise produce anomalies and then take every anomaly, every attempt to evade them, as occasions for further intervention to bring the anomalies under the scientific norms. This is normalization.

Normalization, according to Foucault, serves not to objectify, exclude, coerce, or punish, but rather to enhance life. Power creates docile bodies and self-absorbed, analytical deep subjects so as to further the range of the human sciences, with no other goal than ever greater welfare for all. It has become self-evident to us that everyone should get the most out of his or her possibilities, and that the human sciences show us the way to do this. The resulting practices Foucault calls biopower. It is a power

working to incite, reinforce, control, monitor, optimize, and organize the forces under it: a power bent on generating forces, making them grow, and ordering them, rather than one dedicated to impending them, making them submit, or destroying them.[45]

Their common critique of technology/biopower does not lead either Heidegger or Foucault to oppose the use of technological devices and specific welfare practices. Heidegger is clear that it is the *technological understanding of Being*, not *technology*, that causes our distress. That the technological understanding of Being can be dissociated from technological devices is clear if one looks at contemporary Japan, where a traditional, non-technological understanding of Being—or, perhaps better, no understanding of Being at all, since it seems that

---

[44]   Heidegger, "The Age of the World Picture," 118.
[45]   Foucault, *La Volonte de savoir*, 179/*The History of Sexuality*, vol. 1, 136.

the Japanese have no single unified understanding of reality—exists alongside the most advanced high-tech production and consumption.

[T]he essence of technology is by no means anything technological. Thus we shall never experience our relationship to the essence of technology so long as we merely conceive and push forward the technological, put up with it, or evade it. Everywhere we remain unfree and chained to technology, whether we passionately affirm or deny it.[46]

Heidegger uses and depends upon modern technological devices like anyone else, and he does not advocate a return to the pre-technological world of ancient Greece. Foucault, like Heidegger, is, of course, not opposed to modern medical technology, and specific welfare practices such as mass vaccination. He is, however, opposed to taking it for granted that welfare practices, based on the human sciences, should, in the name of efficiency and optimization, be extended without critical questioning to all aspects of our lives.

What Resists and Why

Whereas Foucault is concerned solely with what is happening to *people*, Heidegger is concerned almost exclusively with what is happening to *things*.[47] And each sees what is endangered as at the same time a source of resistance.

Heidegger is not against modern science, but he is critical of the way its methods, legitimate and successful for dealing with physical reality, are carried over into other aspects of human practices so that all things become mere resources for more and more flexible and total organisation. Yet he holds that things can never be completely understood by science, nor totally controlled. Their resistance is not the passive resistance of prime matter, but an active withdrawal. Heidegger calls this function "earth":

Earth... shatters every attempt to penetrate into it. It causes every merely calculating importunity upon it to turn into a destruction. This destruction may herald itself under

---

[46] Heidegger, "The Question Concerning Technology," 4.

[47] Occasionally in passing Heidegger notes the social consequences of the technological understanding of Being. He once speaks of practices dedicated to "the organized establishment of a uniform state of happiness for all men" (*What Is Called Thinking?* (New York: Harper & Row, 1968), 30) and adds that in this pursuit man is turned into yet another resource:

Man, who no longer conceals his character of being the most important raw material, is also drawn into this process.
  Since man is the most important raw material, one must reckon with the fact that some day factories will be built for the artificial breeding of human material. ("Overcoming Metaphysics," in *The End of Philosophy* (New York: Harper & Row, 1973), 104, 106).

the appearance of mastery and of progress in the form of the technical-scientific objecti-
vation of nature, but this mastery nevertheless remains an impotence of will. The earth
appears openly cleared as itself only when it is perceived and preserved as that which is by
nature undisclosable, that which shrinks from every disclosure and constantly keeps itself
closed up.[48]

This refusal of things to fit into some preordained total plan reveals things not
just as anomalies but as the source of other ways of seeing things. Just as for Kuhn
anomalies sometimes contain a resistance that forces a revolution in science in
which the anomaly is no longer an anomaly but a paradigm case of a new truth,
so for Heidegger the resistance intrinsic to things holds open the possibility of a
saving breakdown of the total ground plan of modern culture, provided we are
open to things in their resistance.

When and in what way do things appear as things? They do not appear *by means of*
human making. But neither do they appear without the vigilance of mortals. The first step
toward such vigilance is the step back from the thinking that merely represents.[49]

Instead we must preserve the endangered marginal and local element: "Here and
now...in simple things...we may foster the saving power in its increase."[50]

   People, however, unlike things, organize themselves, and Foucault not only
shows us in detail how human beings come to impose norms on themselves; he
finds in them a resistance to biopower parallel to the one that Heidegger finds in
things:

[T]here is indeed always something in the social body, in classes, groups and individuals
themselves which in some sense escapes relations of power, something which is by no
means a more or less docile or reactive primal matter, but rather a centrifugal movement,
an inverse energy, a discharge. There is certainly no such thing as "the" plebs; rather there
is, as it were, a certain plebeian quality or aspect. There is plebs in bodies, in souls, in
individuals, in the proletariat, in the bourgeoisie, but everywhere in a diversity of forms
and extensions, of energies and irreducibilities. This measure of plebs is not so much what
stands outside relations of power as their limit, their underside, their counter-stroke, that
which responds to every advance of power by a movement of disengagement.[51]

For both Heidegger and Foucault these strange notions are presumably meant to
encourage us to pay attention to what remains of the different, the local, and the
recalcitrant in our current practices. But Heidegger and Foucault are faced with a
dilemma concerning the status of those marginal practices that have escaped or

---

[48] Heidegger, "The Origin of the Work of Art," in *Poetry, Language, Thought*, 47.
[49] Heidegger, "The Thing," in *Poetry, Language, Thought*, 181.
[50] Heidegger, "The Question Concerning Technology," 33.
[51] Michel Foucault, "Power and Strategies," in *Power/Knowledge*, p. 138.

successfully resisted the spread of technology/biopower. While they remain dispersed, these practices escape totalization but offer little resistance to its further spread. However, if Heidegger or Foucault were to focus on them in an ordered way, even in the name of counter-tradition or resistance, they would risk being taken over and normalized.

When it comes to the difficult question of just why and how, then, we should resist, Heidegger and Foucault finally take quite different paths, each of which has its advantages and drawbacks. Heidegger, unlike Foucault, has an account of why the technological understanding of Being causes human beings distress. For Heidegger human beings, whether they realize it or not, are the recipients of all understandings of Being. Human practices have been receptive to at least two radically different understandings of Being in our culture, and could receive many others. Human beings who explicitly see and reflect on this happening Heidegger calls "thinkers," but all human beings are essentially receptive. Although the current understanding of Being as the total ordering of everything for its own sake conceals the fact that it is received, not controlled, human beings none the less remain recipients. Heidegger holds that realizing this would weaken the hold of our technological understanding of reality, but because technology actively blocks the possibility of this realization and its expression in our practices, we experience distress.

In the last analysis Foucault is more radical than Heidegger in that, consistent with his opposition to *all* totalizing, he avoids any account of what human beings essentially are and are called to do, whether that be Nietzsche's call to constant self-overcoming or Heidegger's claim that Being demands total receptivity. Although Foucault does attempt to be receptive to the problematizations in our current practices "through which being offers itself as having to be thought," he does not claim that in so doing he is fulfilling his human essence. This, of course, denies him any account of why biopower should be felt as distressing and so be resisted, but it enables him to avoid adding one more universal norm, while still engaging in active resistance to current leveling or totalizing practices.

PART IV

Nihilism and the Technological Age

10

Heidegger on the Connection between Nihilism, Technology, Art, and Politics (1992)

Martin Heidegger's major work, *Being and Time*, is usually considered the culminating work in a tradition called existential philosophy. The first person to call himself an existential thinker was Søren Kierkegaard, and his influence is clearly evident in Heidegger's thought. Existential thinking rejects the traditional philosophical view, which goes back to Plato at least, that philosophy must be done from a detached, disinterested point of view. Kierkegaard argues that our primary access to reality is through our involved action. The way things show up for a detached thinker is a partial and distorted version of the way things show up to a committed individual.

Kierkegaard defines the self as a relation that relates itself to itself. That means that who I am depends on the stand I take on being a self. Moreover, how I interpret myself is not a question of what I think but of what I do. I have to take up what is the given or factical part of my self and, by acting on it, define who I am. I understand myself as being a student, a teacher, the lover of a specific person, or the follower of a specific cause. Thus, the self defines itself by taking up its past by means of present actions that make sense in terms of its future. For Kierkegaard, then, the self can be understood as a temporal structure.

Given his emphasis on involvement, Kierkegaard was convinced that philosophical reflection has undermined commitment in the West. In his book *The Present Age*,[1] written in 1846, he gave a prophetic description of how all authority was disappearing, all concrete differences were being leveled, everything was becoming indifferent, giving rise to alternate fits of lethargy and excitement. Such was the victory of critical detachment over involved commitment. His whole work was devoted to the question: How can we get meaning and commitment back into our lives once we have gotten into the passionless, reflective attitude we are now in?

---

[1] Søren Kierkegaard, *The Present Age*, trans. Alexander Dru (New York: Harper & Row, 1962).

Heidegger calls the basic structure of human being—that each human being's way of being is an issue for it—*Dasein*. In his "existentialist" phase, during the twenties, Heidegger was interested in the ahistorical, cross-cultural structures of everyday involved experience. He worked out an interpretation of three basic ways of being (availableness, or "readiness-to-hand"; occurrence, or "presence-at-hand"; as well as Dasein) and their general structure (temporality) grounded in Dasein's ability to take a stand on its own being. These existential structures, Heidegger demonstrated, provided the conditions of the possibility of all modes of intelligibility. He also investigated the way the conformity to norms necessary for intelligibility opens up the possibility of flight into conformism, which levels down all meaningful distinctions.

But whereas Kierkegaard thought that leveling and lack of commitment had been accentuated to nihilistic proportions by the media, Heidegger in *Being and Time* writes as if leveling has been with humankind as long as tools have, and he sees nothing special in the present age. Around 1930, however, Heidegger began to investigate the understanding of being peculiar to modern Western culture. As he put it, in *Being and Time* "'phenomenology' and all hermeneutical-transcendental questions had not yet been thought in terms of the history of being."[2] His early interest in the existential structure of the self had shifted to another Kierkegaardian concern—the lack of meaning and seriousness in the present age.

Nihilism

In his lectures on Nietzsche in 1936 Heidegger quotes with approval Nietzsche's Kierkegaardian condemnation of the present age:

Around the year 1882 [Nietzsche] says regarding his times, "Our age is an agitated one, and precisely for that reason, not an age of passion; it heats itself up continuously, because it feels that it is not warm—basically it is freezing. . . . In our time it is merely by means of an echo that events acquire their 'greatness'—the echo of the newspaper."[3]

Heidegger agrees with Nietzsche that "there is no longer any goal in and through which all the forces of the historical existence of peoples can cohere and in the direction of which they can develop."[4]

---

[2] Martin Heidegger, *The End of Philosophy*, trans. Joan Stambaugh (New York: Harper & Row, 1973), 15.
[3] Martin Heidegger, *Nietzsche*, vol. 1: *The Will to Power as Art*, ed. David E. Krell (New York: Harper & Row, 1979), 47.
[4] Heidegger, *Nietzsche*, vol. 1, 157.

Nihilism is Nietzsche's name for this loss of meaning or direction. Both Kierkegaard and Nietzsche agree that if nihilism were complete, there would be no significant private or public issues. Nothing would have authority for us, would make a claim on us, would demand a commitment from us. In a non-nihilistic age there is something at stake; there are questions that all can agree are important, even if they violently disagree as to what the answers to these questions are. But in our age, everything is in the process of becoming equal. There is less and less difference among political parties, among religious communities, among social causes, among cultural practices—everything is on a par, all meaningful differences are being leveled.

Kierkegaard thought that the answer to nihilism was to make one's own individual absolute commitment. If you can commit yourself unconditionally—in love, for instance—then that becomes a focus for your whole sense of reality. Things stand out or recede into insignificance on the basis of that ultimate concern. You do not discover a significance that is already there. There is no basis for this commitment in the cosmos. Indeed, such a commitment is exactly the opposite of belief in an objective truth. You are called by some concrete concern—either a person or a cause—and when you define yourself by your dedication to that concern, your world acquires seriousness and significance.

The only way to have a meaningful life in the present age, then, is to let your involvement become definitive of reality for you, and what is definitive of reality for you is not something that is in any way provisional—although it certainly is vulnerable. That is why, once a society like ours becomes rational and reflective, such total commitments begin to look like a kind of dangerous dependency. The committed individual is identified as a workaholic or a woman who loves too much. This suggests that to be recognized and appreciated, individual commitment requires a shared understanding of what is worth pursuing. But as our culture comes more and more to celebrate critical detachment, self-sufficiency, and rational choice, there are fewer and fewer shared commitments. So commitment itself begins to look like craziness.

Heidegger comes to see the recent undermining of commitment as due not so much to a failure of the individual as to a lack of anything in the modern world that could solicit commitment from us and sustain us in it. The things that once evoked commitment—gods, heroes, the God-man, the acts of great statesmen, the words of great thinkers—have lost their authority. As a result, individuals feel isolated and alienated. They feel that their lives have no meaning because the public world contains no guidelines.

When everything that is material and social has become completely flat and drab, people retreat into their private experiences as the only remaining place to find significance. Heidegger sees this move to private experience as characteristic of the modern age. Art, religion, sex, education—all become varieties of experience. When all our concerns have been reduced to the common denominator of "experience," we will have reached the last stage of nihilism. One then sees "the plunge into frenzy and the disintegration into sheer feeling as redemptive. The 'lived experience' as such becomes decisive."[5] That is, when there are no shared examples of greatness that focus public concerns and elicit social commitment, people become spectators of fads and public lives, just for the excitement. When there are no religious practices that call forth sacrifice, terror, and awe, people consume everything from drugs to meditation practices to give themselves some kind of peak experience. The peak experience takes the place of what was once a relation to something outside the self that defined the real and was therefore holy. As Heidegger puts it, "The loss of the gods is so far from excluding religiosity that rather only through that loss is the relation to the gods changed into mere 'religious experience'."[6] Of course, private experience seems attractive only once the shared public world has lost its meaning and reality. Then one thinks (as if somehow it had always been the case and one had just discovered it) that, after all, it is the experience that matters. But sooner or later one finds that although private experience may have "energy" or "spontaneity" or "zing," it provides nothing in terms of which one can give consistency, meaning, and seriousness to one's life.[7] In Nietzsche's words "God is dead, and we have killed him."

Nietzsche, however, unlike Heidegger, finds the death of God liberating. He foresees a new stage of our culture that he calls "positive nihilism," in which each "free spirit" will posit, that is, create, his or her own values. Heidegger is not so sanguine. He sets out to investigate the history of the understanding of being in the West in order to understand how we did the terrible deed of killing God. One way he tells the story of the loss of meaning is by tracing the history of the very idea of values taken over uncritically by Nietzsche. Heidegger argues that to think of nihilism as a state in which we have forgotten or betrayed our values is part of the problem. Thinking that we once had values but that we do not have values now, and that we should regain our values or choose new ones, is just another

[5] Heidegger, *Nietzsche*, vol. 1, 86.

[6] Martin Heidegger, *The Question Concerning Technology and Other Essays*, trans. William Lovitt (New York: Harper & Row, 1977), 117/*Holzwege*, *Gesamtausgabe* vol. 5 (Frankfurt am Main: Klostermann, 1977), 76.

[7] For evidence that Heidegger is right on this point, see Robert N. Bellah, Richard Madsen, William M. Sullivan, Ann Swidler, and Steven M. Tipton, *Habits of the Heart* (Berkeley and Los Angeles, CA: University of California Press, 1985).

symptom of the trouble. Heidegger claims that thinking about our deepest concerns as values *is* nihilism.

The essence of a value is that it is something that is completely independent of us. It is perceived, and then chosen or rejected. Values have an interesting history. Plato starts with the claim that they are what shows us what is good for us independent of our interests and desires. The idea of the good shines on us and draws us to it. Only with the Enlightenment do we arrive at the notion that values are objective—passive objects standing over against us—and we must *choose* our values. These values have no claim on us until we *decide* which ones we want to adopt. Once we get the idea that there is a plurality of values and that we choose which ones will have a claim on us, we are ripe for the modern idea, first found in the works of Nietzsche, especially in *Thus Spoke Zarathustra*, that we *posit* our values—that is, that valuing is something we do and value is the result of doing it. But once we see that we posit values, we also see that we can equally "unposit" them. They thus lose all authority for us. So, far from giving meaning to our lives, thinking of what is important to us in terms of values shows us that our lives have no intrinsic meaning. As long as we think in terms of value positing rather than being gripped by shared concerns, we will not find anything that elicits our commitment. As Heidegger says, "No one dies for mere values."[8]

Once we see how thinking of the problem of nihilism in terms of lacking values perpetuates rather than combats the problem, we are ready to diagnose and seek a cure for our condition. According to Heidegger our trouble begins with Socrates' and Plato's claim that true moral knowledge, like scientific knowledge, must be explicit and disinterested. Heidegger questions both the possibility and the desirability of making our everyday understanding totally explicit. He introduces the idea that the shared everyday skills, concerns, and practices into which we are socialized provide the conditions necessary for people to make sense of the world and of their lives. All intelligibility presupposes something that cannot be fully articulated—a kind of knowing-how rather than a knowing-that. At the deepest level such knowing is embodied in our social skills rather than in our concepts, beliefs, and values. Heidegger argues that our cultural practices can direct our activities and make our lives meaningful only insofar as they are and stay unarticulated, that is, as long as they stay the soil out of which we live. If there is to be seriousness, it must draw on these unarticulated background practices. As Heidegger puts it in a later work, "The Origin of the Work of Art," "Every decision...bases itself on something not mastered, something concealed, confusing; else it would never

[8] Heidegger, *The Question Concerning Technology*, 142/*Holzwege*, 102.

be a decision."[9] Critical reflection is necessary in some situations where our ordinary way of coping is insufficient, but such reflection cannot and should not play the central role it has played in the philosophical tradition. What is most important and meaningful in our lives is not and should not be accessible to critical reflection.

The cultural know-how that embodies our concerns is certainly not conscious, but neither does it appear to be unconscious. To get a sense of what this know-how is like, let us take a very simple case. People in various cultures stand different distances from an intimate, a friend, a stranger. Furthermore, the distances vary when these people are chatting, doing business, or engaging in courtship. Each culture, including our own, embodies an incredibly subtle shared pattern of social distancing. Yet no one explicitly taught this pattern to each of us. Our parents could not possibly have consciously instructed us in it since they do not know the pattern any more than we do. We do not even know we have such know-how until we go to another culture and find, for example, that in North Africa strangers seem to be oppressively close while in Scandinavia friends seem to stand too far away. This makes us uneasy, and we cannot help backing away or moving closer. It is through such responses that we got this know-how in the first place. As small children, when we began to interact with other people, we sometimes got the distances wrong. This made our parents and friends uneasy, and they either backed away or moved closer so that we gradually picked up the whole pattern. It was never made explicit. As a skill or *savoir faire* it is not something like a set of rules that could be made explicit.[10] Yet it embodies rudiments of an understanding of what it is to be a human being—hints of how important body contact is, and the relative importance of intimacy and independence.

Now practices like how far to stand from people are not all that are passed on by training and imitation. Our everyday know-how involves an understanding of what it is to be a person, a thing, a natural object, a plant, an animal, and so on. Our understanding of animals these days, for example, is in part embodied in our skill in buying pieces of them, taking off their plastic wrapping, and cooking them in microwave ovens. In general, we deal with things as resources to be used and then disposed of when no longer needed. A styrofoam cup is a perfect example. When we want a hot or cold drink it does its job, and when we are through with it we throw it away. This understanding of an object is very different from what

---

[9] Martin Heidegger, *Poetry, Language, Thought*, trans. Albert Hofstadter (New York: Harper & Row, 1971), 55/*Holzwege*, 43.

[10] See Hubert L. Dreyfus and Stuart Dreyfus, *Mind over Machine* (New York: Free Press, 1982).

we can suppose to be the Japanese understanding of a delicate, painted teacup, which does not do as good a job of maintaining temperature and which has to be washed and protected, but which is preserved from generation to generation for its beauty and its social meaning. Or, to take another example, an old earthenware bowl, admired for its simplicity and its ability to evoke memories of ancient crafts, such as is used in a Japanese tea ceremony, embodies a unique understanding of things. It is hard to picture a tea ceremony around a styrofoam cup.

Note that an aspect of the Japanese understanding of what it is to be human (passive, contented, gentle, social, etc.) fits with an understanding of what it is to be a thing (evocative of simpler times, pure, natural, simple, beautiful, traditional, etc.). It would make no sense for us, who are active, independent, and aggressive—constantly striving to cultivate and satisfy our desires—to relate to things the way the Japanese do; or for the Japanese (before their understanding of being was interfered with by ours) to invent and prefer styrofoam teacups. In the same vein *we* tend to think of politics as the negotiation of individual desires, while the Japanese seek consensus. In sum, the practices containing an understanding of what it is to be a human being, those containing an interpretation of what it is to be a thing, and those defining society fit together. Social practices thus transmit not only an implicit understanding of what it is to be a human being, an animal, or an object, but, finally, an understanding of what it is for anything to be at all.

The shared practices into which we are socialized, moreover, provide a background understanding of what matters and what it makes sense to do, on the basis of which we can direct our actions. This understanding of being creates what Heidegger calls a *clearing* in which things and people can show up as mattering and meaningful for us. We do not produce the clearing. It produces us as the kind of human *beings* we are. Heidegger describes the clearing as follows:

Beyond what is, not away from it but before it, there is still something else that happens. In the midst of beings as a whole an open place occurs. There is a clearing, a lighting. . . . This open center is . . . not surrounded by what is; rather, the lighting center itself encircles all that is. . . . Only this clearing grants and guarantees to human beings a passage to those entities that we ourselves are not, and access to the being that we ourselves are.[11]

As we have noted, our cultural practices and the understanding of being they embody allow us to direct our activities and make sense of our lives only insofar as they are and stay unarticulated, that is, stay the atmosphere in which we live.

---

[11] Heidegger, *Poetry, Language, Thought*, 53/*Holzwege*, 39–40.

These background practices are the concealed and unmastered that Heidegger tells us give seriousness to our decisions. Mattering lies not in what we choose, but in "that on the basis of which" we choose. The more our know-how is formulated and objectified as knowing-that, the more it is called up for critical questioning, the more it loses its grip on us. This is part of what Kierkegaard saw in his attack on modern critical reflection, and Heidegger in his attack on value thinking.

But this cannot be the whole story about nihilism. For there must always be a clearing—background practices containing an understanding of being—in order for things and people to be intelligible at all. And these will never be fully accessible to reflection. So there must be a deeper problem that Heidegger is pointing to. There must be something wrong with our current background practices that leads us to ignore them, causing us to seek meaning by choosing objective values and finally by positing personal values for ourselves. So Heidegger raises new questions: What is it to have a nihilistic clearing, how did we come to have one, and what can we do about it? Only when we have answered these, he holds, can we ask: Are there still left in our practices some remnants of shared meaningful concerns? If so, where are such remnants to be found? The strongest argument that some meaningful practices must have survived is that without some remnant of them we would not be distressed by nihilism. But before we can answer these questions, we must ask a prior one: How do practices give shared meaning to the lives of those who practice them?

The Work of Art (World and Earth)

For everyday practices to give meaning to our lives and to unite us in a community, they must be focused and held up to the practitioners. Clifford Geertz and Charles Taylor have discussed this important phenomenon. Geertz, for example, describes the role of the cockfight in Balinese society:

It provides a metasocial commentary upon the whole matter of assorting human beings into fixed hierarchical ranks and then organizing the major part of collective existence around that assortment. Its function, if you want to call it that, is interpretive: it is a Balinese reading of Balinese experience, a story they tell themselves about themselves.[12]

Heidegger calls that interpretive function "truth setting itself to work," and anything that performs this function he calls a work of art. As his illustration of an artwork, Heidegger takes the Greek temple. The temple held up to the

---

[12] Clifford Geertz, *The Interpretation of Cultures* (New York: Harper Colophon Books, 1973), 448.

Greeks what was important, and so let there be meaningful differences such as victory and disgrace, disaster and blessing:

It is the templework that first fits together and at the same time gathers around itself the unity of those paths and relations in which birth and death, disaster and blessing, victory and disgrace, endurance and decline acquire the shape of destiny for human beings. The all-governing expanse of this open relational context is the world of this historical people.[13]

The Greeks whose practices were manifested and focused by the temple lived in a moral space of gods, heroes, and slaves, a moral space that gave direction and meaning to their lives. In the same way, the medieval cathedral made it possible to be a sinner or a saint and showed Christians the dimensions of salvation and damnation.[14] In either case, one knew where one stood and what one had to do. Heidegger would say that the understanding of what it is to be changes each time a culture gets a new artwork. Then different sorts of human beings and things show up. For the Greeks, what showed up were heroes and slaves and marvelous things; for the Christians, saints and sinners, rewards and temptations. There could not have been saints in ancient Greece. At best there could only have been weak people who let everybody walk all over them. Likewise, there could not have been Greek-style heroes in the Middle Ages. Such people would have been regarded as pagans—prideful sinners who disrupted society by denying their dependence on God.

Generalizing the idea of a work of art, Heidegger holds that "there must always be some being in the open [the clearing], something that is, in which the openness takes its stand and attains its constancy."[15] Let us call such special things cultural paradigms. Talking of a paradigm focusing the practices seems almost inevitable. Compare Geertz: "It is this kind of bringing of assorted experiences of everyday life to focus that the cockfight...accomplishes, and so creates what, better than typical or universal, could be called a paradigmatic human event."[16]

A cultural paradigm collects the scattered practices of a group, unifies them into coherent possibilities for action, and holds them up to the people who can then act and relate to each other in terms of that exemplar. Works of art, when performing this function, are not merely representations or symbols, but actually

---

[13] Heidegger, *Poetry, Language, Thought*, 42/*Holzwege*, 29.

[14] For a description of the dimensions and directions of moral space see Charles Taylor, *Sources of the Self* (Cambridge, MA: Harvard University Press, 1989).

[15] Heidegger, *Poetry, Language, Thought*, 61/*Holzwege*, 48.

[16] Geertz, *The Interpretation of Cultures*, 450.

produce a shared understanding. As Geertz put it: "Quartets, still lifes, and cockfights are not merely reflections of a pre-existing sensibility analogically represented; they are positive agents in the creation and maintenance of...sensibility."[17]

Charles Taylor makes the same point when he distinguishes *shared meanings*, which he calls intersubjective meanings, from *common meanings* "whose being shared is a collective act":

> It is part of the meaning of a common aspiration, belief, celebration, etc. that it be not just shared but part of the common reference world. Or to put it another way, its being shared is a collective act...
>
> Common meanings are the basis of community. Inter-subjective meanings give a people a common language to talk about social reality and a common understanding of certain norms, but only with common meaning does this common reference world contain significant common actions, celebrations, and feelings. These are objects in the world that everybody shares. This is what makes community.[18]

In *The Structure of Scientific Revolutions*, Thomas Kuhn shows that scientists engaged in what he calls normal science operate in terms of such an exemplar or paradigm—an outstanding example of a good piece of work. The paradigm for modern science was Newton's *Principia*. All agreed that Newton had seen exemplary problems, given exemplary solutions, and produced exemplary justifications for his claims. Thus, for more than two centuries natural scientists knew that, insofar as their work resembled Newton's, they were doing good science.

The Newtonian paradigm was later replaced by the Einsteinian paradigm. Such a paradigm shift constitutes a scientific revolution. After such a revolution scientists see and do things differently. As Kuhn puts it, they work in a different world. They also believe and value different things, but this is less important. Kuhn is quite Heideggerian in holding that it is the paradigm that guides the scientists' practices and that the paradigm cannot be explained as a set of beliefs or values and so cannot be stated as a criterion or rule. As Kuhn notes: "That scientists do not usually ask or debate what makes a particular problem or solution legitimate tempts us to suppose that, at least intuitively, they know the answer. But it may only indicate that neither the question nor the answer is felt to be relevant to their research. Paradigms may be prior to, more binding, and more complete than any set of rules for research that could be unequivocally abstracted

---

[17] Geertz, *The Interpretation of Cultures*, 451.

[18] Charles Taylor, "Interpretation and the Sciences of Man," in *Philosophy and the Human Sciences* (Cambridge: Cambridge University Press, 1985), 39.

from them."[19] Kuhn further points out that "the concrete scientific achievement, as a locus of professional commitment, [is] prior to the various concepts, laws, theories, and points of view that may be abstracted from it." He adds that the paradigm cannot be rationalized: "The shared paradigm [is] a fundamental unit for the student of scientific development, a unit that cannot be fully reduced to logically atomic components which might function in its stead."[20] That the paradigm cannot be rationalized but only imitated is crucial to the paradigm's authority. It requires that the paradigm work by way of the background practices, in terms of which the scientists have a world. It also makes it possible for the scientists to agree without having to spell out their agreement.

At the time of a scientific revolution, however, Kuhn tells us that the paradigm itself becomes the focus of conflicting interpretations, each interpretation trying to rationalize and justify itself. Similarly, Heidegger holds that a working artwork is so important to a community that people must try to make the work clear and coherent and to make everyone follow it in all aspects of their lives. But the artwork, like the scientific paradigm, exhibits a resistance to such rationalization. Any paradigm could be paraphrased and rationalized only if the concrete thing that serves as an exemplar symbolized or represented an underlying system of beliefs or values abstractable from the particular exemplar. But the whole point of needing an exemplar is that there is no such system, there are only shared practices. Heidegger calls the way the artwork solicits the culture to make the artwork explicit, coherent, and encompassing the *world* aspect of the work. He calls the way the artwork and its associated practices resist such totalization the *earth*.

Heidegger points out that world and earth are both necessary for an artwork to work. The temple must clarify and unify the practices—it must be "all-governing"—but being a concrete thing it resists rationalization. Such resistance is manifest in the very materiality of the artwork. Such materiality is not accidental. The temple requires the stone out of which it is made in order to do its job of showing man's place in the natural world, so that a temple made out of steel would not work. Likewise a tragedy requires the sound of poetry to create a shared mood and thus open up a shared world. Since it is made out of rock or sounds, the artwork shows that what is at stake cannot be captured in a system of beliefs and values. All those aspects of a cultural paradigm and the practices it organizes that resist being rationalized and totalized are included in Heidegger's

---

[19] Thomas Kuhn, *The Structure of Scientific Revolutions*, 2nd edn. (Chicago, IL: University of Chicago Press, 1970), 46.
[20] Kuhn, *The Structure of Scientific Revolutions*, 11.

notion of the earth. Earth is not passive matter, but comes into being precisely as what resists the attempt to abstract and generalize the point of the paradigm. And since no interpretation can ever completely capture what the work means, the work of art sets up a struggle between earth and world. This struggle is a necessary aspect of the way meaning inheres in human practices. It is a fruitful struggle in that the conflict of interpretations it sets up generates a culture's history.

Next Heidegger generalizes the notion of a cultural paradigm from a work of art to any being in the clearing that can refocus and so renew cultural practices:

One essential way in which truth establishes itself in the beings it has opened up is truth setting itself into work. Another way in which truth occurs is the act that founds a political state. Still another way in which truth comes to shine forth is the nearness of that which is not simply a being, but the being that is most of all. Still another way in which truth grounds itself is the essential sacrifice. Still another way in which truth becomes is the thinker's questioning, which, as the thinking of being, names being in its question-worthiness.[21]

One can recognize an allusion to the covenant of God with the Jews and the crucifixion. There is also a reference to the political act that founds a state. For example, the U.S. Constitution, like a work of art, has necessarily become the focus of attempts to make it explicit and consistent and to make it apply to all situations, and, of course, it is fecund just insofar as it can never be interpreted once and for all. The founding of a state could also refer to the act of a charismatic leader such as Hitler. This possibility will concern us later in this essay.

Technology

Cultural paradigms do not, however, always establish meaningful differences. There can be nihilistic paradigms. Such paradigms, instead of showing forth the earth on the basis of which our actions can matter to us, conceal the struggle between earth and world and celebrate our ability to get everything clear and under control. Thus, the current paradigms that hold up to us what our culture is dedicated to and is good at are examples of flexibility and efficiency, not for the sake of some further end, but just for the sake of flexibility and efficiency themselves. We admire the way computers are getting faster and faster and at the same time cheaper and cheaper, without knowing how we will use the incredibly flexible computing power they give us. Likewise, fast-food chains

---

[21] Heidegger, *Poetry, Language, Thought*, 61–2/*Holzwege*, 49.

that give us cheap and instant service at any time of day or night stand out as technological triumphs of efficiency and adaptability. Heidegger's example is the power station of the Rhine:

The hydroelectic plant is set into the current of the Rhine. It sets the Rhine to supplying its hydraulic pressure, which then sets the turbines turning. This turning sets those machines in motion whose thrust sets going the electric current for which the long-distance power station and its network of cables are set up to dispatch electricity.... the energy concealed in nature is unlocked, what is unlocked is transformed, what is transformed is stored up, what is stored up is, in turn, distributed, and what is distributed is switched about ever anew. In the context of the interlocking processes pertaining to the orderly disposition of electrical energy, even the Rhine itself appears as something at our command.[22]

All such paradigms deny that an understanding of being necessarily involves receptivity and mystery, and so they deny Heideggerian seriousness.

Again, a comparison with Kuhn can help us see Heidegger's point. According to Kuhn, a science becomes normal when the practitioners in a certain area all agree that a particular piece of work identifies the important problems in a field and demonstrates how certain of these problems can be successfully solved. Thus, a modern scientific paradigm sets up normal science as an activity of puzzle solving. It is the job of normal science to eliminate anomalies by showing how they fit into the total theory the paradigm sketches out in advance. In a similar way, the technological paradigm embodies and furthers our technological understanding of being according to which what does not fit in with our current paradigm—that is, that which is not yet at our disposal to use efficiently (e.g., the wilderness, friendship, and stars)—will finally be brought under our control, and turned into a resource. The contrast with the Greek temple is obvious. The temple is not a totalizing paradigm that makes everything clear and promises to bring it under control. The temple not only shows people what they stand for, but shows them that there is an earthy aspect of things that withdraws and that can never be articulated and dominated.

In the face of the totalizing tendency of the technological artwork, the earth's resistance to total ordering shows up as a source of what Kuhn calls anomalies. What cannot be ordered is treated as recalcitrant human beings who are deviant and must be reformed or as natural forces that have yet to be understood and mastered. All cultures inculcate norms of human behavior and find some order in nature, but ours is the only culture that tries to make the social and natural order total by transforming or destroying all exceptions. Kierkegaard already saw that

---

[22] Heidegger, *The Question Concerning Technology*, 16/*Vorträge und Aufsätze* (Pfullingen: Neske, 1959), 23.

the individual or exceptional was menaced by leveling. Heidegger sees that all our marginal practices are in danger of being taken over and normalized. It looks to us, of course, as if this is for our own good.

Heidegger, however, sees in these marginal practices the only possibility of resistance to technology. Greek practices such as friendship and the cultivation of the erotic are not efficient. When friendship becomes efficient networking, it is no longer the mutual trust and respect the Greeks admired. Likewise, the mystical merging power of the erotic is lost when we turn to private sexual experience. Similarly, Greek respect for the irrational in the form of music and Dionysian frenzy do not fit into an efficiently ordered technological world. Indeed, such "pagan" practices did not even fit into the Christian understanding of being and were marginalized in the name of disinterested agapê—love and peace. These Christian practices in turn were seen as trivial or dangerous given the Enlightenment's emphasis on individual maturity, self-control, and autonomy.

In order to combat modern nihilism Heidegger attempts to point out to us the peculiar and dangerous aspects of our technological understanding of being. But Heidegger does not oppose technology. In "The Question Concerning Technology" he hopes to reveal the essence of technology in a way that "in no way confines us to a stultified compulsion to push on blindly with technology or, what comes to the same thing, to rebel helplessly against it." Indeed, he promises that "when we once open ourselves expressly to the *essence* of technology, we find ourselves unexpectedly taken into a freeing claim."[23]

We will need to explain opening, essence, and freeing before we can understand Heidegger here. But already Heidegger's project should alert us to the fact that he is not announcing one more reactionary rebellion against technology, although many take him to be doing just that. Nor is he doing what progressive thinkers would like to do: proposing a way to get technology under control so that it can serve our rationally chosen ends. The difficulty in locating just where Heidegger stands on technology is no accident. Heidegger has not always been clear about what distinguishes his approach from a romantic reaction to the domination of nature, and when he does finally arrive at a clear formulation of his own original view, it is so strange that in order to understand it we are tempted to translate it into conventional platitudes. Thus, Heidegger's ontological concerns are mistakenly assimilated to ecologically minded worries about the devastation of nature.

Those who want to make Heidegger intelligible in terms of current anti-technological banalities can find support in his texts. During the war he attacked

---

[23] Heidegger, *The Question Concerning Technology*, 25–6/*Vorträge und Aufsätze*, 33.

consumerism: "The circularity of consumption for the sake of consumption is the sole procedure which distinctively characterizes the history of a world which has become an unworld."[24] And as late as 1955, in an address to the Schwarzwald peasants, he points out: "The world now appears as an object open to the attacks of calculative thought.... Nature becomes a gigantic gasoline station, an energy source for modern technology and industry."[25] In this address he also laments the appearance of television antennas on the peasants' dwellings and gives his own version of an attack on the leveling power of the media:

Hourly and daily they are chained to radio and television.... All that with which modern techniques of communication stimulate, assail, and drive man—all that is already much closer to man today than his fields around his farmstead, closer than the sky over the earth, closer than the change from night to day, closer than the conventions and customs of his village, than the tradition of his native world.[26]

Such quotes make it seem Heidegger is a Luddite who would like to return from consumerism, the exploitation of the earth, and mass media to the world of the pre-Socratic Greeks or the good old Schwarzwald peasants.

Nevertheless, although Heidegger does not deny that technology presents us with serious problems, as his thinking develops he comes to the surprising and provocative conclusion that focusing on loss and destruction is still technological: "All attempts to reckon existing reality...in terms of decline and loss, in terms of fate, catastrophe, and destruction, are merely technological behavior."[27] Seeing our situation as posing a problem that must be solved by appropriate action is technological too: "The instrumental conception of technology conditions every attempt to bring man into the right relation to technology.... The will to mastery becomes all the more urgent the more technology threatens to slip from human control."[28] Heidegger is clear this approach will not work. "No single man, no group of men," he tells us, "no commission of prominent statesmen, scientists, and technicians, no conference of leaders of commerce and industry, can brake or direct the progress of history in the atomic age."[29]

Heidegger's view is both darker and more hopeful. He thinks there is a more dangerous situation facing modern man than the technological destruction of

---

[24] Heidegger, *The End of Philosophy*, 107/*Vorträge und Aufsätze*, 96.

[25] Martin Heidegger, *Discourse on Thinking*, trans. John M. Anderson and E. Hans Freund (New York: Harper & Row, 1966), 50/Martin Heidegger, *Gelassenheit* (Pfullingen: Neske, 1959), 19–20.

[26] Heidegger, *Discourse on Thinking*, 50/*Gelassenheit*, 17.

[27] Heidegger, *The Question Concerning Technology*, 48/Martin Heidegger, *Die Technik und die Kehre* (Pfullingen: Neske, 1962), 45–6.

[28] Heidegger, *The Question Concerning Technology*, 5/*Vorträge und Aufsätze*, 14–15.

[29] Heidegger, *Discourse on Thinking*, 52/*Gelassenheit*, 22.

nature and civilization, yet this is a situation about which something *can* be done—at least indirectly. Heidegger's concern is the human *distress* caused by the *technological understanding of being*, rather than the *destruction* caused by *specific technologies*. Consequently, he distinguishes the current problems caused by technology—ecological destruction, nuclear danger, consumerism, and so on—from the devastation that would result should technology solve all our problems:

What threatens man in his very nature is . . . that man, by the peaceful release, transform-ation, storage, and channeling of the energies of physical nature, could render the human condition . . . tolerable for everybody and happy in all respects.[30]

The "greatest danger" is that

the approaching tide of technological revolution in the atomic age could so captivate, bewitch, dazzle, and beguile man that calculative thinking may someday come to be accepted and practiced *as the only way* of thinking.[31]

The danger, then, is not the destruction of nature or culture but certain totalizing kinds of practices—a leveling of our understanding of being. This threat is not a *problem* for which we must find a *solution*, but an *ontological condition* that requires a *transformation of our understanding of being*.

What, then, is the essence of technology—that is, the technological under-standing of being, or the technological clearing—and how does opening ourselves to it give us a free relation to technological devices? To begin with, when he asks about the essence of technology we must understand that Heidegger is not seeking a definition. His question cannot be answered by defining our concept of technology. Technology is as old as civilization. Heidegger notes that it can be correctly defined as "a means and a human activity." But if we ask about the *essence* of technology (the technological understanding of being) we find that modern technology is "something completely different and . . . new."[32] It even goes beyond using styrofoam cups to satisfy our desires. The essence of modern technology, Heidegger tells us, is to seek to order everything so as to achieve more and more flexibility and efficiency: "Expediting is always itself directed from the beginning . . . towards driving on to the maximum yield at the minimum expense."[33] That is, our only goal is optimal ordering, *for its own sake*: "Every-where everything is ordered to stand by, to be immediately at hand, indeed to

[30]   Heidegger, *Poetry, Language, Thought*, 116/*Vorträge und Aufsätze*, 294.
[31]   Heidegger, *Discourse on Thinking*, Heidegger, *Discourse on Thinking*, 56/*Gelassenheit*, 27.
[32]   Heidegger, *The Question Concerning Technology*, 5/*Vorträge und Aufsätze*, 15.
[33]   Heidegger, *The Question Concerning Technology*, 15/*Vorträge und Aufsätze*, 23.

stand there just so that it may be on call for a further ordering. Whatever is ordered about in this way has its own standing. We call it standing-reserve."[34] No more do we have subjects turning nature into an object of exploitation: "The subject–object relation thus reaches, for the first time, its pure 'relational,' i.e., ordering, character in which both the subject and the object are sucked up as standing-reserves."[35] Heidegger concludes: "Whatever stands by in the sense of standing-reserve no longer stands over against us as object."[36] He tells us that a modern airliner, understood in its technological essence, is not a tool we use; it is not an object at all, but rather a flexible and efficient cog in the transportation system. Likewise, we are not subjects who use the transportation system, but rather we are used by it to fill the planes.

In this technological perspective, ultimate goals such as serving God, society, our fellows, or even ourselves no longer make sense to us. Human beings, on this view, become a resource to be used—but more important, to be enhanced—like any other: "Man, who no longer conceals his character of being the most important raw material, is also drawn into this process."[37] In the film *2001*, the robot HAL, when asked if he is happy on the mission, says: "I'm using all my capacities to the maximum. What more could a rational entity want?" This is a brilliant expression of what anyone would say who is in touch with our current understanding of being. We pursue the development of our potential simply for the sake of further growth. We have no specific goals. The human potential movement perfectly expresses this technological understanding of being, as does the attempt to better organize the future use of our natural resources. We thus become part of a system that no one directs but that moves toward the total mobilization and enhancement of all beings, even us. This is why Heidegger thinks the perfectly ordered society dedicated to the welfare of all is not the solution to our problems but the culmination of the technological understanding of being.

Heidegger, however, sees that "it would be foolish to attack technology blindly. It would be shortsighted to condemn it as the work of the devil. We depend on technical devices; they even challenge us to ever greater advances."[38] Instead, Heidegger suggests that there is a way we can keep our technological devices and yet remain true to ourselves as receivers of clearings: "We can affirm the unavoidable use of technical devices, and also deny them the right to dominate

---

[34] Heidegger, *The Question Concerning Technology*, 17/*Vorträge und Aufsätze*, 24.
[35] Heidegger, *The Question Concerning Technology*, 173/*Vorträge und Aufsätze*, 61.
[36] Heidegger, *The Question Concerning Technology*, 17/*Vorträge und Aufsätze*, 24.
[37] Heidegger, *The End of Philosophy*, 104/*Vorträge und Aufsätze*, 90.
[38] Heidegger, *Discourse on Thinking*, 53/*Gelassenheit*, 24.

us, and so to warp, confuse, and lay waste our nature."[39] To understand how this might be possible, we need an illustration of Heidegger's important distinction between technology and the technological understanding of being. Again we can turn to Japan. In contemporary Japan traditional, non-technological practices still exist alongside the most advanced high-tech production and consumption. The television set and the household gods share the same shelf—the styrofoam cup coexists with the porcelain teacup. We thus see that the Japanese, at least, can enjoy technology without taking over the technological understanding of being.

For us to be able to make a similar dissociation, Heidegger holds, we must rethink the history of being in the West. Then we will see that although a technological understanding of being is our destiny, it is not our fate. That is, although our understanding of things and ourselves as resources to be ordered, enhanced, and used efficiently has been building up since Plato, we are not stuck with that understanding. Although the technological understanding of being governs the way things have to show up for us, we can be open to a transformation of our current cultural clearing.

Only those who think of Heidegger as opposing technology will be surprised at his next point. Once we see that technology is our latest understanding of being, we will be grateful for it. Our technological clearing is the cause of our distress, yet if it were not given to us to encounter things and ourselves as resources, nothing would show up *as* anything at all, and no possibilities for action would make sense. And once we realize—in our practices, of course, not just as a matter of reflection—that we *receive* our technological understanding of being, we have stepped out of the technological understanding of being, for we then see that what is most important in our lives is not subject to efficient enhancement—indeed, the drive to control everything is precisely what we do not control. This transformation in our sense of reality—this overcoming of thinking in terms of values and calculation—is precisely what Heideggerian thinking seeks to bring about. Heidegger seeks to make us see that our practices are needed as the place where an understanding of being can establish itself, so we can overcome our restricted modern clearing by acknowledging our essential receptivity to understandings of being:

Modern man must first and above all find his way back into the full breadth of the space proper to his essence. That essential space of man's essential being receives the dimension that unites it to something beyond itself...that is the way in which the safekeeping of being itself is given to belong to the essence of man as the one who is needed and used by being.[40]

---

[39] Heidegger, *Discourse on Thinking*, 54/*Gelassenheit*, 24–5.
[40] Heidegger, *The Question Concerning Technology*, 39/*Die Technik und die Kehre*, 39.

This transformation in our understanding of being, unlike the slow process of cleaning up the environment, which is, of course, also necessary, would take place in a sudden gestalt switch: "The turning of the danger comes to pass suddenly. In this turning, the clearing belonging to the essence of being suddenly clears itself and lights up."[41] The danger—namely that we have a leveled and concealed understanding of being—when grasped *as* the danger, becomes that which saves us. "The selfsame danger is, when it is *as* the danger, the saving power."[42]

This remarkable claim gives rise to two opposed ways of understanding Heidegger's response to technology. Both interpretations agree that once one recognizes the technological understanding of being for what it is—a historical understanding—one gains a free relation to it. We neither push forward technological efficiency as our sole goal nor always resist it. If we are free of the technological imperative we can, in each case, discuss the pros and cons. As Heidegger puts it:

We let technical devices enter our daily life, and at the same time leave them outside, . . . as things which are nothing absolute but remain dependent upon something higher. I would call this comportment toward technology which expresses "yes" and at the same time "no," by an old word, *releasement towards things.*[43]

One natural way of understanding this proposal holds that once we get in the right relation to technology, namely, recognize it as a clearing, it is revealed as just as good as any other clearing.[44] Efficiency—getting the most out of ourselves and everything else, "being all you can be"—is fine, as long as we see that efficiency for its own sake is not the *only* end for man, dictated by reality itself, but is just our current understanding. Heidegger seems to support this acceptance of the technological understanding of being as a way of living with technological nihilism when he says:

That which shows itself and at the same time withdraws [i.e., our understanding of being] is the essential trait of what we call the mystery. I call the comportment which enables us to keep open to the meaning hidden in technology, *openness to the mystery.*

---

[41] Heidegger, *The Question Concerning Technology*, 44/*Die Technik und die Kehre*, 43.

[42] Heidegger, *The Question Concerning Technology*, 39/*Die Technik und die Kehre*, 39.

[43] Heidegger, *Discourse on Thinking*, 54/*Gelassenheit*, 25. Why Heidegger speaks of "things" here is a long and interesting story. In his essay "The Thing" in *Poetry, Language, Thought*, Heidegger spells out the way that certain things, such as a jug of wine, can focus practices and collect people around them. Such things function like local, temporary works of art in giving meaning to human activities, but they do not focus a whole culture and so do not become the locus of a struggle between earth and world. Rather, they produce a moment of stillness and harmony. Albert Borgmann interprets and develops this idea in his account of "focal practices" (see Albert Borgmann, *Technology and the Character of Contemporary Life* (Chicago, IL: University of Chicago Press, 1984)). For an illuminating discussion of the importance for Heidegger of the thing, see also Charles Taylor's "Heidegger, Language and Ecology," in *Heidegger: A Critical Reader*, ed. Hubert Dreyfus and Harrison Hall (Oxford: Basil Blackwell, 1992), 247–69.

[44] See Richard Rorty, "Heidegger, Contingency and Pragmatism," in Dreyfus and Hall, *Heidegger*, 209–30.

Releasement toward things and openness to the mystery belong together. They grant us the possibility of dwelling in the world in a totally different way. They promise us a new ground and foundation upon which we can stand and endure in the world of technology without being imperiled by it.[45]

Nevertheless, such acceptance of the mystery of the gift of an understanding of being cannot be Heidegger's whole story about how to overcome technological nihilism, for he immediately adds, "Releasement toward things and openness to the mystery give us a vision of a new rootedness which *someday* might even be fit to recapture the old and now rapidly disappearing rootedness in a changed form."[46] When we then look back at the preceding remark, we realize releasement gives only a "possibility" and a "promise" of "dwelling in the world in a totally different way"; it does not enable us to do so. Mere openness to technology leaves out much that Heidegger finds essential to overcoming nihilism: embeddedness in nature, or localness, and new shared meaningful differences. Releasement, while giving us a free relation to technology and protecting our nature from being distorted and distressed, cannot by itself give us any of these.

For Heidegger, then, there are two issues. One is clear: "The issue is the saving of man's essential nature. Therefore, the issue is keeping meditative thinking alive."[47] This is a matter of preserving our sense of ourselves as *receivers* of understandings of being. But that is not enough: "If releasement toward things and openness to the mystery awaken within us, then we should arrive at a path that will lead to a new ground and foundation."[48] Releasement, it turns out, is only a stage, a kind of holding pattern we can enter into while we are awaiting a new understanding of being that would give a shared content to our openness—what Heidegger calls a new rootedness. That is why each time Heidegger talks of releasement and the saving power of understanding technology as a gift, he then goes on to talk of the divine: "Only when man, in the disclosing coming-to-pass of the insight by which he himself is beheld ... renounces human self-will ... may [he], as the mortal, look out toward the divine."[49] This is reflected in Heidegger's famous remark in his last interview: "Only a god can save us now."[50] But what does this mean?

---

[45] Heidegger, *Discourse on Thinking*, 55/*Gelassenheit*, 26.

[46] Heidegger, *Discourse on Thinking*, 55/*Gelassenheit*, 26.

[47] Heidegger, *Discourse on Thinking*, 56/*Gelassenheit*, 27.

[48] Heidegger, *Discourse on Thinking*, 56/*Gelassenheit*, 28.

[49] Heidegger, *The Question Concerning Technology*, 47/*Die Technik und die Kehre*, 45.

[50] Martin Heidegger, "Only a God Can Save Us: *Der Spiegel*'s Interview with Martin Heidegger," *Philosophy Today* 20 (1976), 267–84.

To begin with, Heidegger holds that we must learn to appreciate marginal practices—what Heidegger calls the saving power of insignificant things—practices such as friendship, backpacking in the wilderness, and drinking the local wine with friends. All these practices remain marginal precisely because they resist efficiency. These practices can, of course, also be engaged in for the sake of health and greater efficiency. Indeed, the greatest danger is that even the marginal practices will be mobilized as resources. That is why we must protect these endangered practices. But just protecting non-technical practices, even if we could succeed, would still not give us what we need, for these practices by themselves do not add up to a shared moral space of serious, meaningful options.

Of course, one cannot legislate a new understanding of being. But some of our practices could come together in a new cultural paradigm that held up to us a new way of doing things—a new paradigm that opened a world in which these practices and others were central, whereas efficient ordering was marginal. An object or event that would ground such a gestalt switch in our understanding of reality Heidegger calls a new god, and this is why he holds that only a god can save us.

What can we do to get what is still non-technological in our practices in focus in a non-nihilistic paradigm? Once one sees the problem, one also sees that there is not much one can do about it. A new sense of reality is not something that can be made the goal of a crash program like the moon flight—another paradigm of modern technological power. A new paradigm would have to take up practices that are now on the margin of our culture and make them central, while de-emphasizing practices now central to our cultural self-understanding. It would come as a surprise to the very people who participated in it, and if it worked it would become an exemplar of a new understanding of what matters and how to act. There would, of course, be powerful forces tending to take it over and mobilize it for our technological order, and if it failed it would necessarily be measured by our current understanding and so look ridiculous.

A hint of what such a new god might look like is offered by the music of the sixties. Bob Dylan, the Beatles, and other rock groups became for many the articulators of a new understanding of what really mattered. This new understanding almost coalesced into a cultural paradigm in the Woodstock music festival of 1969, where people actually lived for a few days in an understanding of being in which mainline contemporary concerns with order, sobriety, willful activity, and flexible, efficient control were made marginal and subservient to certain pagan practices, such as enjoyment of nature, dancing, and Dionysian ecstasy, along with neglected Christian concerns with peace, tolerance, and nonexclusive love of one's neighbor. Technology was not smashed or denigrated;

rather, all the power of electronic communications was put at the service of the music, which focused the above concerns.

If enough people had recognized in Woodstock what they most cared about and recognized that many others shared this recognition, a new understanding of being might have been focused and stabilized. Of course, in retrospect it seems to us who are still in the grip of the technological understanding of being that the concerns of the Woodstock generation were not organized and total enough to sustain a culture. Still we are left with a hint of how a new cultural paradigm would work. This helps us understand that we must foster human receptivity and preserve the endangered species of pre-technological practices that remain in our culture, in the hope that one day they will be pulled together in a new paradigm, rich enough and resistant enough to give a new meaningful direction to our lives.

Politics

Heidegger's political engagement was predicated upon his interpretation of the situation in the West as technological nihilism, and of National Socialism as a new paradigm that could give our culture a new understanding of being. But the very same interpretation of the history of being that led Heidegger to support Hitler in 1933 provided the ground for his decisive break with National Socialism somewhere between 1935 and 1938. Between 1933 and 1935 Heidegger seems to have thought that following Hitler as a charismatic leader was the only way to save and focus local and traditional practices in the face of global technology as exemplified by the Soviet Union and the United States. In 1935 he says in a lecture course:

From a metaphysical point of view, Russia and America are the same; the same dreary technological frenzy.... Situated in the center, our nation incurs the severest pressure.... If the great decision regarding Europe is not to bring annihilation, that decision must be made in terms of new spiritual energies unfolding historically from out of the center.[51]

But by 1938, in "The Age of the World Picture," Heidegger sees technology as the problem of the *West*, and National Socialism, rather than the USSR and the United States, as the most dangerous form of what he calls, in Nazi terms, "total mobilization."[52] Heidegger also criticized the belief in a *Führer* as the organizer of a total order as an example of faith in technological ordering.

---

[51] Martin Heidegger, *Introduction to Metaphysics*, trans. Ralph Manheim (New Haven, CT: Yale University Press, 1959), 31–2.

[52] Heidegger, *The Question Concerning TechnologyI,* 137/*Holzwege*, 97.

Beings have entered the way of erring in which the vacuum expands which requires a single order and guarantee of beings. Herein the necessity of "leadership," that is, the planning calculation . . . of the whole of beings, is required.[53]

After 1938, then, Heidegger thought of National Socialism not as the answer to technology and nihilism, but as its most extreme expression.

This gets us to one final question: To what extent was Heidegger's support of National Socialism a personal mistake compounded of conservative prejudices, personal ambition, and political naiveté, and to what extent was his engagement dictated by his philosophy? We have seen that Heidegger, like Charles Taylor and Robert Bellah more recently, holds that we can get over nihilism only by finding some set of shared meaningful concerns that can give our culture a new focus. Moreover, Heidegger sees no hope of overcoming nihilism if one accepts the faith in rational autonomy central to the Enlightenment. In fact, he sees the pursuit of autonomy as the cause of our dangerous contemporary condition. He counters the Enlightenment vision with a non-theological version of the Christian message that man cannot be saved by autonomy, maturity, equality, and dignity alone. Heidegger holds that only some shared meaningful concerns that grip us can give our culture a focus and enable us to resist acquiescence to a state that has no higher goal than to provide material welfare for all. This conviction underlies his dangerous claim that only a god—a charismatic figure, or some other culturally renewing event—can save us from nihilism.

To many, however, the idea of *a* god that will give us a unified but open community—one set of concerns that everyone shares if only as a focus of disagreement—sounds either unrealistic or dangerous. Heidegger would probably agree that its open democratic version looks increasingly unobtainable and that we have certainly seen that its closed totalitarian form can be very dangerous. But Heidegger holds that given our historical essence—the kind of beings we became in fifth century BC Greece when our culture gained its identity—such a community is necessary to us or else we will remain in nihilism. It is, he thinks, our only hope or, as he puts it, our destiny.

It follows for Heidegger that our deepest needs will be satisfied and our distress overcome only when our culture gets a new center. Our current condition is defined by the absence of a god:

The era is defined by the god's failure to arrive, by the "default of god." But the default of god . . . does not deny that the Christian relationship with God lives on in individuals and in the churches; still less does it assess this relationship negatively. The default of god

---

[53] Heidegger, *The End of Philosophy*, 105/*Vorträge und Aufsätze*, 93.

means that no god any longer gathers men and things unto himself, visibly and unequivocally, and by such gathering disposes of the world's history and man's sojourn in it.[54]

Heidegger's *personal* mistake comes from having thought that Hitler or National Socialism was such a god. Yet Heidegger had already, in "The Origin of the Work of Art," developed criteria that could serve to determine whether a charismatic leader or movement deserved our allegiance. He stresses there that a true work of art must set up a struggle between earth and world. That is, a true work of art does not make everything explicit and systematic. It generates and supports resistance to total mobilization. Yet Heidegger chose to support a totalitarian leader who denied the truth of all conflicting views and was dedicated to bringing everything under control. Heidegger no doubt interpreted Hitler as setting up some sort of appropriate struggle. Unfortunately, there is no interpretation-free criterion for testing a new god, and such mistakes are always possible. Heidegger's *philosophy*, then, is dangerous because it seeks to convince us that only a god—a charismatic figure or some other culturally renewing event—can save us from falling into contented nihilism. It exposes us to the risk of committing ourselves to some demonic event or movement that promises renewal.

What sort of claim is Heidegger making when he tells us that Enlightenment welfare and dignity are not enough and that only a god can save us? How can one justify or criticize Heidegger when he reads our current condition as the absence of a god and our current distress as a sign of the greatest danger?—for only such a reading of the present age justifies risking commitment to some new cultural paradigm.

The first answer we might try to give is that Heidegger is offering a genealogical interpretation. He will focus on and augment our distress and show that it can be accounted for by telling a story of the progressive narrowing, leveling, and totalizing of the West's understanding of being. Such an interpretation has to make sense of more details of our history and present situation than any rival interpretation, and ultimately it must convince us by the illumination it casts on our current condition, especially on our sense of ontological distress or emptiness, if we have one.

But how could we know that our distress was due to the absence of a god rather than personal and social problems? One answer might be that we will just have to wait for the perfected welfare state and then see how we feel. If defenders of the Enlightenment are right, distress will be eliminated, whereas Heidegger, one might suppose, would expect that, as technology succeeds, the suffering will

---

[54] Heidegger, *Poetry, Language, Thought*, 91/*Holzwege*, 269.

grow. But Heidegger does not make this claim. Heidegger admits and fears the possibility that everyone might simply become healthy and happy, and forget completely that they are receivers of understandings of being. All Heidegger can say is that such a forgetting of our forgetting of being would be the darkest night of nihilism. In such an "unworld," Heidegger could no longer expect to be understood. Only now, and only as long as he can awaken our distress and our sense of our receptivity to a mysterious source of meaning that creates and sustains us, can he hope that we will be able to see the force of his interpretation.

Such thinking is far from the "infallible knowledge"[55] many think Heidegger claims. Indeed, Heidegger goes out of his way to point out that he can claim no infallibility for his interpretation. He writes to a student that "this thinking can never show credentials such as mathematical knowledge can. But it is just as little a matter of arbitrariness."[56] He then goes on to repeat his reading of the West as having lost touch with the saving practices excluded by totalizing technology—practices that are nonetheless all around us:

The default of god and the divinities is absence. But absence is not nothing; rather it is precisely the presence, which must first be appropriated, of the hidden fullness and wealth of what has been and what, thus gathered, is presencing, of the divine in the world of the Greeks, in prophetic Judaism, in the preaching of Jesus.[57]

And he immediately adds that he can claim no special authority: "I can provide no credentials for what I have said...that would permit a convenient check in each case whether what I say agrees with 'reality'."[58] This is an appropriate warning since Heidegger's own political mistake reminds us that any guidelines must always be interpreted, and that if one opts for the charismatic one cannot avoid the risk. Thus, Heidegger's letter to the student fittingly concludes: "Any path always risks going astray.... Stay on the path, in genuine need, and learn the craft of thinking, unswerving, yet erring."[59]

---

[55] Jürgen Habermas, "Work and Weltanschauung: The Heidegger Controversy from a German Perspective," *Critical Inquiry* 15 (Winter 1989), 431–56, 456, reprinted in Dreyfus and Hall, *Heidegger*, 186–208.

[56] Heidegger, *Poetry, Language, Thought*, 184/*Vorträge und Aufsätze*, 183.

[57] Heidegger, *Poetry, Language, Thought*, 184/*Vorträge und Aufsätze*, 183.

[58] Heidegger, *Poetry, Language, Thought*, 186/*Vorträge und Aufsätze*, 184.

[59] Heidegger, *Poetry, Language, Thought*, 186/*Vorträge und Aufsätze*, 185.

11

Highway Bridges and Feasts

Heidegger and Borgmann on How to Affirm Technology (1997)

Hubert L. Dreyfus and Charles Spinosa

Albert Borgmann advances an American frontiersman's version of the question concerning technology that was pursued by Heidegger almost half a century ago among the peasants in the Black Forest.[1] Since the *critique* of technology pioneered by these thinkers has by now become widely known, we would like to address a subsequent question with which each has also struggled. How can we relate ourselves to technology in a way that not only resists its devastation but also gives it a positive role in our lives? This is an extremely difficult question to which no one has yet given an adequate response, but it is perhaps *the* question for our generation. Through a sympathetic examination of the Borgmannian and Heideggerian alternatives, we hope we can show that Heidegger suggests a more coherent and credible answer than Borgmann's.

The Essence of Technology

In writing about technology, Heidegger formulates the goal we are concerned with here as that of gaining a free relation to technology—a way of living with technology that does not allow it to "warp, confuse, and lay waste our nature."[2] According to Heidegger our nature is to be world disclosers. That is, by means of

---

[1] An earlier version of this essay was delivered as the 1996 Bugbee Lecture at the University of Montana. We would like thank Albert Borgmann, David Hoy, and Julian Young for their helpful comments on earlier drafts of this paper.
[2] Martin Heidegger, *Discourse on Thinking*, trans. John M. Anderson and E. Hans Freund (New York: Harper & Row, 1966), 54.

our equipment and coordinated practices we human beings open coherent, distinct contexts or worlds in which we perceive, act, and think. Each such world makes possible a distinct and pervasive way in which things, people, and selves can appear and in which certain ways of acting make sense. The Heidegger of *Being and Time* called a world an understanding of being and argued that such an understanding of being is what makes it possible for us to encounter people and things as such. He considered his discovery of the ontological difference—the difference between the understanding of being and the beings that can show up given an understanding of being—his single great contribution to Western thought.

Middle Heidegger (roughly from the 1930s to 1950) added that there have been a series of total understandings of being in the West, each focused by a cultural paradigm, which he called a work of art.[3] He distinguished roughly six epochs in our changing understanding of being. First things were understood on the model of wild nature as *physis*, i.e., as springing forth on their own. Then on the basis of *poiesis*, or nurturing, things were dealt with as needing to be helped to come forth. This was followed by an understanding of things as finished works, which in turn led to the understanding of all beings as *creatures* produced by a creator God. This religious world gave way to the modern one in which everything was organized to stand over against and satisfy the desires of autonomous and stable subjects. In 1950, Heidegger claimed that we were entering a final epoch, which he called *the technological understanding of being*.

But until late in his development, Heidegger was not clear as to how technology worked. He held for a long time that the danger of technology was that man was dominating everything and exploiting all beings for his own satisfaction, as if man were a subject in control and the objectification of everything were the problem. Thus, in 1940 he says:

Man is what lies at the bottom of all beings; and that is, in modern terms, at the bottom of all objectification and representability.[4]

To test this early claim we turn to the work of Albert Borgmann, since he has given us the best account of this aspect of Heidegger's thinking. Rather than doing an exegesis of Heidegger's texts, Borgmann does just what Heidegger wants his readers to do. He follows Heidegger on his path of thought, which always means finding the phenomena about which Heidegger is thinking. In *Technology*

---

[3] Heidegger's main example of cultural paradigms are works of art, but he does allow that there can be other kinds of paradigm. Truth, or the cultural paradigm, can also establish itself through the actions of a god, a statesman, or a thinker.

[4] Martin Heidegger, *Nietzsche*, vol. 4 (New York: Harper & Row, 1982), 28.

and the Character of Contemporary Life, Borgmann draws attention to the phenomenon of the technological device. Before the triumph of technological devices, people primarily engaged in practices that nurtured or crafted various things. So gardeners developed the skills and put in the effort necessary for nurturing plants, musicians acquired the skill necessary for bringing forth music, the fireplace had to be filled with wood of certain types and carefully maintained in order to provide warmth for the family. Technology, as Borgmann understands it, belongs to the last stage in the history of the understandings of being in the West. It replaces the worlds of *poiesis*, craftsmen, and Christians with a world in which subjects control objects. In such a world the things that call for and focus nurturing, craftsmanly, or praising practices are replaced by devices that offer a more and more transparent or commodious way of satisfying a desire. Thus the wood-burning fireplace as the foyer or focus of family activity is replaced by the stove and then by the furnace.

As Heidegger's thinking about technology deepened, however, he saw that even objects cannot resist the advance of technology. He came to see this in two steps. First, he saw that the nature of technology does not depend on subjects understanding and using objects. In 1946 he said that exploitation and control are not the subject's doing; "that man becomes the subject and the world the object, is a consequence of technology's nature establishing itself, and not the other way around."[5] And in his final analysis of technology, Heidegger was critical of those who, still caught in the subject/object picture, thought that technology was dangerous because it embodied instrumental reason. Modern technology, he insists, is "something completely different and therefore new."[6] The goal of technology Heidegger then tells us, is the more and more flexible and efficient ordering of resources, not as objects to satisfy our desires, but simply for the sake of ordering. He writes:

Everywhere everything is ordered to stand by, to be immediately at hand, indeed to stand there just so that it may be on call for a further ordering. Whatever is ordered about in this way...we call...standing-reserve....Whatever stands by in the sense of standing-reserve no longer stands over against us as object.[7]

Like late Heidegger, recent Borgmann sees that the direction technology is taking will eventually get rid of objects altogether. In his latest book, *Crossing*

---

[5] Martin Heidegger, "What Are Poets For?" in *Poetry, Language, Thought* (New York: Harper & Row, 1971), 112.

[6] Martin Heidegger, "The Question Concerning Technology," in *The Question Concerning Technology and Other Essays*, trans. William Lovitt (New York: Harper & Row, 1977), 5.

[7] Heidegger, "The Question Concerning Technology," 17.

the Postmodern Divide, Borgmann takes up the difference between *modern* and *postmodern* technology. He distinguishes *modern hard* technology from *postmodern soft* technology. On Borgmann's account, modern technology, by rigidity and control, overcame the resistance of nature and succeeded in fabricating impressive structures such as railroad bridges as well as a host of standard durable devices. Postmodern technology, by being flexible and adaptive, produces instead a diverse array of quality goods such as high-tech athletic shoes designed specifically for each particular athletic activity.

Borgmann notes that as our postmodern society has moved from production to service industries our products have evolved from sophisticated goods to information. He further sees that this postmodern instrumental reality is giving way in its turn to the hyperreality of simulators that seek to get rid of the limitations imposed by the real world. Taken to the limit the simulator puts an improved reality completely at our disposal. Thus the limit of postmodernity, as Borgmann understands it, would be reached, not by the total objectification and exploitation of nature, but by getting rid of natural objects and replacing them with simulacra that are completely under our control. The essential feature of such hyperreality on Borgmann's account is that it is "entirely subject to my desire."[8] Thus for Borgmann the *object* disappears precisely to the extent that the *subject* gains total control. But Borgmann adds the important qualification that in gaining total control, the postmodern subject is reduced to "a point of arbitrary desires."[9] In the end, Borgmann's postmodern hyperreality would eliminate both objects and modernist subjects who have long-term identities and commitments. Nevertheless, Borgmann still remains within the field of subjectivity by maintaining that hyperreality is driven by the satisfaction of desires.

Even though he wrote almost half a century ago, Heidegger already had a similar account of the last stage of modernity. Like Borgmann he saw that information is replacing objects in our lives, and Heidegger and Borgmann would agree that information's main characteristic is that it can be easily transformed. But, whereas Borgmann sees the goal of these transformations as serving a minimal subject's desires, Heidegger claims that "both the subject and the object are sucked up as standing-reserve."[10] To see what he means by this, we can begin by examining Heidegger's half-century-old example. Heidegger describes the hydroelectric power station on the Rhine as his paradigm

---

[8] Albert Borgmann, *Crossing the Postmodern Divide* (Chicago, IL: University of Chicago Press, 1992), 88.

[9] Borgmann, *Crossing the Postmodern Divide*, 108.

[10] Martin Heidegger, "Science and Reflection," in *The Question Concerning Technology and Other Essays*, 173.

technological device because for him electricity is the paradigm technological stuff. He says:

> The revealing that rules throughout modern technology has the character of a setting-upon, in the sense of a challenging-forth. That challenging happens in that the energy concealed in nature is unlocked, what is unlocked is transformed, what is transformed is stored up, what is stored up is, in turn, distributed, and what is distributed is switched about *ever anew.*[11]

But we can see now that electricity is not a perfect example of technological stuff because it ends up finally turned into light, heat, or motion to satisfy some subject's desire. Heidegger's intuition is that treating everything as standing reserve or, as we might better say, resources, makes possible *endless* disaggregation, redistribution, and reaggregation *for its own sake.* As soon as he sees that information is truly endlessly transformable Heidegger switches to computer manipulation of information as his paradigm.[12]

As noted, when Heidegger says that technology is not instrumental and objectifying but "something entirely new," he means that, along with objects, subjects are eliminated by this new mode of being. Thus for Heidegger postmodern technology is not the culmination of the modern subject's controlling of objects but a new stage in the understanding of being. Heidegger, standing on Nietzsche's shoulders, gains a glimpse of this new understanding when he interprets Nietzsche as holding that the will to power is not the will to gain control for the sake of satisfying one's desires—even arbitrary ones—but the tendency in the practices to produce and maintain flexible ordering so that the fixity of even the past can be conquered; this cashes out as flexible ordering for the sake of more ordering and reordering without limit, which, according to Heidegger, Nietzsche expresses as the eternal return of the same.[13] Thanks to Nietzsche, Heidegger could sense that, when everything becomes standing reserve or resources, people and things will no longer be understood as having essences or identities or, for people, the goal of satisfying arbitrary desires, but back in 1955 he could not yet make out just how such a world would look.

Now, half a century after Heidegger wrote "The Question Concerning Technology," the new understanding of being is becoming evident. A concrete

---

[11] Heidegger, "The Question Concerning Technology," 16 (emphasis ours).

[12] See Martin Heidegger, "On the Way to Language" (1959), trans. Peter D. Hertz, in *On the Way to Language* (New York: Harper & Row, 1971), 132. See also Martin Heidegger, "Memorial Address" (1959), in *Discourse on Thinking*, trans. John M. Anderson and E. Hans Freund (New York: Harper, 1966), 46.

[13] Martin Heidegger, *What Is Called Thinking?*, trans. Fred D. Wieck and J. Glenn Gray (New York: Harper & Row, 1968), 104–9.

example of this change and of an old-fashioned subject's resistance to it can be seen in a recent *New York Times* article entitled "An Era When Fluidity Has Replaced Maturity" (March 20, 1995). The author, Michiko Kakutani, laments that "for many people ... shape-shifting and metamorphosis seem to have replaced the conventional process of maturation." She then quotes a psychiatrist, Robert Jay Lifton, who notes in his book *The Protean Self* that "We are becoming fluid and many-sided. Without quite realizing it, we have been evolving a sense of self appropriate to the restlessness and flux of our time."[14] Kakutani then comments:

Certainly signs of the flux and restlessness Mr. Lifton describes can be found everywhere one looks. On a superficial cultural level, we are surrounded by images of shape-shifting and reinvention, from sci-fi creatures who "morph" from form to form, to children's toys [she has in mind Transformers that metamorphose from people into vehicles]; from Madonna's ever expanding gallery of ready-to-wear personas to New Age mystics who claim they can "channel" other people or remember "previous" lives.[15]

In a quite different domain, in a talk at Berkeley on the difference between the modern library culture and the new information-retrieval culture, Terry Winograd notes a series of oppositions that, when organized into a chart, show the transformation of the modern into the postmodern along the lines that Heidegger described. A few of the oppositions that Winograd found are shown in Table 11.1.

Table 11.1 Modern and postmodern paradigms for the organization of knowledge

Library Culture	*Information-Retrieval Culture*
Careful selection:	Access to everything:
a. quality of editions	a. inclusiveness of editions
b. perspicuous descriptions on cards to enable judgment	b. operational training on search engines to enable coping
c. authenticity of the text	c. availability of texts
Classification:	Diversification:
a. disciplinary standards	a. user friendliness
b. stable, organized, defined by specific interests	b. hypertext—following all lines of curiosity
Permanent collections:	Dynamic collections:
a. preservation of a fixed text	a. intertextual evolution
b. browsing	b. surfing the web

[14] Robert Jay Lifton, as quoted by Michiko Kakutani, "When Fluidity Replaces Maturity," *New York Times* (March 20, 1995), C 11.
[15] Kakutani, "When Fluidity Replaces Maturity."

It is clear from these opposed lists that more has changed than the move from control of objects to flexibility of storage and access. What is being stored and accessed is no longer a fixed body of objects with fixed identities and contents. Moreover, the user seeking the information is not a subject who desires a more complete and reliable model of the world, but a protean being ready to be opened up to ever new horizons. In short, the postmodern human being is not interested in collecting but is constituted by connecting.

The perfect postmodern artifact is, thus, the Internet, and Sherry Turkle has described how the Net is changing the background practices that determine the kinds of selves we can be. In her recent book, *Life on the Screen: Identity in the Age of the Internet*, she details "the ability of the Internet to change popular under-standings of identity." On the Internet, she tells us, "we are encouraged to think of ourselves as fluid, emergent, decentralized, multiplicitous, and ever in process."[16] Thus "the Internet has become a significant social laboratory for experimenting with the constructions and reconstructions of self that characterize postmodern life."[17] Precisely what sort of identity does the Net encourage us to construct?

There seem to be two answers that Turkle does not clearly distinguish. She uses as her paradigm Net experience the MUD, which is an acronym for Multi-User Dungeon—a virtual space popular with adults that has its origin in a teenagers' role-playing game. A MUD, she says, "can become a context for discovering who one is and wishes to be."[18] Thus some people explore roles in order to become more clearly and confidently themselves. The Net then functions in the old subject/object mode "to facilitate self knowledge and personal growth."[19] But, on the other hand, although Turkle continues to use the outdated, modernist language of personal growth, she sees that the computer and the Internet promote something totally different and new. "MUDs," she tells us, "make possible the creation of an identity so fluid and multiple that it strains the limits of the notion."[20] Indeed, the MUD's disembodiment and lack of commitment enables people to be many selves without having to integrate these selves or to use them to improve a single identity. As Turkle notes:

In MUDs you can write and revise your character's self-description whenever you wish. On some MUDs you can even create a character that "morphs" into another with the command "morph."[21]

---

[16] Sherry Turkle, *Life on the Screen: Identity in the Age of the Internet* (New York: Simon & Schuster, 1995), 263–4.

[17] Turkle, *Life on the Screen*, 180. [18] Turkle, *Life on the Screen*, 180.

[19] Turkle, *Life on the Screen*, 185. [20] Turkle, *Life on the Screen*, 12.

[21] Turkle, *Life on the Screen*, 192.

Once we become accustomed to the age of the Net, we shall have many different skills for identity construction, and we shall move around virtual spaces and real spaces seeking ways to exercise these skills, powers, and passions as best we can. We might imagine people joining in this or that activity with a particular identity for so long as the identity and activity are exhilarating and then moving on to new identities and activities. Such people would thrive on having no home community and no home sense of self. The promise of the Net is that we will all develop sufficient skills to do one kind of work with one set of partners and then move on to do some other kind of work with other partners. The style that would govern such a society would be one of intense, but short, involvements, and everything would be done to maintain and develop the flexible disaggregation and reaggregation of various skills and faculties. Desires and their satisfaction would give way to having the thrill of the moment.

Communities of such people would not seem like communities by today's standards. They would not have a core cadre who remained in them over long periods of time. Rather, tomorrow's communities would live and die on the model of rock groups. For a while there would be an intense effort among a group of people and an enormous flowering of talent and artistry, and then that activity would get stale, and the members would go their own ways, joining other communities.[22] If you think that today's rock groups area special case, consider how today's businesses are getting much work done by so-called hot groups. Notoriously, the Apple Macintosh was the result of the work of such group. More and more products are appearing that have come about through such efforts. In such a world not only fixed identities but even desiring subjects would, indeed, have been sucked up as standing reserve.

Heidegger's Proposal

In order to explain Heidegger's positive response to technological things, we shall generalize Heidegger's description of the gathering power of mostly Black Forest things[23] by using Borgmann's American account of what he calls focal practices. We will then be in a position to see how, given their shared view of how things and their local worlds resist technology, Borgmann's understanding of technological practices as still enmeshed with subjectivity leads him to the conclusion

---

[22] In his account of brief habits, Nietzsche describes a life similar to moving from one hot group to another. Brief habits are neither like long-lasting habits that produce stable identities, nor like constant improvisation. For Nietzsche, the best life occurs when one is fully committed to acting out of one brief habit until it becomes irrelevant and another takes over. See Friedrich Nietzsche, *The Gay Science*, trans. Walter Kaufmann (New York: Vintage, 1974), §295, 236–7.

[23] Martin Heidegger, "The Thing," in *Poetry, Language, Thought*, 182.

that technological things cannot solicit focal practices, while Heidegger's account of postmodern technological practices as radically different from modern subject/object practices enables him to see a positive role for technological things, and the practices they solicit.

In "The Thing" (1949) and "Building Dwelling Thinking" (1951), Heidegger explores a kind of gathering that would enable us to resist postmodern technological practices. In these essays, he turns from the cultural gathering he explored in "The Origin of the Work of Art" (which sets up shared meaningful differences and thereby unifies an entire culture) to local gatherings that set up local worlds. Such local worlds occur around some everyday thing that temporarily brings into their own both the thing itself and those involved in the typical activity concerning the use of the thing. Heidegger calls this event a *thing thinging* and the tendency in the practices to bring things and people into their own, *appropriation*. Albert Borgmann has usefully called the practices that support this local gathering *focal practices*.[24] Heidegger's examples of things that focus such local gathering are a wine jug and an old stone bridge. Such things gather Black Forest peasant practices, but, as Borgmann has seen, the family meal acts as a focal thing when it draws on the culinary and social skills of family members and solicits fathers, mothers, husbands, wives, children, familiar warmth, good humor, and loyalty to come to the fore in their excellence, or in, as Heidegger would say, their ownmost.

Heidegger describes such focal practices in general terms by saying that when things thing they bring together earth and sky, divinities and mortals. When he speaks this way, his thinking draws on Holderlin's difficult poetic terms of art; yet, what Heidegger means has its own coherence so long as we keep the phenomenon of a thing thinging before us. Heidegger, thinking of the taken-for-granted practices that ground situations and make them matter to us, calls them *earth*. In the example of the family meal we have borrowed from Borgmann, the grounding practices would be the traditional practices that produce, sustain, and develop the nuclear family. It is essential to the way these earthy practices operate that they make family gathering matter. For families, such dining practices are not simply options for the family to indulge in or not. They are the basis upon which all manifest options appear. To ground mattering such practices must remain in the background. Thus, Heidegger conceives of the earth as being fruitful by virtue of being withdrawing and hidden.

---

[24] Albert Borgmann, *Technology and the Character of Contemporary Life* (Chicago, IL: University of Chicago Press, 1984), 196–210.

By *sky*, Heidegger means the disclosed or manifest stable possibilities for action that arise in focal situations.[25] When a focal situation is happening, one feels that certain actions are appropriate. At dinner, actions such as reminiscences, warm conversation, and even debate about events that have befallen family members during the day, as well as questions to draw people out, are solicited. But, lecturing, impromptu combat, private jokes, and brooding silence are discouraged. What particular possibilities are relevant is determined by the situation itself.

In describing the cultural works of art that provide unified understandings of being, Heidegger was content with the categories of earth and world, which map roughly on the thing's earth and sky. But when Heidegger thinks of focal practices, he also thinks in terms of *divinities*. When a focal event such as a family meal is working to the point where it has its particular integrity, one feels extraordinarily in tune with all that is happening, a special graceful ease takes over, and events seem to unfold of their own momentum—all combining to make the moment all the more centered and more a gift. A reverential sentiment arises; one feels thankful or grateful for receiving all that is brought out by this particular situation. Such sentiments are frequently manifested in practices such as toasting or in wishing others could be joining in such a moment. The older practice for expressing this sentiment was, of course, saying grace. Borgmann expresses a similar insight when, in speaking of a baseball game as attuning people, he says:

Given such attunement, banter and laughter flow naturally across strangers and unite them into a community. When reality and community conspire this way, divinity descends on the game.[26]

Our sense that we did not and could not make the occasion a center of focal meaning by our own effort, but rather that the special attunement required for such an occasion to work has to be granted to us, is what Heidegger wants to capture in his claim that when a thing things the divinities must be present. How the power of the divinities will be understood will depend on the understanding of being of the culture but the phenomenon Heidegger describes is cross-cultural.

The fourth element of what Heidegger calls the fourfold is the *mortals*. By using this term, Heidegger is describing us as disclosers and he thinks that death primarily reveals our disclosive way of being to us. When he speaks of death, he does not mean demise or a medically defined death. He means an attribute of the way human practices work that causes mortals (later Heidegger's word for people who are inside a focal practice) to understand that they have no fixed identity and

---

[25] Martin Heidegger, "Building Dwelling Thinking," in *Poetry, Language, Thought*, 149.
[26] Borgmann, *Crossing the Postmodern Divide*, 135.

so must be ready to relinquish their current identity in order to assume the identity that their practices next call them into attunement with.[27] Of course, one needs an account of how such a multiplicity of identities and worlds differs from the morphing and hot groups we have just been describing. We will come back to this question shortly.

So far, following Borgmann, we have described the phenomenon of a thing thinging in its most glamorized form where we experience the family coming together as an integrated whole at a particular moment around a particular event. Heidegger calls this heightened version of a thing thinging a thing "shining forth."[28] But if we focus exclusively on the glamorized version, we can easily miss two other essential features of things that Heidegger attends to in "Building Dwelling Thinking." The first is that things thing even when we do not respond to them with full attention. For instance, when we walk off a crowded street into a cathedral, our whole demeanor changes even if we are not alert to it. We relax in its cool darkness that solicits meditativeness. Our sense of what is loud and soft changes, and we quiet our conversation. In general, we manifest and become centered in whatever reverential practices remain in our post-Christian way of life. Heidegger claims that such things as bridges and town squares establish location and thereby thing even if in ways more privative than our cathedral example. He seems to mean that so long as people who regularly encounter a thing are socialized to respond to it appropriately, their practices are organized around the thing, and its solicitations are taken into account even when no one notices.

Instead of cathedrals, Heidegger uses various sorts of bridges as examples of things thinging but not shining. His list of bridges includes a bridge from almost every major epoch in his history of the Western understandings of being. Heidegger's account could begin with the *physis* bridge—say some rocks or a fallen tree—which just flashes up to reward those who are alert to the offerings of nature. But he, in fact, begins his list with a bridge from the age of *poiesis*: "the river bridge near the country town [that] brings wagon and horse teams to the surrounding villages."[29] Then there is the bridge from high medieval times, when being was understood as *createdness*. It "leads from the precincts of the castle to the cathedral square." Oddly enough there is no bridge from the subject/object days but Borgmann has leapt into the breach with magnificent accounts of the heroic effort involved in constructing railroad bridges,

---

[27] Heidegger, "The Thing," *Poetry, Language, Thought*, 178–9.
[28] Heidegger, "The Thing," 182.
[29] Heidegger, "Building Dwelling Thinking," 152.

and poets, starting with Walt Whitman, have seen in the massive iron structure of the Brooklyn Bridge an emblem of the imposing power and optimism of America.[30] Such a modern bridge is solid and reliable but it is rigid and locks into place the locations it connects.

After having briefly and soberly mentioned the *poiesis* bridge, Heidegger redescribes it in the style of Black Forest kitsch for which he is infamous. "The old stone bridge's humble brook crossing gives to the harvest wagon its passage from the fields into the village and carries the lumber cart from the field path to the road." Passages like this one seem to support Borgmann's contention that "an inappropriate nostalgia clings to Heidegger's account"[31] and that the things he names are "scattered and of yesterday."[32] And it is true that Heidegger distrusts typewriters,[33] phonographs, and television.[34] Borgmann finds "Heidegger's reflections that we have to seek out pre-technological enclaves to encounter focal things...misleading and dispiriting."[35]

While Borgmann shares Heidegger's distrust of technological *devices*, he, nonetheless, sees himself as different from Heidegger in that he finds a positive place for what he calls technological *instruments* in supporting traditional things and the practices they focus. He mentions the way hi-tech running shoes enhance running,[36] and one might add in the same vein that the dishwasher is a transparent technological instrument that supports, rather than interferes with or detracts from, the joys of the "great meal of the day." Still, according to Borgmann, what gets supported can never be technological devices since such devices, by satisfying our arbitrary desires as quickly and transparently as possible, cannot focus our practices and our lives but only disperse them.[37]

---

[30] Borgmann, *Crossing the Postmodern Divide*, 27–34.

[31] Borgmann, *Technology and the Character of Contemporary Life*, 196.

[32] Borgmann, *Technology and the Character of Contemporary Life*, 199.

[33] Martin Heidegger, *Parmenides*, trans. Andre Schuwer and Richard Rojecewicz (Bloomington, IN: Indiana University Press, 1992), 85.

[34] See footnote 42.

[35] Borgmann, *Technology and the Character of Contemporary Life*, 200.

[36] Borgmann, *Technology and the Character of Contemporary Life*, 221.

[37] In an attempt to overcome the residual nostalgia in any position that holds that technological devices can never have a centering role in a meaningful life, Robert Pirsig has argued in *Zen and the Art of Motorcycle Maintenance* that, if properly understood and maintained, technological devices can focus practices that enable us to live in harmony with technology. Although the motorcycle is a technological device, understanding and caring for it can help one to resist the modern tendency to use whatever is at hand as a commodity to satisfy one's desires and then dispose of it. But, as Borgmann points out, this saving stance of understanding and maintenance is doomed as our devices, for example computers, become more and more reliable while being constructed of such minute and complex parts that understanding and repairing them is no longer an option.

But if there were a way that technological devices could thing and thereby gather us, then one could be drawn into a positive relationship with them without becoming a resource engaged in this disaggregation and reaggregation of things and oneself and thereby losing one's nature as a discloser. Precisely in response to this possibility, Heidegger, while still thinking of bridges, overcomes his Black Forest nostalgia and suggests a radical possibility unexplored by Borgmann. In reading Heidegger's list of bridges from various epochs, each of which things inconspicuously "in its own way," no one seems to have noticed the last bridge in the series. After his kitschy remarks on the humble old stone bridge, Heidegger continues: "The highway bridge is tied into the network of long-distance traffic, paced as calculated for maximum yield."[38] Clearly Heidegger is thinking of the postmodern autobahn interchange, in the middle of nowhere, connecting many highways so as to provide easy access to as many destinations as possible. Surely, one might think, Heidegger's point is that such a technological artifact could not possibly thing. Yet Heidegger continues:

Ever differently the bridge escorts the lingering and hastening ways of men to and fro...The bridge *gathers*, as a passage that crosses, before the divinities—whether we explicitly think of, and visibly *give thanks for*, their presence, as in the figure of the saint of the bridge, or whether that divine presence is hidden or even pushed aside.[39]

Heidegger is here following out his sense that different things thing with different modes of revealing, that is, that each "*gathers* to itself in *its own way* earth and sky, divinities and mortals."[40] Figuring out what Heidegger might mean here is not a question of arcane Heidegger exegesis but an opportunity to return to the difficult question we raised at the beginning: How can we relate ourselves to technology in a positive way while resisting its devastation of our essence as world disclosers? In Heidegger's terms we must ask, How can a technological artifact like the highway bridge, dedicated as it is to optimizing options, gather the fourfold? Or, following Borgmann's sense of the phenomenon, we can ask how could a technological device like the highway bridge give one's activity a temporary focus? Granted that the highway bridge is a flexible resource, how can we get in tune with it without becoming flexible resources ourselves? How can mortals morph?

To answer this question about how we can respond to technology as disclosers or mortals, we must first get a clear picture of exactly what it is like to be turned

---

[38] Heidegger, "Building Dwelling Thinking," 152.
[39] Heidegger, "Building Dwelling Thinking," 152–3.
[40] Heidegger, "Building Dwelling Thinking," 153.

into resources responding to each situation according to whichever of our disaggregated skills is solicited most strongly. We can get a hint of what such optimizing of disaggregated skills looks like if we think of the relations among a pack of today's teenagers. When a group of teenagers wants to get a new CD, the one with the car (with the driving skills and capacity) will be most important until they get to the store; then the one with the money (with purchasing skills and capacity) will lead; and then when they want to play the CD, the one with the CD player (with CD playing skills and capacity) will be out front. In each moment, the others will coordinate themselves to bring out maximally whatever other relevant skills (or possessions) they have, such as chatting pleasantly, carrying stuff, reading maps, tuning the car radio, making wisecracks, and scouting out things that could be done for free. Consequently, they will be developing these other skills too.

If people lived their whole lives in this improvising mode, they would understand themselves only in terms of the skills that made the most sense at the moment. They would not see themselves as having a coordinated network of skills, but only in being led by chance to exercise some skill or other. Hence, they would not experience themselves as satisfying desires so much as getting along adaptably. Satisfying a desire here and there might be some small part of that.

If we now turn back to the autobahn "bridge" example, we can see the encounter with the interchange as a chance to let different skills be exercised. So on a sunny day we may encounter an interchange outside of Freiburg as we drive to a meeting in town as soliciting us to reschedule our meeting at Lake Constance. We take the appropriate exit and then use our cellular phone to make sure others do the same.

We can begin to understand how Heidegger thinks we can respond to technological things without becoming a collection of disaggregated skills, if we ask how the bridge could gather the fourfold. What is manifest like the *sky* are multiple possibilities. The interchange connects anywhere to anywhere else—strictly speaking it does not even connect two banks. All that is left of *earth* is that it matters that there are such possibilities, although it does not matter that there are these specific ones. But what about the *divinities*? Heidegger has to admit that they have been pushed aside. As one speeds around a clover leaf one has no premodern sense of having received a gift. Neither is there a modern sense, such as one might experience on a solid, iron railroad bridge, that human beings have here achieved a great triumph. All one is left with is a sense of flexibility and excitement. One senses how easy it would be to go anywhere. If one is in tune with technological flexibility, one feels *lucky* to be open to so many possibilities.

We can see that for Heidegger the interchange bridge is certainly not the best kind of bridge but it does have its style, and one can be sensitive to it in the way it solicits. The next question is, whether in getting in tune with the thinging of the highway bridge one is turned into a resource with no stable identity and no world that one is disclosing or whether one still has some sense of having an identity and of contributing to disclosing. This is where Heidegger's stress on our being *mortals* becomes essential. To understand oneself as mortal means to understand one's identity and world as fragile and temporary and requiring one's active engagement. In the case of the highway bridge, it means that, even while getting in tune with being a flexible resource, one does not understand oneself as being a resource all the time and everywhere. One does not always feel pressured, for instance, to optimize one's vacation possibilities by refusing to get stuck on back roads and sticking to the interstates. Rather, as one speeds along the overpass, one senses one's mortality, namely that one has other skills for bringing out other sorts of things, and therefore one is never wholly a resource.[41]

We have just described what may seem to be a paradox. We have said that even a technological thing may gather together earth, sky, mortals, and maybe even divinities, which are supposed to be the aspects of practices that gather people, equipment, and activities into local worlds, with roles, habitual practices, and a style that provide disclosers with a sense of integrity or centeredness. But technological things notoriously disperse us into a bunch of disaggregated skills with a style of flexible dispersion. So what could they gather into a local world? There is only one answer here. Neither equipment nor roles could be

---

[41] If we take the case of writing implements, we can more clearly see both the positive role that can be played by technological things as well as the special danger they present to which Borgmann has made us sensitive. Like bridges, the style of writing implements reflects their place in the history of being. The fountain pen solicits us to write to someone for whom the personality of our handwriting will make a difference. When involved in the practices that make the fountain pen seem important, we care about such matters as life plans, stable identities, character, views of the world, and so on. We are subjects dealing with other subjects. A typewriter, however, will serve us better if we are recording business matters or writing factual reports simply to convey information. A word processor hooked up to the Net with its great flexibility solicits us to select from a huge number of options in order to produce technical or scholarly papers that enter a network of conversations. And using a word processor one cannot help but feel lucky that one does not have to worry about erasing, retyping, literally cutting and pasting to move text around, and mailing the final product. But, as Borgmann points out, a device is not neutral; it affects the possibilities that show up for us. If one has a word processor and a modem, the text no longer appears to be a piece of work that one finishes and then publishes. It evolves through many drafts none of which is final. Circulating texts on the Net is the culmination of the dissolution of the finished object, where different versions (of what would have before been called a single text) are contributed to by many people. With such multiple contributions, not only is the physical work dispersed but so is the author. Such authorial dispersion is a part of the general dispersion of identity that Sherry Turkle describes.

gathered, but the skills for treating ourselves as disaggregated skills and the world as a series of open possibilities are what are drawn together so that various dispersed skillful performances become possible.

But if we focus on the skills for dispersing alone, then the dangerous seduction of technology is enhanced. Because the word processor makes writing easy for desiring subjects and this ease in writing solicits us to enter discourses rather than produce finished works, the word processor attached to the Net solicits us to substitute it for pens and typewriters, thereby eliminating the equipment *and the skills* that were appropriate for modern subject/object practices. It takes a real commitment to focal practices based on stable subjects and objects to go on writing personal letters with a fountain pen and to insist that papers written on the word processor must reach an elegant finish. If the tendency to rely completely on the flexibility of technological devices is not resisted, we will be left with only one kind of writing implement promoting one style of practice, namely those of endless transformation and enhancement. Likewise, if we live our lives in front of our home entertainment centers where we can morph at will from being audiophiles to sports fans to distance learners, our sense of being mortals who can open various worlds and have various identities will be lost as we, indeed, become pure resources.[42]

Resistance to technological practices by cultivating focal practices is the primary solution Borgmann gives to saving ourselves from technological devastation. Borgmann cannot find anything more positive in technology—other than indulging in good running shoes and a Big Mac every now and then—because he sees technology as the highest form of subjectivity. It may fragment our identities, but it maintains us as desiring beings not world disclosers. In contrast, since Heidegger sees technology as disaggregating our identities into a contingently built-up collection of skills, technological things solicit certain skills without requiring that we take ourselves as having one style of identity or another. This absence of identity may make our mode of being as world disclosers impossible for us. This would be what Heidegger calls the greatest danger. But this absence of an identity also allows us to become sensitive to the various identities we have when we are engaged in disclosing the different worlds focused by different styles

---

[42] Heidegger writes in "The Thing":

Man ... now receives instant information, by radio, of events which he formerly learned about only years later, if at all. The germination and growth of plants, which remained hidden throughout the seasons, is now exhibited publicly in a minute, on film. Distant sites of the most ancient cultures are shown on film as if they stood this very moment amidst today's street traffic.... The peak of this abolition of every possibility of remoteness is reached by television, which will soon pervade and dominate the whole machinery of communication. (165)

of things. For, although even dispersive technological skills will always gather in some fashion as they develop, the role of mortals as active world disclosers will only be preserved if it is at least possible for the gathering of these background skills to be experienced as such. And this experience will only be possible in technology if one can shift back and forth between pre-technological identities with their style of coping and a technological style. As such disclosers we can then respond to technological things as revealing one kind of world among others. Hence, Heidegger's view of technology allows him to find a positive relation to it, but only so long as we maintain skills for disclosing other kinds of local worlds. Freeing us from having a total fixed identity so that we may experience ourselves as multiple identities disclosing multiple worlds is what Heidegger calls technology's saving power.[43]

We have seen that for Heidegger being gathered by and nurturing non-technological things makes possible being gathered by technological things. Thus, living in a plurality of local worlds is not only desirable, as Borgmann sees, but is actually necessary if we are to give a positive place to technological devices. Both thinkers must, therefore, face the question that Borgmann faces in his recent book, as to how to live in a plurality of communities of focal celebration. If we try to organize our lives so as to maximize the number of focal worlds we dwell in each day, we will find ourselves teaching, then running, then making dinner, then clearing up just in time to play chamber music. Such a controlling approach will produce a subject that is always outside the current world, planning the next. Indeed such willful organization runs against the responsiveness necessary for dwelling in local worlds at all. But if, on the other hand, one goes from world to world fully absorbed in each and then fully open to whatever thing grabs one next, one will exist either as a collection of unrelated selves or as no self at all, drifting in a disoriented way among worlds. To avoid such a morphing or empty identities, one wants a life where engaging in one focal practice leads naturally to engaging in another—a life of affiliations such that one regularly is solicited to do the next focal thing when the current one is becoming irrelevant. Borgmann has intimations of such a life:

Musicians recognize gardeners; horse people understand artisans.... The experience of this kinship ... opens up a wider reality that allows one to refocus one's life when failing strength or changing circumstances withdraw a focal thing.[44]

---

[43] Martin Heidegger, "The Turning," in *The Question Concerning Technology and Other Essays*, 43, where he claims that our turning away from a technological understanding of being will, at least initially, be a matter of turning to multiple worlds where things thing.

[44] Borgmann, *Crossing the Postmodern Divide*, 122.

Such a plurality of focal skills not only enables one to move from world to world; it gives one a sort of poly-identity that is neither the identity of an arbitrary desiring subject nor the rudderless adaptability of a resource.

Such a kinship of mortals opens new possibilities for relations among communities. As Borgmann says:

People who have been captivated by music...will make music themselves, but they will not exclude the runners or condemn the writers. In fact, they may run and write themselves or have spouses or acquaintances who do. There is an interlacing of communities of celebration.[45]

Here, we suspect, we can find a positive place for technological devices. For there is room in such interconnecting worlds not only for a joyful family dinner, writing to a lifelong friend, and attending the local concert but also for surfing on the Internet and happily zipping around an autobahn cloverleaf in tune with technology and glad that one is open to the possibilities of connecting with each of these worlds and many others.

But Borgmann does not end with his account of the interlacing of communities, which is where Heidegger, when he is thinking of things thinging, would end. Borgmann writes:

To conclude matters in this way...would suppress a profound need and a crucial fact of communal celebration, namely religion. People feel a deep desire for comprehensive and comprehending orientation.[46]

Borgmann thinks that, fortunately, we postmoderns are more mature than former believers who excluded communities other than their own. Thus we can build a world that promotes both local worlds and a "community of communities" that satisfies everyone's need for comprehensiveness. To accept the view that our concerns form what Borgmann calls a *community of communities* is to embrace one, overarching understanding of being of the sort that Heidegger in his middle period hoped might once again shine forth in a unifying cultural paradigm. So we find that Borgmann, like middle Heidegger, entertains the possibility that "a hidden center of these dispersed focuses may emerge some day to unite them."[47] Moreover, such a focus would "surpass the peripheral ones in concreteness, depth, and significance."[48]

---

[45] Borgmann, *Crossing the Postmodern Divide*, 141.
[46] Borgmann, *Crossing the Postmodern Divide*, 144.
[47] Borgmann, *Technology and the Character of Contemporary Life*, 199.
[48] Borgmann, *Technology and the Character of Contemporary Life*, 218.

Heidegger's thinking until 1955, when he wrote "The Question Concerning Technology," was like Borgmann's current thinking in that for him preserving things was compatible with awaiting a single God.[49] Heidegger said as early as 1946 that the divinities were traces of the lost godhead.[50] But Heidegger came to think that there was an essential antagonism between a unified understanding of being and local worlds. Of course, he always realized that there would be an antagonism between the style set up by a cultural paradigm and things that could only be brought out in their ownness in a style different from the dominant cultural style. Such things would inevitably be dispersed to the margins of the culture. There, as Borgmann so well sees, they will shine in contrast to the dominant style but will have to resist being considered irrelevant or even wicked.[51] But, if there is a single understanding of being, even those things that come into their own in the dominant cultural style will be inhibited as things. Already in his "Thing" essay Heidegger goes out of his way to point out that, even though the original meaning of 'thing' in German is a gathering to discuss a matter of concern to the community, in the case of the thing thinging, the gathering in question must be self-contained. The focal occasion must determine which community concerns are relevant rather than the reverse.[52]

Given the way local worlds establish their own internal coherence that resists any imposition from outside, there is bound to be a tension between the glorious cultural paradigm that establishes an understanding of being for a whole culture and the humble inconspicuous things. The shining of one would wash out the shining of the others. The tendency toward one unified world would impede the gathering of local worlds. Given this tension, in a late seminar Heidegger abandoned what he had considered up to then his crucial contribution to philosophy, the notion of a single understanding of being and its correlated notion of the ontological difference between being and beings. He remarks that "from the perspective of appropriation [the tendency in the practices to bring things out in their ownmost] it becomes necessary to free thinking from the

---

[49]   Heidegger, "The Question Concerning Technology," 33–5.

[50]   Heidegger, "What Are Poets For?" 97.

[51]   Borgmann, *Technology and the Character of Contemporary Life*, 212.

[52]   To put this in terms of meals, we can remember that in Virginia Woolfe's *To the Lighthouse* arguments about politics brought in from outside almost ruin Mrs. Ramsey's family dinner, which only works when the participants become so absorbed in the food that they stop paying attention to external concerns and get in tune with the actual occasion. The same thing happens in the film *Babette's Feast*. The members of an ascetic religious community go into the feast resolved to be true to their dead founder's principles and not to enjoy the food. Bickering and silence ensues until the wine and food makes them forget their founder's concerns and attunes them to the past and present relationships that are in accord with the gathering.

ontological difference." He continues, "From the perspective of appropriation, [letting-presence] shows itself as the relation of world and thing, a relation which could in a way be understood as the relation of being and beings. But then its peculiar quality would be lost."[53] What presumably would be lost would be the self-enclosed local character of worlds focused by things thinging. It follows that, as mortal disclosers of worlds in the plural, the only integrity we can hope to achieve is our openness to dwelling in many worlds and the capacity to move among them. Only such a capacity allows us to accept Heidegger's and Borgmann's criticism of technology and still have Heidegger's genuinely positive relationship to technological things.

---

[53] Martin Heidegger, "Summary of a Seminar on the Lecture 'Time and Being,'" in *On Time and Being*, trans. Joan Stambaugh (New York: Harper & Row, 1972), 37.

12

Nihilism on the Information Highway

Anonymity versus Commitment in the Present Age (2004)

> Oh God said to Abraham, "Kill me a son." ...
> Well Abe says, "Where do you want this killin' done?"
> God says, "Out on Highway 61."
> Well Mack the Finger said to Louie the King
> I got forty red, white, and blue shoe strings
> And a thousand telephones that don't ring
> Do you know where I can get rid of these things
> And Louie the King said let me think for a minute son.
> And he said yes, I think it can be easily done
> Just take everything down to Highway 61.
> Now the rovin' gambler he was very bored
> He was tryin' to create a next world war
> He found a promoter who nearly fell off the floor
> He said I never engaged in this kind of thing before
> But yes I think it can be very easily done
> We'll just put some bleachers out in the sun
> And have it on Highway 61.
>
> Bob Dylan, "Highway 61 Revisited"

In his essay *The Present Age*,[1] written in 1846, Kierkegaard warns that his age is characterized by a disinterested reflection and curiosity that levels all differences of status and value. In his terms, this detached reflection levels all qualitative distinctions. Everything is equal in that nothing matters enough that one would be willing to die for it. Nietzsche gave this modern condition a name; he called it nihilism.

---

[1] Søren Kierkegaard, *The Present Age*, trans. Alexander Dru (New York: Harper & Row, 1962).

Kierkegaard blames this leveling on what he calls "the Public." He says that "in order that everything should be reduced to the same level, it is first of all necessary to produce a phantom, its spirit a monstrous abstraction . . . and that phantom is *the Public*."[2] But the real villain behind the Public, Kierkegaard claims, is "the Press." He warned: "Europe will come to a standstill at the Press and remain at a standstill as a reminder that the human race has invented something which will eventually overpower it,"[3] and he adds: "Even if my life had no other significance, I am satisfied with having discovered the absolutely demoralizing existence of the daily press."[4]

But why blame leveling on the public rather than on democracy, technology, consumerism, or loss of respect for the tradition, to name a few candidates? And why this monomaniacal demonizing of the Press? Kierkegaard says in his journals that "it is the Press, more specifically the daily newspaper . . . which make[s] Christianity impossible."[5] This is an amazing claim. Clearly, Kierkegaard saw the Press as a unique cultural/religious threat, but it will take a little while to explain why.

It is no accident that, writing in 1846, Kierkegaard chose to attack the Public and the Press. To understand why he did so, we have to begin a century earlier. In *The Structural Transformation of the Public Sphere*, Jürgen Habermas locates the beginning of what he calls the "public sphere" in the middle of the eighteenth century.[6] He explains that, at that time, the press and coffeehouses became the locus of a new form of political discussion. This new sphere of discourse was radically different from the ancient polis or republic; the modern public sphere understood itself as being outside political power. This extrapolitical status was not just defined negatively as a lack of political power, but seen positively. Just because public opinion is not an exercise of political power, it is protected from any partisan spirit. Enlightenment intellectuals saw the public sphere as a space in which the rational, disinterested reflection that should guide government and human life could be institutionalized and refined. Such disengaged discussion came to be seen as an essential feature of a free society. As the Press extended public debate to a wider and wider readership of ordinary citizens, Burke exalted that "in a free country, every man thinks he has a concern in all public matters."[7]

---

[2] Kierkegaard, *The Present Age*, 59.

[3] Søren Kierkegaard, *Journals and Papers*, vol. 2, ed. and trans. H. V. Hong and E. H. Hong (Bloomington, IN: Indiana University Press, 1967), 483.

[4] Kierkegaard, *Journals and Papers*, vol. 2, 163.

[5] Kierkegaard, *Journals and Papers*, vol. 2, 163.

[6] Jürgen Habermas, *The Structural Transformation of the Public Sphere* (Cambridge: MIT Press, 1989).

[7] Habermas, *Structural Transformation*, 94.

Over the next century, thanks to the expansion of the daily press, the public sphere became increasingly democratized until this democratization had a surprising result that, according to Habermas, "altered [the] social preconditions of 'public opinion' around the middle of the [nineteenth] century."[8] "[As] the Public was expanded...by the proliferation of the Press...the reign of public opinion appeared as the reign of the many and mediocre."[9] Many people, including J. S. Mill and Alexis de Tocqueville, feared "the tyranny of public opinion,"[10] and Mill felt called on to protect "nonconformists from the grip of the Public itself."[11] According to Habermas, Tocqueville insisted that "education and powerful citizens were supposed to form an *elite public* whose critical debate determined public opinion."[12]

The Present Age shows just how original Kierkegaard was. While Tocqueville and Mill claimed that the masses needed elite philosophical leadership and, while Habermas agrees with them that what happened around 1850 with the democratization of the public sphere by the daily press is an unfortunate decline into conformism from which the public sphere must be rescued, Kierkegaard sees the public sphere as a new and dangerous cultural phenomenon in which the nihilism produced by the Press brings out something that was deeply wrong with the Enlightenment idea of detached reflection from the start. Thus, while Habermas wants to recapture the moral and political virtues of the public sphere, Kierkegaard warns that there is no way to salvage the public sphere because, unlike concrete and committed groups, it was from the start the source of leveling.

This leveling was produced in several ways. First, the new massive distribution of desituated information was making every sort of information immediately available to anyone, thereby producing a desituated, detached spectator. Thus, the new power of the Press to disseminate information to everyone in a nation led its readers to transcend their local, personal involvement and overcome their reticence about what didn't directly concern them. As Burke had noted with joy, the Press encouraged everyone to develop an opinion about everything. This is seen by Habermas as a triumph of democratization, but Kierkegaard saw that the public sphere was destined to become a detached world in which everyone had an opinion about and commented on all public matters without needing any first-hand experience, and without having or wanting any responsibility.

---

[8] Habermas, *Structural Transformation*, 130.
[9] Habermas, *Structural Transformation*, 131, 133.
[10] Habermas, *Structural Transformation*, 138.
[11] Habermas, *Structural Transformation*, 134.
[12] Habermas, *Structural Transformation*, 137.

The Press and its decadent descendant, the talk show, are bad enough, but this demoralizing effect was not Kierkegaard's main concern. For Kierkegaard, the deeper danger is just what Habermas applauds about the public sphere—as Kierkegaard puts it, "a public...destroys everything that is relative, concrete and particular in life."[13] The public sphere thus promotes ubiquitous commentators who deliberately detach themselves from the local practices out of which specific issues grow and in terms of which these issues must be resolved through some sort of committed action. What seems a virtue to detached Enlightenment reason, therefore, looks like a disastrous drawback to Kierkegaard. Even the most conscientious commentators don't have to have first-hand experience or take a concrete stand. Rather, as Kierkegaard complains, they justify their views by citing principles. Since the conclusions such abstract reasoning reaches are not grounded in the local practices, its proposals would presumably not enlist the commitment of the people involved, and consequently would not work even if enacted as laws. As Kierkegaard puts it in *The Present Age*: "A public is neither a nation, nor a generation, nor a community, nor a society, nor these particular men, for all these are only what they are through the concrete; *no single person who belongs to the Public makes a real commitment*."[14]

More basically still, that the public sphere lies outside of political power meant, for Kierkegaard, that one could hold an opinion on anything without having to act on it. He notes with disapproval that the public's "ability, virtuosity and good sense consists in trying to reach a judgment and a decision without ever going so far as action."[15] This opens up the possibility of endless reflection. If there is no need for decision and action, one can look at all things from all sides and always find some new perspective. Accumulating information thus postpones decision indefinitely because, as one finds out more, it is always possible that one's picture of the world and, therefore, of what one should do will have to be revised. Kierkegaard saw that, when everything is up for endless critical commentary, action can always be postponed. "At any moment reflection is capable of explaining everything quite differently and allowing one some way of escape."[16] Thus one need never act.

All that a reflective age like ours produces is more and more knowledge. As Kierkegaard put it, "by comparison with a passionate age, an age without passion gains in *scope what it loses in intensity*."[17] He adds: "We all know...the different

---

[13] Kierkegaard, *The Present Age*, 62.
[14] Kierkegaard, *The Present Age*, 63 (my italics).
[15] Kierkegaard, *The Present Age*, 33.
[16] Kierkegaard, *The Present Age*, 42.
[17] Kierkegaard, *The Present Age*, 68.

ways we can go, but nobody is willing to move."[18] No one stands behind the views the Public holds, so no one is willing to act. Kierkegaard is clear that "reflection by transforming the capacity for action into a means of escape from action, is both corrupt and dangerous."[19] He wrote in his journal: "Here...are the two most dreadful calamities which really are the principal powers of impersonality—the Press and anonymity."[20] Therefore, the motto Kierkegaard suggested for the Press was: "Here men are demoralized in the shortest possible time on the largest possible scale, at the cheapest possible price."[21]

In *The Present Age*, Kierkegaard succinctly sums up his view of the relation of the Press, the public sphere, and the leveling going on in his time. The desituated and anonymous press and the lack of passion or commitment in our reflective age combine to produce the Public, the agent of the nihilistic leveling: "The Press is an abstraction...which in conjunction with the passionless and reflective character of the age produces that abstract phantom: a public which in its turn is really the leveling power."[22] Kierkegaard would surely have seen in the Internet—with its websites full of anonymous information from all over the world and its interest groups that anyone in the world can join without qualifications, and where one can discuss any topic endlessly without consequences—the hi-tech synthesis of the worst features of the newspaper and the coffee house.[23] Indeed, thanks to the Internet, Burke's dream has been realized.

---

[18] Kierkegaard, *The Present Age*, 77.   [19] Kierkegaard, *The Present Age*, 68.

[20] Kierkegaard, *Journals and Papers*, vol. 2, 480.

[21] Kierkegaard, *Journals and Papers*, vol. 2, 489. Kierkegaard would no doubt have been happy to transfer this motto to the Web, for just as no individual assumes responsibility for the consequences of the information in the Press, no one assumes responsibility for even the accuracy of the information on the Web. Of course, no one really cares if it is reliable because no one is going to act on it. All that matters is that everyone passes the word along by forwarding it to other users. The information has become so anonymous that no one knows or cares where it came from. Just to make sure no one can be held responsible, in the name of protecting privacy, identification codes are being developed that will ensure that even the sender's address will remain secret. Kierkegaard could have been speaking of the Internet when he said of the Press: "It is frightful that someone who is no one...can set any error into circulation with no thought of responsibility and with the aid of this dreadful disproportioned means of communication" (*Journals and Papers*, vol. 2, 481).

[22] Kierkegaard, *The Present Age*, 64.

[23] Although Kierkegaard does not mention it, what is striking about such interest groups is that no experience or skill is required to enter the conversation. Indeed, a serious danger of the public sphere, as illustrated on the Internet, is that it undermines expertise. As I've argued in "How Far is Distance Learning from Education?," in Hubert Dreyfus, *On the Internet* (New York: Routledge, 2001), acquiring a skill requires interpreting the situation as being of a sort that requires a certain action, taking that action, and learning from the results. As Kierkegaard understood, there is no way to gain practical wisdom other than by making risky commitments and thereby experiencing both success and failure, otherwise the learner will be stuck at the level of competence and never achieve mastery. Thus the heroes of the public sphere who appear on serious radio and TV programs have a view on every issue, and can justify their view by appeal to abstract principles.

In newsgroups, anyone, anywhere, anytime can have an opinion on anything. All are only too eager to respond to the equally deracinated opinions of other anonymous amateurs who post their views from nowhere. Such commentators do not take a stand on the issues they speak about. Indeed, the very ubiquity of the Net tends to make any such local stand seem irrelevant.

What Kierkegaard envisaged as a consequence of the Press's indiscriminate and uncommitted coverage is now fully realized on the World Wide Web. Thanks to hyperlinks, meaningful differences have, indeed, been leveled. Relevance and significance have disappeared. And this is an important part of the attraction of the Web. Nothing is too trivial to be included. Nothing is so important that it demands a special place. In his religious writing, Kierkegaard criticized the implicit nihilism in the idea that God is equally concerned with the salvation of a sinner and the fall of a sparrow. "For God there is nothing significant and nothing insignificant," he said. On the Web, the attraction and the danger is that everyone can take this godlike point of view. One can view a coffeepot in Cambridge or the latest supernova, look up references in a library in Alexandria, find out what fellowships are available to his specific profile, or direct a robot to plant and water a seed in Austria, not to mention plow through thousands of ads, all with equal ease and equal lack of any sense of what is important. The highly significant and the absolutely trivial are laid out together on the information highway in just the way Abraham's sacrifice of Isaac, red, white, and blue shoe strings, a thousand telephones that don't ring, and the next world war are laid out on Dylan's nihilistic Highway 61.

Kierkegaard even foresaw that the ultimate activity the Internet would encourage would be speculation on how big it is, how much bigger it will get, and what, if anything, all this means for our culture. This sort of discussion is, of course, in danger of becoming part of the very cloud of anonymous speculation Kierkegaard abhorred. Ever sensitive to his own position as a speaker, Kierkegaard concluded his analysis of the dangers of the present age and his dark predictions of what was ahead for Europe with the ironic remark that: "In our times, when so little is done, an extraordinary number of prophecies, apocalypses, glances at and studies of the future appear, and there is nothing to do but to join in and be one with the rest."[24]

However, they do not have to act on the principles they defend and therefore lack the passionate perspective that alone can lead to egregious errors and surprising successes and so to the gradual acquisition of practical wisdom.

[24] Kierkegaard, *The Present Age*, 85.

The only alternative Kierkegaard saw to the Public's leveling and paralyzing reflection was for one to plunge into some kind of activity—any activity—as long as one threw oneself into it with passionate commitment. In *The Present Age*, he exhorts his contemporaries to make such a leap:

There is no more action or decision in our day than there is perilous delight in swimming in shallow waters. But just as a grown-up, struggling delightedly in the waves, calls to those younger than himself: "Come on, jump in quickly"—the decision in existence… calls out…. Come on, leap cheerfully, even if it means a lighthearted leap, so long as it is decisive. If you are capable of being a man, then danger and the harsh judgment of existence on your thoughtlessness will help you become one.[25]

Such a lighthearted leap out of the shallow, leveled present age into deeper water is typified for Kierkegaard by people who leap into what he calls the *aesthetic sphere of existence*. Each sphere of existence, as we shall see, represents a way of trying to get out of the leveling of the present age by taking the risk of making some way of life absolute.[26] In the aesthetic sphere, people make enjoyment of what is interesting the center of their lives.

Such an aesthetic response is characteristic of the Netsurfer, for whom information gathering has become a way of life. Such a surfer is curious about everything and ready to spend every free moment visiting the latest hot spots on the Web. He or she enjoys the sheer range of possibilities. For such a person, just visiting as many sites as possible and keeping up on the cool ones is an end in itself. The qualitative distinction that staves off leveling for the aesthete is the distinction between those sites that are *interesting* and those that are *boring*, and, thanks to the Net, something interesting is always only a click away. Life consists of fighting off boredom by being a spectator of everything interesting in the universe and of communicating with everyone else so inclined. Such a life produces what we would now call a postmodern self—a self that has no defining content or continuity, and so is open to all possibilities and to constantly taking on new roles.

[25] Kierkegaard, *The Present Age*, 36–7.
[26] Given Kierkegaard's use of the term "Sphere," precisely because reflection is the opposite of taking any decisive action, and therefore the opposite of making anything absolute, what Habermas calls the public sphere is not a sphere at all. A related non-sphere, worth noting because it has become popular on the Net, is de Chardin's Noosphere, which has been embraced by the Extropians and others who hope that, thanks to the World Wide Web, our minds will one day leave behind our bodies. The Noosphere, or mind sphere (in Ionian Greek *noos* means "mind"), is supposed to be the convergence of all human beings in a single giant mental network that would surround the earth to control the planet's resources and shepherd a world of unified love. According to Teilhard, this would be the Omega or End-Point of time. From Kierkegaard's perspective, the Noosphere—where risky, embodied locality and individual commitment would have been replaced by safe and detached ubiquitous contemplation and love—would be a confused Christian version of the public sphere.

But we have still to explain what makes this use of the Web attractive. Why is there a thrill in being able to be up on everything no matter how trivial? What motivates a passionate commitment to curiosity? Kierkegaard thought that in the last analysis, people were addicted to the Press, and we can now add the Web, because the anonymous spectator *takes no risks*. The person in the aesthetic sphere keeps open all possibilities and has no fixed identity that could be threatened by disappointment, humiliation, or loss.

Life on the Web is ideally suited to such a mode of existence. On the Internet, commitments are at best virtual commitments. Sherry Turkle has described how the Net is changing the background practices that determine what kinds of selves we can be. In *Life on the Screen*, she details "the ability of the Internet to change popular understandings of identity." On the Internet, she tells us, "We are encouraged to think of ourselves as fluid, emergent, decentralized, multiplicitous, flexible, and ever in process."[27] Thus, "the Internet has become a significant social laboratory for experimenting with the constructions and reconstructions of self that characterize postmodern life."[28]

Chat rooms lend themselves to the possibility of playfully inhabiting many selves, none of whom is recognized as one's true identity, and this possibility actually introduces new social practices. Turkle tells us: "The rethinking of human...identity is not taking place just among philosophers but 'on the ground,' through a philosophy in everyday life that is in some measure both proved and carried by the computer presence."[29]

She notes with approval that the Net encourages what she calls "experimentation" because what one does on the Net has no consequences. For that very reason, the Net frees people to develop new and exciting selves. The person living in the aesthetic sphere of existence would surely agree, but according to Kierkegaard, "As a result of knowing and being everything possible, one is in

---

[27] Sherry Turkle, *Life on the Screen: Identity in the Age of the Internet* (New York: Simon and Schuster, 1995), 263–4.

[28] Turkle, *Life on the Screen*, 180. A year after the publication of her book, Turkle seems to be having doubts about the value of such experiments. She notes: "Many of the people I have interviewed claim that virtual gender-swapping (pretending to be the opposite sex on the Internet) enables them to understand what it's like to be a person of the other gender, and I have no doubt that this is true, at least in part. But as I have listened to this boast, my mind has often traveled to my own experiences of living in a woman's body. These include worry about physical vulnerability, fears of unwanted pregnancy and infertility, fine-tuned decisions about how much makeup to wear to a job interview, and the difficulty of giving a professional seminar while doubled over with monthly cramps. Some knowledge is inherently experiential, dependent on physical sensations" ("Virtuality and its Discontents: Searching for Community in Cyberspace," *The American Prospect* 24 (Winter 1996)).

[29] Turkle, *Life on the Screen*, 26.

contradiction with oneself."[30] When he is speaking from the point of view of the next higher sphere of existence, Kierkegaard tells us that the self requires not "variableness and brilliancy," but "firmness, balance, and steadiness."[31]

We would therefore expect the aesthetic sphere to reveal that it was ultimately unlivable. Indeed, Kierkegaard held that if one leapt into the aesthetic sphere with total commitment, expecting it to give meaning to one's life, it was bound to break down. Without some way of telling the significant from the insignificant and the relevant from the irrelevant, everything becomes equally interesting and equally boring, and one finds oneself back in the indifference of the present age. Writing from the perspective of an aesthete experiencing the despair that signals the breakdown of the aesthetic sphere, he laments: "My reflection on life altogether lacks meaning. I take it some evil spirit has put a pair of spectacles on my nose, one glass of which magnifies to an enormous degree, while the other reduces to the same degree."[32]

This inability to distinguish the trivial from the important eventually stops being thrilling and leads to the very boredom the aesthete Netsurfer dedicates his life to avoiding. So, if one throws oneself into it fully, one eventually sees that the aesthetic way of life just doesn't work to overcome leveling. Kierkegaard calls such a realization *despair*. Thus, Kierkegaard concludes: "Every aesthetic view of life is despair, and everyone who lives aesthetically is in despair whether he knows it or not. But when one knows it, a higher form of existence is an imperative requirement."[33]

That higher form of existence Kierkegaard calls *the ethical sphere*. In it, one has a stable identity and one engages in involved action. Information is not played with, but is sought and used for serious purposes. As long as information gathering is not an end in itself, whatever reliable information there is on the Web can be a valuable resource serving serious concerns. Such concerns require that people have life plans and take up serious tasks. They then have goals that determine what needs to be done and what information is relevant for doing it.

Insofar as the Internet can reveal and support making and maintaining commitments for action, it supports life in the ethical sphere. But Kierkegaard would probably hold that the huge number of interest groups on the Net committed to various causes, and the ease of joining such groups, would eventually bring about the breakdown of the ethical sphere. The multiplicity of causes

---

[30] Kierkegaard, *The Present Age*, 68.

[31] Søren Kierkegaard, *Either/Or*, trans. D. E. Swenson and L. M. Swenson (Princeton, NJ: Princeton University Press, 1959), vol. 2, 16, 17.

[32] Kierkegaard, *Either/Or*, vol. 1, 46.   [33] Kierkegaard, *Either/Or*, vol. 2, 197.

and the ease of making commitments, which should have supported action, will eventually lead either to paralysis or an arbitrary choice as to which commitments to take seriously.

To avoid arbitrary choice, one might—similar to Judge William, Kierkegaard's pseudonymous author of the description of the ethical sphere in *Either/Or*—turn to facts about one's life to limit one's commitments. Thus, Judge William says that his range of possible relevant commitments is constrained by his abilities and his social roles as judge and husband. Or to take a more contemporary example, one could choose which interest groups to join on the basis of certain facts about one's life situation. After all, there are not merely interest groups devoted to everything from bottle caps to such cultural stars as Kierkegaard.[34] There are interest groups, for example, for the parents of children with rare and incurable diseases. So the ethical Net enthusiast might argue that to avoid leveling, all one need do is to choose to devote one's life to something that matters based on some accidental condition in one's life.

But the goal of the person in the ethical sphere, as Kierkegaard defines it, is to be morally mature, and Kant held that moral maturity consists in the ability to act lucidly *and freely*. To live ethically, then, one cannot base the meaning of one's life on what accidental facts impose their importance. Judge William is proud of the fact that, as an autonomous agent, he is free to give whatever meaning he chooses to his talents and his roles and all other facts about himself. He claims that, in the end, his freedom to give his life meaning is not constrained by his talents and social duties, unless he chooses to make them important.

Judge William sees that the choice as to which facts about his life are important is based on a more fundamental choice of what is worthy and not worthy, what is good and what is evil, and that choice is up to him. As Judge William puts it: "The good *is* for the fact that I will it, and apart from my willing, it has no existence. This is the expression for freedom.... By this the distinctive notes of good and evil are by no means belittled or disparaged as merely subjective distinctions. On the contrary, the absolute validity of these distinctions is affirmed."[35]

But, Kierkegaard would respond, if everything were up for choice, including the standards on the basis of which one chooses, there would be no reason for choosing one set of standards rather than another.[36] Besides, if one were totally free, choosing the guidelines for one's life would never make any serious difference, as one could always choose to rescind one's previous choice. A commitment does

---

[34] When I typed in Søren Kierkegaard, Google found 3450 hits; Alta Vista found 7452.

[35] Kierkegaard, *Either/Or*, vol. 2, 228.

[36] Jean-Paul Sartre develops the idea of the absurdity of fully free choice in *Being and Nothingness*.

not get a grip on me if I am always free to revoke it.[37] Indeed, commitments that are freely chosen can and should be revised from minute to minute as new information comes along. The ethical thus ends up in despair because either I am stuck with whatever happens to be imposed on me as important in my life (for example, some life-threatening disease) and so I'm not free, or else the pure power of the freedom to make and unmake commitments undermines itself. As Kierkegaard puts the latter point: "If the despairing self is *active*... it is constantly relating to itself only experimentally, no matter what it undertakes, however great, however amazing and with whatever perseverance. It recognizes no power over itself; therefore in the final instance it lacks seriousness.... The self can, at any moment, start quite arbitrarily all over again."[38]

Thus the *choice* of qualitative distinctions that was supposed to support serious action undermines it, and one ends up in what Kierkegaard calls the "despair of the ethical." One can take over some accidental fact about one's life and make it one's own only by freely *deciding* that it is crucially important, but then one can equally freely decide it is not, so in the ethical sphere all meaningful differences are leveled by one making one's freedom absolute.

According to Kierkegaard, one can only stop the leveling of commitments by being *given* an individual identity that opens up an individual world. Fortunately, the ethical view of commitments as freely entered into and always open to being revoked does not seem to hold for those commitments that are most important to us. These special commitments are experienced as gripping our whole being. Political and religious movements can grip us in this way, as can romantic relationships and, for certain people, such vocations as science or art. When we respond to such a summons with what Kierkegaard calls infinite passion, that is, when we respond by accepting an *unconditional commitment*, this commitment determines what will be the significant issue for us for the rest of our life. Such an unconditional commitment thus blocks leveling by establishing qualitative distinctions between what is important and trivial, relevant and irrelevant, serious and playful in my life. Living by such an irrevocable commitment puts one in what Kierkegaard called the "Christian Sphere of Existence."[39]

---

[37] Sartre gives the example in *Being and Nothingness* of a gambler who, having freely decided in the evening that he will gamble no more, must, the next morning, freely decide whether to abide by his previous decision.

[38] Søren Kierkegaard, *Sickness unto Death*, trans. Walter Lowrie (Princeton, NJ: Princeton University Press, 1941), 100.

[39] There are two forms of Christianity for Kierkegaard. One is Platonic and disembodied. It is best expressed in St. Augustine. It amounts to giving up the hope of fulfilling one's desires in this life and trusting in God to take care of us. Kierkegaard calls this "Religiousness A," and says it is not the true meaning of Christianity. True Christianity, or Religiousness B, for Kierkegaard, is based on the

Of course, such a commitment makes one vulnerable. One's cause may fail. One's lover may leave. The detached reflection of the present age, the hyperflexibility of the aesthetic sphere, and the unbounded freedom of the ethical sphere are all ways of avoiding one's vulnerability. But it turns out, Kierkegaard claims, that, for that very reason, they level all qualitative distinctions and end in the despair of meaninglessness. Only a risky unconditioned commitment and the strong identity it produces can give an individual a world organized by that individual's unique qualitative distinctions.

This leads to the perplexing question: What role, if any, can the Internet play in encouraging and supporting unconditional commitments? A first suggestion might be that the movement from stage to stage would be facilitated by living experimentally on the Web, just as flight simulators help us learn to fly. One would be solicited to throw oneself into enjoying Netsurfing until it became boring, then into freely choosing which interest group was important until that choice revealed its absurdity. Finally, one would be driven to let oneself be drawn into a risky unconditional commitment as the only way out of despair. Indeed, at any stage, from looking for all sorts of interesting websites as one surfs the Net, to striking up a conversation in a chat room, to joining an interest group to deal with an important problem in one's life, one might just find oneself being drawn into a lifetime commitment. No doubt this might happen—people do meet in chat rooms and fall in love—but it is relatively rare.

Kierkegaard would surely argue that, while the Internet, like the public sphere and the Press, does not *prohibit* unconditional commitments, in the end, it *undermines* them. Like a simulator, the Net manages to capture everything but the risk.[40] Our imaginations can be drawn in, as they are in playing games and watching movies, and no doubt, if we are sufficiently involved to feel as if we are taking risks, such simulations can help us acquire skills. But insofar as games

Incarnation and consists in making an unconditional commitment to something finite, and having the faith-given courage to take the risks required by such a commitment. Such a committed life gives one a meaningful life in this world.

[40] An attempt at inducing a sense of online risk was made in Ken Goldberg's telerobotic art project Legal Tender (www.counterfeit.org). Remote viewers were presented with a pair of purportedly authentic U.S. $100 bills. After registering for a password sent to their email address, participants were offered the opportunity to "experiment" with the bills by burning or puncturing them at an online telerobotic laboratory. After choosing an experiment, participants were reminded that it is a Federal crime to knowingly deface U.S. currency, punishable by up to six months in prison. If, in spite of the threat of incarceration, participants click a button indicating that they "accept responsibility," the remote experiment is performed and the results shown. Finally, participants were asked if they believed the bill and the experiment were real. Almost all responded in the negative. So they either never believed the bills were real or were setting up an alibi if they were accused of defacing the bills. In either case, they hadn't experienced any risk and taken any responsibility after all.

work by temporarily capturing our imaginations in limited domains, they cannot simulate serious commitments in the real world. Imagined commitments hold us only when our imaginations are captivated by the simulations before our ears and eyes. And that is what computer games and the Net offer us. But the risks are only imaginary and have no long-term consequences.[41] The temptation is to live in a world of stimulating images and simulated commitments and thus to lead a simulated life. As Kierkegaard says of the present age, "It transforms the real task into an unreal trick and reality into a play."[42]

The test as to whether one had acquired an unconditional commitment would come only if one had the passion and courage to transfer what one had learned on the Net to the real world. Then one would confront what Kierkegaard calls "the danger and the harsh judgment of existence." But precisely the attraction of the Net, like that of the Press in Kierkegaard's time, inhibits that final plunge. Indeed, anyone using the Net who was led to risk his or her real identity in the real world would have to act against the grain of what attracted him or her to the Net in the first place.

So it looks as though Kierkegaard may be right. The Press and the Internet are the ultimate enemy of unconditional commitment, and only the unconditional commitment of what Kierkegaard calls the religious sphere of existence can save us from the nihilistic leveling launched by the Enlightenment, promoted by the Press and the public sphere, and perfected in the World Wide Web.

---

[41] As Turkle puts it: "Instead of solving real problems—both personal and social—many of us appear to be choosing to invest ourselves in unreal places. Women and men tell me that the rooms and mazes on MUDs are safer than city streets, virtual sex is safer than sex anywhere, MUD friendships are more intense than real ones, and when things don't work out you can always leave" ("Virtuality and its Discontents").

[42] Kierkegaard, The Present Age, 38.

13

Christianity without Onto-Theology

Kierkegaard's Account of the Self's Movement from Despair to Bliss (2003)

Kierkegaard belongs right after Mark Wrathall's eloquent explanation and defense of the later Heidegger's account of the fourfold:[1] the local earth, the seasons, our mortality, and the remnants of the pagan gods. Wrathall presented the fourfold as an attempt to answer the question: Why do we need the divine and the sacred in our lives and how should we preserve and promote them?

If he had read Martin Heidegger, Kierkegaard would have answered that any attempt to preserve the local is doomed; that technicity, the drive toward optimization and efficiency, will sooner or later wipe out traditional practices, just as it has already wiped out the last stage of onto-theology, the metaphysics of the subject, and is turning us all into resources.

Heidegger was all too aware of this possibility, which he expresses in his lament that "the wasteland grows," that what is so dangerous about technology is that it is a drive toward the total efficient ordering of *everything*. The wilderness is turning into a resource—the Alaskan resource—human beings are no longer personnel, but rather material for the Human Resources Departments, and a recent advertisement proclaimed that children "are our most precious resource." What Robert Pippin called "farmer metaphysics" is on the way out. Heidegger sadly notes the television antennas on the peasants' huts and feels that we are already failing to dwell, and that our culture is rushing into the "longest night."

---

[1] Mark Wrathall, "Between the Earth and the Sky: Heidegger on Life after the Death of God," in *Religion after Metaphysics* (Cambridge: Cambridge University Press, 2004), 69–87; reprinted in Mark Wrathall, *Heidegger and Unconcealment: Truth, Language, and History* (Cambridge: Cambridge University Press, 2010), 195–211.

For Heidegger, all we can do is carry out a holding action trying to preserve the endangered species of practices while awaiting a new God.

What Heidegger does not consider is that losing our appreciation of the jug of local wine, the seasons, our mortal vulnerability, and our local religious traditions might be a good thing; that these pagan practices might be standing in the way of a more intensely rewarding religious life.

This is where Kierkegaard comes in. He had a similar despairing analysis of the present age as nihilistic, and saw all meaningful differences being leveled by what he called "reflection." That was his name for the fact that more and more people in his time were becoming spectators and critics and fewer and fewer were willing to take the risk of making a serious commitment. He claimed that thanks to the media, this spectator attitude and the leveling it produces would get worse and worse, until, like a bonfire, it would "consume everything."[2] That is, it would level all meaningful differences between the trivial and the important.

But Kierkegaard, the radical Christian, has an entirely different response than Heidegger, the conservative pagan. Kierkegaard thinks that clearing away the local rootedness and the local gods is a good thing; when the bonfire has consumed everything local, we shall be left only with the choice between the meaningless distractions of the present age and what Kierkegaard calls the "decision in existence." If we heed the call, he says, we shall be able to leap over "the sharp scythe of the leveler ... into the arms of God."[3] That would be to discover a new and better way of finding meaning, and mattering in our lives. As he puts it in the culminating exhortation of The Present Age:

There is no more action or decision in our day than there is perilous delight in swimming in shallow waters. But just as a grown-up, struggling delightedly in the waves, calls to those younger than himself: "Come on, jump in quickly"—the decision in existence ... calls out ... Come on, leap cheerfully, even if it means a lighthearted leap, so long as it is decisive. If you are capable of being a man, then danger and the harsh judgment of existence on your thoughtlessness will help you become one.[4]

The leap into the deep water refers to a series of total commitments, first to the enjoyment of possibility (the aesthetic), then to the universal ethical, and then to the mystical life of self-annihilation before God. Each opens what Kierkegaard calls a sphere of existence. But Kierkegaard also claims that if one lives passionately in each sphere, each sphere will break down and land one back in the leveling of the present age. In Sickness unto Death, Kierkegaard describes these breakdowns and presents the only sphere of existence that he claims will work.

---

[2] Søren Kierkegaard, The Present Age, trans. Alexander Dru (London: Collins, 1962), 56.
[3] Kierkegaard, The Present Age, 82.   [4] Kierkegaard, The Present Age, 36-7.

He does so by giving an account of the structure of the self that explains the breakdowns and also what is required for a meaningful life. He then shows how only Christianity, the religion of the God-man, meets this requirement.

What Is a Self?

According to Kierkegaard, a human being is a combination of two sets of factors:

The human being is spirit. But what is spirit? Spirit is the self. But what is the self? The self is a relation which relates to itself, or that in the relation which is its relating to itself. The self is not the relation but the relation's relating to itself. A human being is a synthesis of the infinite and the finite, of the eternal and the temporal, of possibility and necessity... A synthesis is a relation between two factors. Looked at in this way a human being is not yet a self.[5]

How can Kierkegaard argue for such an essentialist view? How can he say more than what Charles Taylor and Richard Rorty agree on, that anyone can have any relation to God or to the sacred that he or she feels called upon to have, as long as he or she does not seek to impose it on others? How can Kierkegaard claim, in this fractured world, to know the essential structure of the self, and consequently that one kind of religion is what every human being is called to have, whether he or she knows it or not?

We must try to understand what kind of claim this is. I used to think that it was a modest claim concerning how the self has come to be constituted in the Judeo-Christian tradition; that Christianity created the disease for which it is the cure. But, if that were so, I would have to agree with Rorty that it's high time we chose a new vocabulary. But now I think it's clear that Kierkegaard thinks that Christianity *discovered* the essential truth about the self—that it was sick unto death, not that Christianity produced this sick self.

---

[5] Søren Kierkegaard, *The Sickness unto Death*, trans. Alastair Hannay (London: Penguin Books, 1989), 43. I have made several changes in the text in order to clarify what I believe to be its meaning. First, I have substituted Walter Lowrie's term "factors" for Hannay's "terms" in the definition of the self, because it provides a convenient shorthand for describing the constituents of the synthesis. Second, I have changed the word "freedom" to "possibility." In other passages in *The Sickness unto Death*, and in *The Concept of Anxiety*, Kierkegaard uses the word "freedom" to refer to the self-defining nature of human beings. He uses the word "possibility" to refer to one factor of the synthesis that a human being defines. Though Kierkegaard is inconsistent in his use of terminology, the distinction between the two concepts is clear. Thus, I have changed the terminology in order to preserve the clear distinction between the two concepts. Finally, I have reversed the order of the possibility/necessity and eternal/temporal factors, since Kierkegaard discusses them in this order in the remainder of *The Sickness unto Death*, and I have changed the order temporal/eternal to eternal/temporal to make it symmetrical with Kierkegaard's presentation of the other sets of factors.

But how can Kierkegaard claim to know the essential nature of the self? He doesn't claim a Husserlian *Wesenschau*, nor is he simply appealing to revelation. I think that his argument has the form introduced by Heidegger in *Being and Time* and worked out by Saul Kripke in *Naming and Necessity*.[6] Heidegger calls it "formal indication"; Kripke calls it "rigid designation." People also call it "black box essentialism."

The idea is that whether there are essences is an experimental question, and so cannot be decided a priori. The way natural science is practiced, we assume provisionally that there are natural kinds like water and gold with essential properties; we then designate such supposed kinds by some property and investigate, in the appropriate way, whether we have picked out a kind and found its essential property. So, to take a few Kripkean examples, we designate gold as that yellow stuff and then it finally turns out that yellowness is not essential but that gold has the atomic number 79. Or we designate heat as what feels warm to the touch and then discover that it is essentially molecular motion. We think that we've got it right, i.e., that we have found the essential property, when we can use it to explain all the other properties and account for all the anomalies that seem to contradict our essentialist account.

Heidegger had a similar idea. Taking his cue from Kierkegaard, he said in *Being and Time* that he would provisionally formally indicate[7] human beings as *Dasein*, i.e., as essentially beings that have to take a stand on their own being. He then did a lot of appropriate investigation, in this case hermeneutic and phenomenological investigation, and it turned out that this account of the self enabled him to understand a lot about human beings, and this confirmed his provisional designation, which of course could still run into problems later on and turn out to be wrong.[8]

[6] Saul A. Kripke, *Naming and Necessity* (Cambridge, MA: Harvard University Press, 1980).

[7] See Martin Heidegger, *Being and Time*, trans. John Macquarrie and Edward Robinson (New York: HarperCollins, 1962), 152, 274.

[8] Surprisingly, it seems that black box essentialism works for human beings but not for natural kinds such as gold. As Rorty points out, the determination of an essence involves a judgment as to which properties are important, e.g., that the color and ductility of gold are important and need to be explained, but not where it was mined or that it shines with divine radiance. Such judgments depend on one's culture. Thus, the essence that explains the important properties of a natural kind is relative to a background understanding of being. That the atomic number of gold is 79 is, indeed, true everywhere and for all times, but in other cultures, and other epochs in our culture, that might not be understood to be *the* essential property.

But, as we shall see, Kierkegaard points to all human beings' susceptibility to despair, namely, that anyone in any culture might someday feel despair, as an important cross-cultural characteristic of the self, and argues that only his account of the self can explain this fact. So it seems that rigid designation might allow us to discover the essential structure of the self, even if it does not justify modern science's claim to be able to determine the unique essence of each natural kind.

Kierkegaard wants to discover the essential structure of the self. He is not the first to try. The self was designated by Plato and many others as some sort of combination of body and soul. Kierkegaard thinks that this approach fails to explain the possibility of despair, an important aspect of human life. He provisionally suggests that the self's essential property is that it is a relation that relates itself to itself, and that such a relation has a complex structure, which he calls a "synthesis" of two sets of factors. Of course, whether this self is a kind, and whether this is its essential structure, indeed, whether there are any kinds with essences at all, will have to be answered by a description of human experience. The appropriate test is how much of human experience Kierkegaard can order and understand, and how he can account for anomalies that seem to contradict alternative accounts.

The Greeks called the two sets of factors you see in Figure 13.1 the soul and the body respectively. According to the ancients, the self begins with these factors in conflict, but once one realizes that *only one set of factors is essential*—that one is an eternal soul, and not a temporal body, or vice versa—the conflict and instability are overcome. Life is a voyage from confusion to clarity and from conflict to harmony. Since the self is potentially whole and harmonious, all one has to do is realize its true nature, find and satisfy its true needs rather than its superficial desires, and one can experience peace and fulfillment.

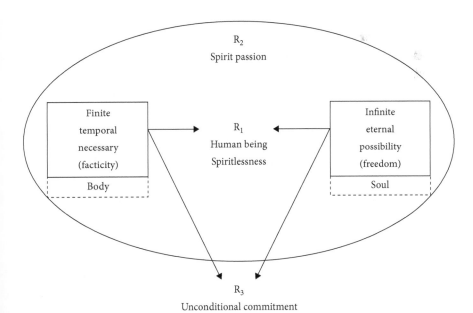

Figure 13.1 Kierkegaard's definition of the self.

On the Greek account, if both sets of factors were equally essential the self would be in hopeless self-contradiction. It could not fully express all its bodily, finite, temporal needs and capacities while at the same time fully expressing all its intellectual, infinite, eternal needs and capacities. It seems, in fact, that the more you express one set of factors, the less you are able to express the other set. So it would seem that the factors were merely *combined*, and only one set of factors could be essential.

Starting with Pascal, however, Christian thinkers realized that according to Christianity, both sets of factors *were* essential and the self was, indeed, a contradiction. As Pascal put it: "What a chimera then is man! What a novelty! What a monster, what a chaos, what a contradiction!"[9]

According to Pascal, a person's highest achievement was not to deny or overcome this contradiction—by getting rid of half the self—but to live in such a way as to express the tension of the contradiction fully. "We do not display greatness by going to one extreme, but in touching both extremes at once, and filling all the intervening space."[10]

Kierkegaard agrees that, according to the Judeo-Christian tradition, the self is a contradictory *synthesis* between two sets of factors and that *each set is essential* and requires the other. He calls this a dialectical relation. That means that both sets of factors are aspects of one whole. You can't satisfy one set of factors without satisfying the other.

Let us now look at this claim in more detail.

Ways of Attempting to be a Self

R_1—This is what Kierkegaard calls spiritlessness. One has a sense that the self is a contradiction that has to be faced, but one lives in what Pascal called distraction, so that one never has to take a stand in thought or action as to how to get the factors together. Pascal gives as examples of distraction playing tennis and sitting alone in one's room solving hard philosophical problems. (No doubt he had Descartes in mind.) Kierkegaard thought that the most important distraction in his time was the public sphere, where one could discuss events and people anonymously without ever having to take responsibility for one's views. One could debate, on the basis of principles, how the world should be run, without running the risk of testing these principles in action. This form of distraction is now perfected in chat rooms and news groups on the Internet, but, of course,

---

[9] Blaise Pascal, *Pascal's Pensées*, trans. W. F. Trotter (New York: Dutton, 1958), number 434.
[10] Pascal, *Pensées*, number 353.

there are many other ways to avoid facing the contradictory nature of the self besides surfing the net.

R_2—If a human being acts only as a combination of factors, he or she is not yet a self. To be a self, the relation must relate itself to itself, by taking a stand on both sets of factors through its actions. It must manifest that something about the self is essential by making something in its life absolute. This can take a negative and a positive form.

Negative R—"In a relation between two things the relation is the third term in the form of a negative unity, and the two relate to the relation, and in the relation to that relation; this is what it is from the point of view of soul for soul and body to be in relation."[11] When the relation is a negative unity, the relation relates to itself in the Greek way; denying one of the sets of factors and acting as if only the other aspect of the self were the essential one. One can, for example, take the soul to be eternal at the expense of the body, as Plato did, or do the opposite, as Lucretius did.

Positive R_2—Such selves try, by themselves, to express fully both sets of factors in thought and action, but this turns out to be impossible. For example, if one makes possibility absolute and lives for constant change, constantly open to new possibilities, one is in the aesthetic sphere—Kierkegaard's anticipation of Nietzsche and the postmoderns—but that gives no expression to the necessary and the eternal. Or, if one tries to make the infinite and the eternal absolute, one loses the finite and the temporal. As Kierkegaard puts it, such mystical types can't bring their God-relationship together with a decision whether or not to take a walk in the park.

Once he has worked through all the first three spheres of existence in this way, Kierkegaard claims to have shown that "the self cannot by itself arrive at or remain in equilibrium and rest."[12] His Christian view is that the self is unable to solve its own problem. It does not have the truth in it, that is, it does not have in itself the resources to live a stable and meaningful life.

Despair: The Sickness unto Death

In *Sickness unto Death*, Kierkegaard tries to show that every possible attempt to combine the factors by essentializing one or the other of each pair of factors leads to despair, as does every way of trying to do justice to both. And, according to Kierkegaard, everyone who has not managed to perform the impossible task of getting his or her self together in a stable, meaningful life is in despair.

[11] Kierkegaard, *Sickness unto Death*, 43.   [12] Kierkegaard, *Sickness unto Death*, 44.

You might well think that this is all ridiculous, since you, at least, are not in despair. You may feel that you are having a great time enjoying all your possibilities, or living a fulfilling life taking care of your family, or that your life is worth living because you are working to eliminate suffering, and so forth. In general, that you are fulfilling your capacities and everything is working out fine.

Kierkegaard would say that you might think you are living a life worth living, but in fact you are in despair. What right does he have to say this? His answer is in *Sickness unto Death*:

Despair differs dialectically from what one usually calls sickness, because it is a sickness of the spirit. And this dialectical aspect, properly understood, brings further thousands under the category of despair. If at any time a physician is convinced that so and so is in good health, and then later that person becomes ill, then the physician may well be right about his *having been* well at the time but now being sick. Not so with despair. Once despair appears, what is apparent is that the person was in despair. In fact, it's never possible at any time to decide anything about a person who is not saved through having been in despair. For when whatever causes a person to despair occurs, it is immediately evident that he has been in despair his whole life.[13]

Kierkegaard is pointing out that despair is not like sadness, regret, disappointment, depression, etc. Rather, unlike these downers, despair exhibits what Kierkegaard calls "the dialectic of eternity." If you are sad, you know that it is temporary. Even if something so terrible happens to you that you feel that you were happy once but that whatever has happened makes it impossible for you ever to be happy again, that is certainly misery, but it is not despair. Despair is the feeling that life isn't working for you and, given the kind of person you are, it is impossible for things to work for you; that a life worth living is, in your case, literally impossible.

That means that once a person experiences despair, "it will be evident that his [previous] success was an illusion"[14]—i.e., all that person's past joys *must have been* self-deceptions. That in turn means that, if you ever experience despair, you realize that you have always been in despair and you always will be. So Kierkegaard concludes that, since the self is a contradiction, even though you now feel that things are going well for you, you must right now be in despair and not know it. Only if you have faced your despair—the sickness unto death—and been cured can you be sure that you are not now in despair. So, given the contradictory nature of the self, all of us, with the exception of those who have faced despair and been healed, must right now be in despair.

---

[13] Kierkegaard, *Sickness unto Death*, 54.   [14] Kierkegaard, *Sickness unto Death*, 51.

The ultimate despair, Kierkegaard contends, is denying that one is in despair by denying the demand that we express the two sets of factors in our lives in a way that enables them to reinforce each other. This is not the distraction of the present age where one represses the call to be a self. Rather, someone in this ultimate form of despair sees that in our religious tradition the self has, indeed, been constituted as having two sets of essential but incompatible factors, but claims that this is merely a traditional, essentialist view that we should opt out of. Since the traditional Judeo-Christian understanding of the self leads people to despair, we should simply give it up and adopt a vocabulary and practices that are healthier and more useful to us now.

How can we decide who is right here, Kierkegaard or the pragmatist? I think that this is a question we can only approach experimentally. In *Sickness unto Death*, Kierkegaard tries to show that the Christian claim that the self is a contradiction is confirmed by a purportedly exhaustive categorization of all the ways of being a self available to us and how each fails.

How the Factors Reinforce Each Other in an Unconditional Commitment

If Kierkegaard is right, not being in despair must mean having been somehow cured of it for good. He says:

The possibility of this sickness is man's advantage over the beast; to be aware of this sickness is the Christian's advantage over natural man; to be cured of this sickness is the Christian's blessedness.[15]

Consequently, Kierkegaard proposed to preface *Sickness unto Death* with a prayer to Jesus as Savior:

O Lord Jesus Christ, who didst come to earth to heal them that suffer from this sickness...help Thou us in this sickness to hold fast to Thee, to the end that we may be healed of it.[16]

According to Kierkegaard, Jesus is "God in time as [an] individual man."[17] But how that enables him to cure us of despair is rather a long story. To begin with, Kierkegaard tells us that the self can only succeed in relating itself to itself by

---

[15] Kierkegaard, *Sickness unto Death*, 45.

[16] Søren Kierkegaard, *Sickness unto Death*, trans. Walter Lowrie (Princeton, NJ: Princeton University Press, 1941), 534.

[17] Søren Kierkegaard, *Concluding Unscientific Postscript*, trans. David F. Swenson and Walter Lowrie (Princeton, NJ: Princeton University Press, 1971), 498.

relating to another. Only when the self "in relating to itself relates to something else,"[18] Kierkegaard contends, can it get the two sets of factors into equilibrium. Only then is each factor defined in such a way as to support rather than be in conflict with the others. But how is this possible?

Whether you can get the factors together or whether they form a contradiction depends on how you define them. Or, to put it another way, the Greeks found that, if you define the factors from the point of view of detachment, you can't get them together. Kierkegaard tries to show that only if you define the factors in terms of a total involvement that gives you your identity do you get a positive synthesis.

This is the claim illustrated in *Fear and Trembling*. The story starts with Abraham the Father of the faith, who "believed he would...[be] blessed in his kin, eternally remembered in Isaac."[19] Isaac was obviously essential to Abraham's identity. To illustrate what is at stake in having an identity, Kierkegaard draws on the chivalric romances. The example on which he says "everything turns" is the case of "A young lad [who] falls in love with a princess, [so that] the content of his whole life lies in this love."[20] Kierkegaard adds in a footnote that "any other interest whatever in which an individual concentrates the whole of life's reality"[21] would do as well.

The lad who loves the princess relates himself to himself by way of this relation. Thanks to it, he knows who he is and what is relevant and important in his world. Any such unconditional commitment to some specific individual, cause, or vocation whereby a person gets an identity and a sense of reality would do to make the point Kierkegaard is trying to make. In such a case the person becomes an individual defined by his or her relation to the object of his or her unconditional commitment. The lad is the lover of the princess, Martin Luther King Jr. is the one who will bring justice to the American blacks, Steve Jobs identifies himself with Apple Computers, etc.

Kierkegaard's model for such a commitment is the knight whose life gets its meaning by his devotion to his lady. This is not a compulsion, an infatuation, or an obsession. That would not be an expression of freedom. Kierkegaard says that the knight is free to "forget the whole thing," but in so doing the knight would "contradict himself," since it is "a contradiction to forget the whole of one's life's content and still be the same."[22]

[18] Kierkegaard, *Sickness unto Death*, trans. Hannay, 43.
[19] Søren Kierkegaard, *Fear and Trembling*, trans. Alastair Hannay (London: Penguin, 1985), 54.
[20] Kierkegaard, *Fear and Trembling*, 70.   [21] Kierkegaard, *Fear and Trembling*, 71.
[22] Kierkegaard, *Fear and Trembling*, 72.

According to Kierkegaard, if and only if you let yourself be drawn into a defining commitment can you achieve that which, while you were in despair, looked impossible, i.e., that the two sets of factors reinforce each other, so that the more you manifest one the more you manifest the other. By responding to the call of such an unconditional commitment and thereby getting an identity, a person becomes what Kierkegaard, following the Bible, calls "a new creation."[23] Thus, Jesus gave those who were saved from despair by being unconditionally committed to him new names, and they called him their Savior.

But just how does this work?

The Temporal and the Eternal

For one to live fully in time, some moment must be absolutely important and make other moments significant relative to it. The moment when one is reborn is obviously such a moment. Kierkegaard, drawing on the biblical saying that we shall be changed in the twinkling of an eye, calls this moment the *Augenblick*. Moreover, after the transformation, other moments become significant since one's unconditional commitment must be expressed in one's day-to-day activity.

But the eternal is also absolutely important in one's life. Not the disinterested, abstract eternity of Plato, but the passionately involved eternity that Kierkegaard calls "eternity in time." Normally, the significance of events in one's life is subject to retroactive reinterpretation,[24] but, in an unconditional commitment that defines the self, one's identity is as eternal as a definition. The lad will henceforth always be the lover of the princess:

He first makes sure that this really is the content of his life, and his soul is too healthy and proud to squander the least thing on an infatuation. He is not cowardly, he is not afraid to let his love steal in upon his most secret, most hidden thoughts, to let it twine itself in countless coils around every ligament of his consciousness—if the love becomes unhappy he will never be able to wrench himself out of it.[25]

Further events will be interpreted in the light of the content given the self in the *Augenblick*, not vice versa. The way a commitment can produce a privileged

---

[23] Kierkegaard, *Fear and Trembling*, 70.

[24] Sartre gives the example of a person who has an emotional crisis as an adolescent; he interprets it as a religious calling and acts on it by becoming a monk. Then, later, he comes to interpret the experience as just a psychological upset during adolescence, and leaves the monastery to become a businessman. But on his deathbed, he feels that it was a religious calling after all, and repents. Sartre's point is that our past is constantly up for reinterpretation, and the final interpretation is an accidental result of what we happen to think as we die.

[25] Kierkegaard, *Fear and Trembling*, 71, translation modified.

moment is not something disinterested thought can understand. Kierkegaard says: "A concrete eternity within the existing individual is the maximum degree of his passion," and "the proposition inaccessible to thought is that one can become eternal although one was not such."[26]

In sum, if you define eternity in an involved way as that which remains constant throughout your life, then what is eternal is your identity. That is, if you are unconditionally committed to a particular person or cause, that will be your identity forever (for every moment of your life). This is a kind of involved eternity that must, in order to exist, be temporal. The paradoxical fact is that "only in existing do I become eternal."[27] But this does not make me any less temporal. "The existing individual *in time* . . . comes into relation with the eternal *in time*."[28]

The Finite and the Infinite

Kierkegaard calls an unconditional commitment an infinite passion for something finite. But just what makes an infinite passion count as infinite? It can't be just a very strong feeling; rather, it must in some sense transcend the finite. For Kierkegaard, an infinite passion can legitimately be called infinite because it opens up a world. Not only *what actually exists* gets its meaning from its connection with my defining passion; anything that could possibly come into existence would get its meaning for me from my defining commitment. As we saw earlier, according to Kierkegaard, one's commitment defines *reality*.

Of course, the object of my infinite passion is something *finite*. We are interested in the smallest particularities of our beloved. But any such finite being is vulnerable, and yet the meaning of my life depends on it. This makes a defining commitment very risky. It would certainly be safer to define one's life in some sort of theoretical quest or in terms of some abstract idea—say the eventual triumph of the proletariat—but that is not concrete enough to satisfy the need to make the finite absolutely significant. So it follows, as Kierkegaard says, that "without risk there is no faith."[29]

I can't go into details here, but suffice it to say that Kierkegaard holds that, given the risk, to let yourself be more and more involved with something finite, you need to live in a kind of absurdity:

---

[26] Kierkegaard, *Concluding Unscientific Postscript*, 277, 508.
[27] Kierkegaard, *Concluding Unscientific Postscript*, 508.
[28] Kierkegaard, *Concluding Unscientific Postscript*, 508.
[29] Kierkegaard, *Concluding Unscientific Postscript*, 188.

Every moment to see the sword hanging over the loved one's head and yet find, not repose in the pain of resignation, but joy on the strength of the absurd—that is wonderful. The one who does that, he is great, the only great one.[30]

In the context of the Abraham story, Isaac will certainly be sacrificed, the sword will fall, and yet Abraham acts as if he will always have Isaac. The Knight of Faith can do this because he lives in the assurance that "God is the fact that everything is possible, or that everything is possible is God."[31]

In sum, when you have a defining commitment, the finite object of your commitment is infinitely important, i.e., the object of your passion is both something particular and also world-defining. Indeed, it is the condition for anything showing up as meaningful. It thus opens up a horizontal transcendence.

The Necessary and the Possible

We have seen that, when you have a defining commitment, you get an identity. That is what you are, and it is *necessary* that you be it. But, although your identity is fixed, it does not dictate an inflexible way of acting as if it were a compulsion. In anything less than total loss and subsequent world collapse, one has to be able to adapt to even the most radical changes in the defining object. All such adaptive changes will, of course, be changes *in* the world but not changes *of* the world. Kierkegaard calls this freedom because, even though the central concern in one's life is fixed, one is free to adapt it to all sorts of possible situations in all sorts of ways.

There is, however, an even more radical kind of freedom: the freedom to change my world, i.e., to change my identity. To be born again *and again*. Although Kierkegaard does not say so in so many words, once we see that eternity can be in time, we can see that, not only can eternity *begin* at a moment of time (the *Augenblick*), but eternity can *change* in time. In Kierkegaard's terms, Abraham has faith that if he sacrifices Isaac "God could give him a new Isaac."[32] This can happen because God is "that everything is possible,"[33] and that means that even the inconceivable is possible.

Here we are touching on the paradox of mourning. This is a topic too complicated to go into here, but this much is clear. On Kierkegaard's view, one can only change worlds by being totally involved in one, deepening one's

---

[30] Kierkegaard, *Fear and Trembling*, 79.
[31] Kierkegaard, *Sickness unto Death*, 75.
[32] Kierkegaard, *Fear and Trembling*, 65.
[33] Kierkegaard, *Sickness unto Death*, 71.

commitment, and taking all the risks involved, until it breaks down and becomes impossible. As in Thomas Kuhn's *Structure of Scientific Revolutions*, revolutions depend on prior unconditional commitment to a paradigm. One can't be a Christian in Kierkegaard's sense and agree with Nietzsche that "convictions are prisons."[34]

Thus, according to Kierkegaard, the radically impossible only makes sense if one is unconditionally committed to the current world. Otherwise, we have such flexibility that everything is possible, and although some events are highly improbable, they are not inconceivable. For the truly impossible to be possible, we must be able to open radically new worlds, which we can't even make sense of until we are in them. Thus, John Caputo's understanding of religion as dealing with "the impossible" only makes sense if there are worlds, that is, if there are what Rorty once called final vocabularies. Only if one relates steadfastly rather than flexibly to the world established by one's defining commitment can one experience a gestalt switch in which one's sense of reality is transformed.

Kierkegaard concludes from his examination of all types of despairing ways to try to relate the factors that the only sphere of existence that can give equal weight to both sets of factors is a religion based on an infinite passion for something finite. Kierkegaard calls such a paradoxical religion Religiousness B. He is clear that "in Religiousness B the edifying is something outside the individual...The paradoxical edification [of Christianity] corresponds therefore to the determination of God in time as the individual man; for if such be the case, the individual is related to something outside himself."[35]

But, given the logic of Kierkegaard's position, it follows that the object of defining relation does not have to be the God-man. Indeed, in the *Postscript* Kierkegaard says, "Subjectively, reflection is directed to the question whether the individual is related to a something *in such a manner* that his relationship is in truth a God relationship."[36] And even more clearly that "it is the passion of the infinite that is the decisive factor and not its content, for its content is precisely itself."[37]

---

[34] Friedrich Nietzsche, *The Anti-Christ*, number 54, in *Twilight of the Idols/The Anti-Christ*, trans. R. J. Hollingdale (New York: Penguin Books, 1990). Of course, individual world-change needs to be distinguished from cultural or what Heidegger calls epochal change, and also from Kuhn's scientific revolutions, but it is, nonetheless, important to note that all these thinkers share the view that, for there to be genuine world disclosure, there must be total involvement in one's current world.

[35] Kierkegaard, *Concluding Unscientific Postscript*, 498.

[36] Kierkegaard, *Concluding Unscientific Postscript*, 178.

[37] Kierkegaard, *Concluding Unscientific Postscript*, 181.

Conclusion

So now we can see why Kierkegaard claims that, unless the self relates itself to something else with an unconditional commitment, it is in despair; that only if it has an unconditional commitment will the self be able to get the two sets of factors together in such a way that they reinforce each other, and so be in bliss. Kierkegaard says rather obscurely:

> This then is the formula that describes the state of the self when despair is completely eradicated: in relating to itself and in wanting to be itself, the self is grounded transparently in the power that established it.[38]

Grounded transparently means acting in such a way that what gives you your identity comes through in everything you do. But what is the power (lower case) that established the self? I used to think that it was whatever finite and temporal object of infinite passion created you as a new being by giving you your identity. But that would only be the power that established your identity, not the power that established the three sets of contradictory factors to which your identity is the solution. What, then, is the power that established the whole relation?

The power doesn't seem to be an onto-theological God since it is lower case and Kierkegaard doesn't say that the power *created* the relation. But Kierkegaard does say that one could not despair "unless the synthesis were originally in the right relationship from the hand of God."[39] How are we to cash out this metaphor, especially if we remember that "God is that everything is possible"— not an entity at all?

I think we have to say that "the fact that everything is possible" makes possible the contradictory God-man who then says, "He who has seen me has seen the Father." He is the paradoxical Paradigm who saves from despair all sinners— those who have tried to take a stand on themselves by themselves, either by relating only to themselves or by relating to an infinite, absolute, and eternal God. The God-man saves them by calling them to make an unconditional commitment to him—"God in time as an individual man."

Therefore, I think that the claim that God established the factors has to mean that by making it possible for people to have a defining commitment—in the first instance to him—and so be reborn, Jesus revealed that the two sets of factors are equally essential and can (and must) be brought into equilibrium. This is the truth about the essential nature of the self that went undiscovered until Jesus revealed it. In this way he established the Christian understanding of the self in

---

[38] Kierkegaard, *Sickness unto Death*, 44.   [39] Kierkegaard, *Sickness unto Death*, 46.

which we now live. He is the call that demands "a decision in existence," which we cannot reject without despair.

So, on this reading, "to be grounded transparently in the power that established it" would mean that saved Christians (1) relate themselves to themselves by manifesting in all aspects of their lives that both sets of factors are essential; by, that is, relating to someone or something finite with an infinite passion and so becoming eternal in time. Whatever constituted the self as the individual self it is, healing it of despair by giving it its identity and, thereby, making it a new being— that "something" would be its savior; and (2) all such lives are grounded in Jesus, the God-man, who first makes such radical transformation of the person and of the world possible.

In this way Kierkegaard has succeeded in saving Christianity from onto-theology by replacing the creator God, who is metaphysically infinite and eternal, with the God-man who is finite and temporal, yet who is the source of the infinity and eternity required by finite beings like us if we are to be saved from despair. In so doing, Kierkegaard has also shown how leveling and technicity can be positive forces in forcing us to leave behind both metaphysics and paganism's sense of the sacred for a more intense and rewarding form of religion.

Bibliography

Bellah, Robert N., Richard Madsen, William M. Sullivan, Ann Swidler, and Steven M. Tipton (1985), *Habits of the Heart* (Berkeley and Los Angeles, CA: University of California Press).

Benner, Patricia (1984), *From Novice to Expert: Excellence and Power in Clinical Nursing Practice* (Menlo Park, CA: Addison-Wesley).

Blattner, William (1994), "The Concept of Death in *Being and Time*," *Man and World* 27, 49–70.

Blattner, William D. (1994), "Is Heidegger a Kantian Idealist?" *Inquiry* 37, 185–201.

Blattner, William D. (1999), *Heidegger's Temporal Idealism* (Cambridge: Cambridge University Press).

Borgmann, Albert (1984), *Technology and the Character of Contemporary Life* (Chicago, IL: University of Chicago Press).

Borgmann, Albert (1992), *Crossing the Postmodern Divide* (Chicago, IL: University of Chicago Press).

Bourdieu, Pierre (1977), *Outline of a Theory of Practice*, trans. Richard Nice (Cambridge: Cambridge University Press).

Carman, Taylor (1994), "On Being Social: A Reply to Olafson," *Inquiry* 37, 203–23.

Carman, Taylor (2003), *Heideggers Analytic: Interpretation, Discourse, and Authenticity in Being and Time* (Cambridge: Cambridge University Press).

Cerbone, David R. (1995), "World, World-Entry, and Realism in Early Heidegger," *Inquiry* 38, 401–21.

Cetina, Karin Knorr, Theodore R. Schatzki, and Eike von Savigny (2001), *The Practice Turn in Contemporary Theory* (New York: Routledge).

Davidson, Donald (1980), "Mental Events," in *Essays on Actions and Events* (New York: Oxford University Press), 207–25.

Davidson, Donald (1984), "On the Very idea of a *Conceptual* Scheme," in *Inquiries into Truth and Interpretation* (Oxford: Clarendon Press), 183–98.

Davidson, Donald (1991), "Three Varieties of Knowledge," in A. P. Griffiths, ed., *A. J. Ayer: Memorial Essays*, Royal Institute of Philosophy, Supplement 30 (Cambridge: Cambridge University Press), 153–66.

Derrida, Jacques (1990), "Force of Law: The Mystical Foundation of Authority," *Cardozo Law Review*, part 2, 920–1045.

Dreyfus, Hubert (1991), *Being-in-the-World: A Commentary on Heidegger's Being and Time, Division I* (Cambridge, MA: MIT Press).

Dreyfus, Hubert and Harrison Hall, eds. (1992), *Heidegger: A Critical Reader* (Oxford: Blackwell).

Dreyfus, Hubert and Mark Wrathall, eds. (2002), *Heidegger Reexamined*, vol. 1: *Dasein, Authenticity, and Death* (London: Routledge).

Dreyfus, Hubert and Mark Wrathall, eds. (2005), *A Companion to Heidegger* (Oxford: Blackwell, 2005).

Dreyfus, Hubert L. (1979), *What Computers Can't Do* (New York: Harper & Row).

Dreyfus, Hubert L. (2014), *Skillful Coping*, ed. Mark Wrathall (Oxford: Oxford University Press).

Dreyfus, Hubert L. and Stuart Dreyfus (1988), *Mind over Machine* (New York: Free Press).

Edwards, Paul (1976), "Heidegger on Death: A Deflationary Critique," *The Monist* 59: 2, 161–8.

Fell, Joseph (1991), "The Familiar and the Strange: On the Limits of Praxis in the Early Heidegger," in Hubert Dreyfus and Harrison Hall, eds., *Heidegger: A Critical Reader* (Cambridge, MA: Basil Blackwell), 65–80.

Fine, Arthur (1986), *The Shaky Game: Einstein, Realism and the Quantum Theory* (Chicago, IL: University of Chicago Press).

Føllesdal, Dagfinn (1986), "Essentialism and Reference," in *The Philosophy of W. V. O. Quine*, The Library of Living Philosophers, vol. 18 (La Salle, IL: Open Court), 97–116.

Føllesdal, Dagfinn (1996), "Conceptual Change and Reference," in Christoph Hubig, ed., *Cognitio Humana: Dynamik des Wissens und der Werte*, Deutscher Kongreß für Philosophie, Leipzig, September 23–7, 1996, lectures and colloquiums (Leipzig: Universität Leipzig, 1996), 356–9.

Foucault, Michel (1963), *Naissance de la clinique* (Paris: PUF).

Foucault, Michel (1966), *Les Mots et les choses* (Paris: Gallimard).

Foucault, Michel (1971), *L'Ordre du discours* (Paris: Gallimard).

Foucault, Michel (1973), *The Order of Things* (New York: Vintage).

Foucault, Michel (1975), *The Birth of the Clinic* (New York: Vintage).

Foucault, Michel (1975), *Surveiller et punir* (Paris: Gallimard).

Foucault, Michel (1976), *L'Histoire de la* sexualité, vol. 1: *La Volonté de savoir* (Paris: Gallimard).

Foucault, Michel (1977), *Discipline and Punish* (New York: Pantheon).

Foucault, Michel (1977), "Nietzsche, Genealogy, History," in *Language, Counter-Memory, Practice*, trans. Donald F. Bouchard and Sherry Simon (Ithaca, NY: Cornell University Press), 139–64.

Foucault, Michel (1980), *The History of* Sexuality, vol. 1: *An Introduction* (New York: Vintage).

Foucault, Michel (1980), "Power and Strategies," in *Power/Knowledge* (New York: Pantheon), 134–45.

Foucault, Michel (1980), "Two Lectures," in *Power/Knowledge* (New York: Pantheon), 78–108.

Foucault, Michel (1983), "The Subject and Power," Afterword in Hubert L. Dreyfus and Paul Rabinow, *Michel Foucault: Beyond Structuralism and Hermeneutics*, 2nd edn. (Chicago, IL: University of Chicago Press), 208–28.

Foucault, Michel (1984), *L'Usage des plaisirs* (Paris: Gallimard).

Foucault, Michel (1984), "Nietzsche, Genealogy and History," in Paul Rabinow, ed., *Foucault Reader* (New York: Pantheon), 76–100.

Foucault, Michel (1985), "Final Interview," *Raritan* 5:1 (Summer), 1–13.

Foucault, Michel (1986), *The History of Sexuality*, vol. 2: *The Use of Pleasure* (New York: Vintage).

Geertz, Clifford (1973), *The Interpretation of Cultures* (New York: Basic Books).

Guignon, Charles (1983), *Heidegger and the Problem of Knowledge* (Indianapolis, IN: Hackett).

Habermas, Jürgen (1989), *The Structural Transformation of the Public Sphere* (Cambridge, MA: MIT Press).

Habermas, Jürgen (1989), "Work and Weltanschauung: The Heidegger Controversy from a German Perspective," *Critical Inquiry* 15, 431–56.

Haugeland, John (2000), "Truth and Finitude: Heidegger's Transcendental Existentialism," in Mark Wrathall and Jeff Malpas, eds., *Heidegger, Authenticity, and Modernity: Essays in Honor of Hubert L. Dreyfus*, vol. 1. (Cambridge, MA: MIT Press), 43–78.

Haugeland, John (2002), "Heidegger on Being a Person," in *Heidegger Reexamined*, vol. 1: *Dasein, Authenticity, and Death* (London: Routledge), 73–84.

Heidegger, Martin (1958), *The Question of Being*, trans. Jean T. Wilde and William Kluback (New Haven, CT: College & University Press).

Heidegger, Martin (1959), *Discourse on Thinking*, trans. John Anderson and E. Hans Freund (New York: Harper & Row).

Heidegger, Martin (1959), *Gelassenheit* (Pfullingen: Neske).

Heidegger, Martin (1959), *Introduction to Metaphysics*, trans. Ralph Manheim (New Haven, CT: Yale University Press).

Heidegger, Martin (1959), *Vorträge und Aufsätze* (Pfullingen: Neske).

Heidegger, Martin (1961), *Introduction to Metaphysics* (New York: Doubleday).

Heidegger, Martin (1961), *Nietzsche*, vol. 2 (Pfullingen: Gunther Neske).

Heidegger, Martin (1962), *Being and Time*, trans. John Macquarrie and Edward Robinson (New York: Harper & Row).

Heidegger, Martin (1962), *Die Technik und die Kehre* (Pfullingen: Neske).

Heidegger, Martin (1966), *Discourse on Thinking*, trans. John M. Anderson and E. Hans Freund (New York: Harper & Row).

Heidegger, Martin (1966), "Memorial Address," in *Discourse on Thinking*, trans. John M. Anderson and E. Hans Freund (New York: Harper & Row), 43–57.

Heidegger, Martin (1968), *What Is Called Thinking?*, trans. Fred D. Wieck and J. Glenn Gray (New York: Harper & Row).

Heidegger, Martin (1969), *The Essence of Reasons*, trans. Terrence Malick (Evanston, IL: Northwestern University Press, 1969).

Heidegger, Martin (1971), "Building, Dwelling, Thinking," in *Poetry, Language, Thought*, trans. Alfred Hofstadter (New York: Harper & Row), 141–50.

Heidegger, Martin (1971), "On the Way to Language," in *On the Way to Language*, trans. Peter D. Hertz (New York: Harper & Row), 111–38.

Heidegger, Martin (1971), "The Origin of the Work of Art," in *Poetry, Language, Thought*, trans. Albert Hofstadter (New York: Harper & Row), 15–86.

Heidegger, Martin (1971), "The Thing," in *Poetry, Language, Thought*, trans. Alfred Hofstadter (New York: Harper & Row), 161–84.

Heidegger, Martin (1971), "What Are Poets For?" in *Poetry, Language, Thought*, trans. Alfred Hofstadter (New York: Harper & Row), 87–140.

Heidegger, Martin (1972), *On Time and Being*, trans. Joan Stambaugh (New York: Harper & Row).

Heidegger, Martin (1972), "Overcoming Metaphysics," in *The End of Philosophy* (New York: Harper & Row), 84–109.

Heidegger, Martin (1972), "Summary of a Seminar on the Lecture Time and Being," in *On Time and Being*, trans. Joan Stambaugh (New York: Harper & Row), 25–54.

Heidegger, Martin (1975), *Die Grundprobleme der Phänomenologie, Gesamtausgabe*, vol. 24 (Frankfurt am Main: Vittorio Klostermann).

Heidegger, Martin (1975), *Early Greek Thinking* (New York: Harper & Row).

Heidegger, Martin (1976), "Only a God Can Save Us: *Der Spiegel*'s Interview with Martin Heidegger," *Philosophy Today* 20, 267–84.

Heidegger, Martin (1977), "The Age of the World Picture," in *The Question Concerning Technology and Other Essays* (New York: Harper & Row), 115–54.

Heidegger, Martin (1977), "Der Ursprung des Kunstwerkes," in *Holzwege, Gesamtausgabe* vol. 5 (Frankfurt am Main: Klostermann), 1–74.

Heidegger, Martin (1977), *Holzwege, Gesamtausgabe* vol. 5 (Frankfurt am Main: Klostermann).

Heidegger, Martin (1977), "Letter on Humanism," *Basic Writings*, ed. David Farrell Krell (New York: Harper & Row), 213–66.

Heidegger, Martin (1977), *Phänomenologische Interpretation von Kants Kritik der reinen Vernunft, Gesamtausgabe*, vol. 25 (Frankfurt am Main: Vittorio Klostermann).

Heidegger, Martin (1977), "The Question Concerning Technology," in *The Question Concerning Technology and Other Essays*, trans. William Lovitt (New York: Harper & Row), 3–35.

Heidegger, Martin (1977), "Science and Reflection," in *The Question Concerning Technology and Other Essays* (New York: Harper & Row), 155–82.

Heidegger, Martin (1977), *Sein und Zeit* (Tübingen: Niemeyer Verlag).

Heidegger, Martin (1977), "What Is Metaphysics?" in *Basic Writings* (New York: Harper & Row), 89–110.

Heidegger, Martin (1977), "The Word of Nietzsche: God is Dead," in *The Question Concerning Technology and Other Essays*, trans. William Lovitt (New York: Harper & Row), 53–114.

Heidegger, Martin (1979), *Nietzsche*, vol. 1: *The Will to Power as Art*, ed. David E. Krell (New York: Harper & Row).

Heidegger, Martin (1979), *Prolegomena zur Geschichte des Zeitsbegriffs*, ed. Petra Jaeger, *Gesamtausgabe*, vol. 20 (Frankfurt am Main: Vittorio Klostermann).

Heidegger, Martin (1982), *The Basic Problems of Phenomenology*, trans. Albert Hofstadter (Bloomington, IN: Indiana University Press).

Heidegger, Martin (1982), *Nietzsche*, vol. 4, trans. David Farrell Krell (New York: Harper & Row).

Heidegger, Martin (1983), *Die Grundbegriffe der Metaphysik: Welt, Endlichkeit, Einsamkeit* (Frankfurt am Main: Klostermann).

Heidegger, Martin (1984), *Hölderlins Hymne "Der Ister," Gesamtausgabe*, vol. 53 (Frankfurt am Main: Vittorio Klostermann).

Heidegger, Martin (1984), *The Metaphysical Foundations of Logic* (Bloomington, IN: Indiana University Press).

Heidegger, Martin (1985), *The History of the Concept of Time* (Bloomington, IN: Indiana University Press).

Heidegger, Martin (1985), *Phänomenologische Interpretationen zu Aristoteles, Gesamtausgabe*, vol. 61 (Frankfurt am Main: Vittorio Klostermann).

Heidegger, Martin (1985), *Schelling's Treatise on the Essence of Human Freedom* (Athens, OH: Ohio University Press).

Heidegger, Martin (1986), *Seminare, Gesamtausgabe*, vol. 15 (Frankfurt am Main: Vittorio Klostermann).

Heidegger, Martin (1987), *Nietzsche*, vol. 3, trans. David Farrell Krell (New York: Harper & Row).

Heidegger, Martin (1991), *Kant und das Problem der Metaphysik* (Frankfurt am Main: Klostermann).

Heidegger, Martin (1992), *Parmenides* (Frankfurt am Main: Klostermann).

Heidegger, Martin (1996), *Being and Time*, trans. Joan Stambaugh (Albany, NY: State University of New York Press).

Heidegger, Martin (1996), *Wegmarken* (Frankfurt am Main: Klostermann).

Heidegger, Martin (1997), *Kant and the Problem of Metaphysics*, trans. Richard Taft (Bloomington, IN: Indiana University Press).

Heidegger, Martin (1997), *Nietzsche*, vol. 2, *Gesamtausgabe*, vol. 6.2 (Frankfurt am Main: Klostermann).

Heidegger, Martin (1997), *Plato's Sophist* (Bloomington, IN: Indiana University Press).

Heidegger, Martin (1998), *Parmenides*, trans. André Schuwer and Richard Rojcewicz (Bloomington, IN: Indiana University Press).

Heidegger, Martin (1998), "What Is Metaphysics?" in William McNeill, ed., *Pathmarks* (Cambridge: Cambridge University Press), 82–96.

Heidegger, Martin (2000), *Vorträge und Aufsätze* (Frankfurt am Main: Klostermann).

Hoffman, Piotr (2008), "Dasein and its Time," in Hubert L. Dreyfus and Mark A. Wrathall, eds., *A Companion to Heidegger* (Oxford: Blackwell), 325–34.

Kakutani, Michiko (1995), "When Fluidity Replaces Maturity," *New York Times*, March 20, 1995, C 11.

Keller, Evelyn Fox (1987), "The Gender/Science System: or, Is Sex to Gender as Nature Is to Science?" *Hypathia* 2:3, 37–49.

Kierkegaard, Søren (1941), *Sickness unto Death*, trans. Walter Lowrie (Princeton, NJ: Princeton University Press).

Kierkegaard, Søren (1959), *Either/Or*, trans. D. E. Swenson and L. M. Swenson (Princeton, NJ: Princeton University Press).

Kierkegaard, Søren (1962), *The Present Age*, trans. Alexander Dru (New York: Harper & Row).

Kierkegaard, Søren (1967), *Journals and Papers*, ed. and trans. H. V. Hong and E. H. Hong (Bloomington, IN: Indiana University Press).

Kierkegaard, Søren (1971), *Concluding Unscientific Postscript*, trans. David F. Swenson and Walter Lowrie (Princeton, NJ: Princeton University Press).

Kierkegaard, Søren (1985), *Fear and Trembling*, trans. Alastair Hannay (New York: Penguin).

Kierkegaard, Søren (1989), *The Sickness unto Death,* trans. Alastair Hannay (London: Penguin Books).

Kisiel, Theodore (1993), *The Genesis of Heidegger's Being and Time* (Berkeley, CA: University of California Press).

Kripke, Saul (1980), *Naming and Necessity* (Cambridge, MA: Harvard University Press).

Kuhn, Thomas (1970), *The Structure of Scientific Revolutions,* 2nd edn. (Chicago, IL: University of Chicago Press).

Kuhn, Thomas (1987), "Sherman Memorial Lectures," University College, London, unpublished.

Malpas, Jeff (1992), *Donald Davidson and the Mirror of Meaning* (Cambridge: Cambridge University Press).

McDonough, Richard (1995), "Review of *Being-in-the-World,*" *The Journal of Speculative Philosophy* 9:4, 309–14.

Merleau-Ponty, Maurice (2002), *The Phenomenology of Perception,* trans. Colin Smith (New York: Routledge).

Nehamas, Alexander (1985), *Nietzsche: Life as Literature* (Cambridge, MA: Harvard University Press).

Nietzsche, Friedrich (1974), *The Gay Science,* trans. Walter Kaufmann (New York: Vintage).

Nietzsche, Friedrich (1990), *The Anti-Christ,* in *Twilight of the Idols/The Anti-Christ,* trans. R. J. Hollingdale (New York: Penguin Books).

Okrent, Mark (1988), *Heidegger's Pragmatism: Understanding, Being, and the Critique of Metaphysics* (Ithaca, NY: Cornell University Press).

Olafson, Frederick A. (1987), *Heidegger and the Philosophy of Mind* (New Haven, CT: Yale University Press).

Olafson, Frederick A. (1994), "Heidegger *à la* Wittgenstein or Coping with Professor Dreyfus," *Inquiry* 37, 45–64.

Olafson, Frederick A. (1994), "Individualism, Subjectivity, and Presence: A Response to Taylor Carman," *Inquiry* 37, 331–7.

Pascal, Blaise (1958), *Pascal's Pensées,* trans. W. F. Trotter (New York: Dutton).

Philipse, Herman (1998), *Heidegger's Philosophy of Being: A Critical Interpretation* (Princeton, NJ: Princeton University Press).

Pickering, Andrew (1984), *Constructing Quarks* (Chicago, IL: University of Chicago Press).

Postema, Gerald J. (1987), "Protestant Interpretation and Social Practices," *Law and Philosophy* 6, 283–319.

Rorty, Richard (1979), *Philosophy and the Mirror of Nature* (Princeton, NJ: Princeton University Press).

Rorty, Richard (1992), "Heidegger, Contingency and Pragmatism," in Hubert Dreyfus and Harrison Hall, eds., *Heidegger: A Critical Reader* (Oxford: Blackwell), 209–30.

Rouse, Joseph (1987), *Knowledge and Power: Toward a Political Philosophy of Science* (Ithaca, NY: Cornell University Press).

Rouse, Joseph (1996), *Engaging Science: How to Understand its Practices Philosophically* (Ithaca, NY: Cornell University Press).

Sartre, Jean-Paul (1966), *Being and Nothingness: A Phenomenological Essay on Ontology,* trans. Hazel E. Barnes (New York: Pocket Books).

Searle, John (1995), *The Construction of Social Reality* (New York: Free Press).

Spinosa, Charles, Fernando Flores, and Hubert L. Dreyfus (1997), *Disclosing New Worlds* (Cambridge, MA: MIT Press).

Taylor, Charles (1979), "Interpretation and the Sciences of Man," in P. Rabinow and W. Smith, eds., *Interpretive Social Science* (Berkeley, CA: University of California Press), 3–51.

Taylor, Charles (1985), "Interpretation and the Sciences of Man," in *Philosophy and the Human Sciences* (Cambridge: Cambridge University Press), 15–57.

Taylor, Charles (1989), *Sources of the Self* (Cambridge, MA: Harvard University Press).

Taylor, Charles (1992), "Heidegger, Language and Ecology," in Hubert Dreyfus and Harrison Hall, eds., *Heidegger: A Critical Reader* (Oxford: Blackwell Publishers), 247–69.

Turkle, Sherry (1995), *Life on the Screen: Identity in the Age of the Internet* (New York: Simon & Schuster).

Turkle, Sherry (1996), "Virtuality and its Discontents: Searching for Community in Cyberspace," *The American Prospect* 24 (Winter), 50–7.

van Buren, John (1994), *The Young Heidegger: Rumor of the Hidden King* (Bloomington, IN: Indiana University Press).

White, Carol (2005), "Preface" to *Time and Death: Heidegger's Analysis of Finitude* (Burlington, VT: Ashgate).

White, Carol J. (1984), "Dasein, Existence and Death," *Philosophy Today* 28, 52–65.

Wittgenstein, Ludwig (1969), *On Certainty*, edited by G. E. M. Anscombe and G. H. von Wright and translated by Denis Paul and G. E. M. Anscombe (New York: Harper & Row).

Wrathall, Mark (2004), "Between the Earth and the Sky: Heidegger on Life after the Death of God," in *Religion after Metaphysics* (Cambridge: Cambridge University Press), 69–87.

Wrathall, Mark (2010), *Heidegger and Unconcealment: Truth, Language, and History* (Cambridge: Cambridge University Press).

Young, Julian (2001), *Heidegger's Philosophy of Art* (Cambridge: Cambridge University Press).

Index

ability-to-be 40, 57, 59, 63, 69, 73, 74
Abraham 41, 218, 233, 240, 243
absurdity 55, 227, 229, 242
Aeschylus 84, 104, 118
affordance 8
agents 5, 78, 91, 129, 182
analytic philosophy 2, 3, 4, 26, 27
Anaximander 117
anomalies 64–6, 70–3, 86, 117, 166, 168, 185, 234, 235
antirealism 81, 82, 95–7, 105, 106, 109
anxiety 8, 23, 39–41, 44, 56–61, 66, 69, 70, 73, 74, 100, 101, 115, 116, 233
anyone, the 11, 66, 74, 151
appropriation 65, 134, 206, 216, 217
Aristotle 26, 27, 29, 32–8, 84, 103, 104, 106, 107, 117, 118
art 4, 14, 25, 49, 52, 65, 104, 125, 128–36, 139, 140, 153, 180, 181, 183, 184, 196, 199, 207
articulation 11, 128, 129, 130, 134, 137, 138
attunement 74, 139, 207, 208
Augenblick 35–41, 66, 137, 241, 243
authenticity 4, 11, 12, 20, 24, 26, 36, 39, 60, 74
autonomy 52, 136, 138, 186, 195
availableness 83, 97, 100, 104, 114, 174
averageness 22, 28

background
    conditions 91
    familiarity 22, 47
    practices 4, 6, 8–15, 22, 24, 25, 47, 49–51, 53, 81, 88–90, 92, 93, 96, 106, 177, 180, 183, 204, 225
    realism 12, 82, 97
    skills 89, 90, 93, 214
    understanding 9, 10, 44, 80, 88, 125, 156, 179, 234
Befindlichkeit 131
being-in-the-world 22, 26, 33, 56, 72, 74, 111, 133, 142, 149
being-towards-death 39
belief 4, 9, 20, 48, 74, 109–11, 121, 127, 129, 131, 175, 177, 182, 183, 194
Bellah, Robert 195
biopower 14, 155, 162, 166, 168, 169
Blattner, William 56, 114
bodies 6, 84, 103, 117, 166, 168, 224
boredom 32, 224, 226
Borgmann, Albert 191, 198, 199, 206

Bourdieu, Pierre 33, 89
breakdown 57, 58, 66, 71, 72, 73, 113–15, 116, 117, 121, 131, 146, 168

calculation 51, 135, 164, 190, 195
care 23, 55, 106, 139, 145, 146, 154, 194, 209, 212, 222, 228, 238
Carman, Taylor 19, 55, 56, 58
Cartwright, Nancy 81, 92
causality 82, 84, 85, 93, 98, 104, 105, 118
Cerbone, David 114
Christianity 104, 219, 228, 233, 236, 244, 246
circumspection 146
clearing 4, 9, 14, 61, 62, 99, 131, 135, 136, 144, 151, 152, 156–9, 165, 179, 180, 181, 184, 188–91, 214, 232
commitment 4, 15, 33, 58, 60, 63, 70, 74, 173–7, 183, 196, 201, 204, 213, 221, 222, 224–30, 232, 235, 239–45
comportment 21, 49, 77, 93, 127, 157, 191
concept 2, 5, 27, 56, 58, 60, 81, 88, 93, 95, 96, 117, 130, 177, 183, 188, 233
conformism 8, 11, 23, 25, 26, 174, 220
consciousness 12, 73, 241
control 15, 28, 51, 90, 103, 104, 135, 139, 144, 152, 162, 163, 166, 167, 169, 184–7, 190, 193, 196, 199–202, 204
convention 11, 110, 186, 187, 203
coping 22, 28, 30, 31, 38, 39, 42, 47, 48, 109, 112–14, 116, 121, 126, 178, 203, 214
creation 36, 38, 40, 51, 52, 112, 125, 129, 135, 136, 138, 159, 182, 204
culture 4, 10, 12, 14, 29–32, 40–1, 44, 47, 48, 51–3, 58, 60–1, 63–73, 75, 78, 79, 83, 85, 90, 94, 95, 100, 105, 106, 112, 117, 120, 125–40, 155, 158, 160, 165, 168, 169, 174–6, 177–9, 181, 183, 184–96, 199, 203, 206, 207, 213, 216, 227, 234, 244
curiosity 151, 203, 218, 225

danger 31, 162, 163, 165, 167, 186–8, 191, 193–6, 199, 200, 212, 213, 221–4, 230–2
Dasein 19, 20, 21, 22, 23, 24, 25, 28, 29, 33–41, 44, 47, 49, 50, 51, 53–60, 62–74, 81, 83, 96–102, 105, 106, 112, 114, 116, 142, 143, 150, 151, 153, 154, 174
Davidson, Donald 85, 105, 110

death
  cultural 53, 60, 63, 64, 66–8, 70, 72, 73
  existential 55, 57, 59, 63, 64, 66–74, 207
  ontological 56, 67, 68, 69, 73
decision 10, 30–2, 41–4, 74, 131, 177, 178, 180,
    194, 221, 224, 225, 228, 232, 237
decontextualizing 13, 82, 93
demise 54–6, 58, 60, 61, 68, 69, 71–4, 207
Derrida, Jacques 41–4
Descartes, Rene 28, 52, 80, 103, 136 n. 16, 137,
    142–4, 148, 154, 160, 166, 236
despair 127, 226, 228, 229, 232, 234, 235, 237–9,
    241, 244–6
destiny 52, 130, 132, 181, 190, 195
destruction 60, 132, 167, 187, 188
detachment 33, 173, 175, 240
deworlding 98, 114, 116, 117
difference, ontological 199, 216, 217
disclosure 26, 61, 64, 65, 132, 137, 154, 168, 244
dispersion 160, 212
divinities, divine 61, 65, 192, 197, 206, 207,
    210–12, 216, 231, 234
Dreyfus, Stuart 90
Dylan, Bob 139, 193, 218

earth 91, 98, 131, 132, 133, 135, 139, 141, 147,
    148, 151, 153, 167, 168, 183–5, 187, 191,
    196, 206, 207, 210–12, 224, 231, 239
efficiency 10, 163, 167, 184, 185, 187, 191,
    193, 231
ego 61, 62, 101
epochs 14, 38, 46, 51, 58, 61, 64, 69, 73, 126,
    127, 128, 133, 144, 155, 158, 159, 164, 199,
    208, 210, 234, 244
equipment 5, 6, 7, 9, 12, 13, 14, 20, 21, 22, 28,
    37, 47, 80, 97, 104, 113–17, 120, 125,
    141–54, 199, 212, 213
essence 62, 64, 73, 83, 84, 100, 103, 117, 120,
    121, 142, 152–4, 159, 160, 161, 163, 167,
    169, 177, 186, 188, 189, 190, 191, 195, 202,
    210, 234, 235
eternity 238, 241, 242, 243, 246
everydayness, everyday
  coping 28, 109, 114, 121
  intelligibility 19, 26, 28–44, 142
  practices 12, 14, 82, 97, 98, 112, 117, 118,
    120, 121, 126, 128, 156, 180
  skills 126, 177
  understanding 29, 44, 80, 82, 93, 98, 115,
    142, 143, 177
  world 13, 44, 47, 80, 85, 87, 88, 92, 93, 104,
    106, 112, 113, 125
existential, existentialism 1, 19–22, 24, 25,
    51, 54, 55, 59, 64, 67, 68, 70–4, 150,
    173, 174
existentiell 20, 21, 22, 24, 37, 59, 74
expert 29, 32, 34, 35, 39, 42, 43, 44, 48, 90, 222

faith 35, 73, 74, 194, 195, 229, 240, 242, 243
familiarity 13, 22, 28, 47, 54, 66, 112, 120, 121,
    125, 137, 206
Fell, Joseph 100, 101
Feyerabend, Paul 78
Fine, Arthur 81, 95, 96, 109 n. 2
finitude 45, 46, 49–51, 53, 55, 57, 60, 61, 67, 68,
    70, 71, 73, 74
fleeing 20, 33, 55, 58, 119
Flores, Fernando 41, 64
forerunning 57, 59, 64, 74
Foucault, Michel 43, 61, 155, 157–60, 164,
    168, 248
freedom 51, 52, 57, 59, 101, 131, 137, 164, 227,
    228, 229, 233, 235, 240, 243

gathering 64, 65, 196, 205, 214, 216, 224, 226
Geertz, Clifford 128, 129, 180
Gestell 14, 152
gift 49, 89, 90, 92, 93, 148, 192, 207, 211
God 10, 51, 52, 53, 70, 135, 136, 139, 142,
    156, 175, 176, 181, 184, 189, 195, 197,
    199, 216, 218, 223, 232, 233, 237, 239,
    243, 244, 245, 246
Goldberg, Ken 229
Guignon, Charles 55, 59
guilt 39, 40, 50, 59, 60, 138

Habermas, Jürgen 197, 219
Hall, Harrison 115, 191
hammer 13, 21, 47, 77, 83, 100, 115, 116, 125,
    146, 147, 149
Hannay, Alastair 233, 240
Haugeland, John 58, 63
Hegel, G. 28, 50, 130, 152
Heidegger, Martin 1–4, 8–15, 19–29, 33–47,
    49–74, 81–6, 95–121, 125–69, 173–217,
    231–4
history 2–4, 12, 13, 33, 41, 46, 51–3, 55, 63, 67,
    68, 77, 126, 132, 135, 139, 141–6, 153, 154,
    158, 159, 162, 165, 174, 176, 177, 184, 187,
    190, 194, 196, 200
Hitler, Adolf 136, 184, 194, 196
horizon 49, 52, 137, 150, 204, 243
human being 9–12, 20–2, 25, 26, 35, 46, 51, 55,
    56, 63, 65, 68, 69, 78, 81, 82, 83, 86, 88, 90,
    92, 93, 95, 96, 98, 99, 101, 105, 110–12, 114,
    118, 130, 131, 133–5, 137, 142, 156, 158,
    160, 162, 165, 168, 169, 174, 178, 179, 180,
    181, 185, 189, 199, 204, 211, 224, 231,
    233–5, 237
Husserl, Edmund 118, 234

identity 8, 15, 36, 37, 39, 44, 58, 60, 66, 67, 69,
    70, 71, 72, 73, 130, 195, 204, 205, 207, 208,
    212, 213, 214, 215, 225, 226, 228–30, 240,
    241, 242, 243, 245, 246

impossibility 56, 59, 67, 71, 161
inauthenticity 74
individualism 52, 137
intelligibility 7–8, 11, 13, 20, 23, 28–9, 34, 40, 44, 47, 51, 82, 85, 98–9, 105, 112, 121, 134, 142, 174, 177
interpretation 1, 2, 3, 4, 9, 11, 19, 24, 25, 26, 37, 38, 39, 41, 46, 53–6, 59, 60, 64, 66, 71, 74, 80, 81, 84, 85, 86, 90, 91, 93, 98, 102–4, 106, 108, 112, 114, 117, 119, 131, 132, 144, 145, 160, 161, 166, 174, 179, 183, 184, 191, 194, 196, 197, 241

Jesus 36, 41, 61, 138, 197, 239, 241, 245, 246
judgment 42, 50, 88, 90, 91, 203, 221, 224, 230, 232, 234

Kairos 36–8
Kant, Immanuel 3, 50, 52, 61, 68, 80, 81, 95, 96, 101, 110, 114, 131, 136, 138, 160–2, 227
Keller, Evelyn Fox 79, 94
Kierkegaard, Søren 3, 15, 20, 21, 35–8, 41, 58–60, 63, 66, 74, 131, 137, 173–5, 180, 185, 218–46
Kisiel, Theodore 22, 29, 72
knowledge 50, 54, 79, 80, 94, 102, 153, 160, 161, 177, 197, 203, 204, 221, 225
Kripke, Saul 110, 121, 234
Kuhn, Thomas 78, 94, 107, 117, 129, 166, 182, 183, 244

language 7, 9, 28, 29, 41, 54, 85, 106, 110, 111, 121, 128, 135–8, 150, 156, 182, 204
leap 42, 43, 46, 52, 59, 61, 119, 137, 224, 226, 232
leveling 14, 20, 165, 169, 174, 186–8, 196, 219, 220, 222, 226–8, 230, 232, 246
logic 2, 27, 111, 130, 183, 244

Malick, Terrence 150
maturity 52, 87, 186, 195, 227
Merleau-Ponty, Maurice 131
metaphysics 53, 62, 141–3, 160, 231, 246
modernity 160, 162, 201
mortals 64, 65, 168, 192, 206, 207, 210, 213–15, 217, 231, 232

nature 14, 77–80, 82–6, 93–5, 97–108, 111–18, 122, 130, 132, 133, 139, 141, 142, 144–50, 153, 163, 164, 166, 168, 185, 186, 188–90, 192, 193, 199, 201, 202, 208, 210
Nehamas, Alexander 103
Nietzsche, Friedrich 1, 25, 68, 103, 130, 134, 141, 142, 143, 153, 154, 155, 156, 158, 169, 174–7, 202, 205, 218, 237, 244
nihilism 4, 14, 15, 44, 60, 74, 154, 175, 176, 177, 180, 186, 191, 192, 194–6, 218, 220, 223

norms 6, 8, 11, 19–25, 28, 39, 40, 128, 165, 166, 168, 174, 182, 185
nothingness 60, 61, 62, 67

objectivity 88, 143, 154
occurrent, the 82, 83, 97–100, 102, 104, 105, 113, 114, 116, 119, 120
Olafson, Frederick 19
ontic 19, 23, 24, 25, 51, 74, 99, 101, 103, 112, 116, 126, 145, 148, 153
ontology 21, 68, 73, 74, 103, 104, 121, 141–3, 149
ordering 14, 101, 114, 143, 147, 152–4, 162, 163, 164, 166, 169, 185, 188, 189, 193, 194, 200, 202, 231
ownmost 35, 39, 51, 134, 206, 216

paradigm 73, 78, 86, 91, 93, 110, 129, 130, 131, 132, 135, 136, 139, 140, 168, 181–5, 193, 194, 196, 199, 201–4, 215, 216, 244
paradox 72, 98, 113, 121, 161, 212, 242–5
Parmenides 46, 64, 66, 145
Pascal, Blaise 236
phenomenology 1, 25, 27, 34, 36, 49, 54, 73, 93, 99, 144, 174
philosophy 1–4, 21, 38, 83, 93, 95, 130, 136, 159, 161, 173, 195, 196, 216, 225
phronimos, phronesis 11, 29, 33–42
physicalism 102
physis 84, 103, 147, 153, 154, 159, 199, 208
Plato 28, 80, 85, 106, 117, 134, 158, 159, 173, 177, 190, 228, 235, 237, 241
poetry 84, 104, 117, 132, 183
politics 48, 127, 155, 179, 216
power 14, 20, 43, 46, 83–5, 95, 99, 100, 102–5, 132, 139, 148, 155–9, 162, 164–6, 168, 184, 186–7, 191–4, 202, 205, 207, 209, 214, 219–21, 222, 228, 245, 246
practices (general) 4, 6–15, 28, 29, 34, 40, 41, 47–54, 83–6, 88–100, 104–7, 109–22, 125–40, 156, 158, 162, 165–9, 175–84, 186, 188, 190, 191, 193, 194, 197, 199, 200, 202, 204–6, 212, 213, 216, 221, 225, 231, 239
   access 13, 81, 95, 118, 119
   anomalous 69
   constitutive 118
   focal 191, 205–7, 213
   marginal 43, 52, 61, 65, 70, 136, 137, 139, 168, 186, 193
   shared 8, 9, 11, 68, 79, 94, 131, 156, 179, 183
pragmatism 144, 147, 148
projection 39, 42, 58, 59, 103, 117, 122, 137, 166
public sphere 219, 220, 221, 222, 224, 229, 230, 236

rationality 10, 159
ready-to-hand 34, 144, 145, 147–51

realism
  deflationary 109, 110, 115, 116
  hermeneutic 12, 82, 86, 94, 96, 97, 108
  plural 13, 85
  robust 13, 109, 113, 114, 116–18, 120
  scientific 4
referential totality 149–54
religion 176, 215, 233, 244, 246
resistance 32, 85, 105, 131, 132, 146, 147, 154,
  155, 167–9, 183, 186, 196, 201, 203, 213
resolute 12, 20, 23, 25, 33–42, 44, 55, 57, 59, 63,
  64, 74, 119
resources 14, 33, 120, 139, 154, 164, 167, 178,
  189, 190, 193, 200, 202, 210, 211, 213, 224,
  231, 237
responsibility 20, 55, 64, 220, 222, 229, 236
Rilke, Rainer Maria 61, 62, 145, 154, 163
Rorty, Richard 78, 85, 86, 87, 92, 93, 106–8,
  233, 234, 244
Rouse, Joseph 6, 81, 83, 100, 109, 112
rules 4, 6, 11, 30, 31–3, 35, 39, 40, 48, 60, 80,
  83, 89, 90, 92, 93, 129, 178, 182, 202

sacrifice 66, 67, 69, 136, 176, 184, 223, 243
Sartre, Jean-Paul 20, 21, 25, 55, 101, 131, 227,
  228, 241
science 12, 13, 51, 63, 67, 77–97, 99–100, 102,
  103, 105–11, 113, 115–18, 122, 126, 129,
  131, 142, 143, 144, 161, 163, 165, 166, 185,
  228, 234
sex, sexuality 158, 159, 164, 176, 186, 225, 230
shining 133, 208, 216
significance 2, 21, 27, 28, 81, 90, 95, 103, 130,
  148–51, 154, 175, 176, 215, 219, 223, 241
situation
  concrete 34, 35, 36, 37, 39, 40, 42, 44
  general 34
skill 4–9, 13, 15, 21, 23, 28–34, 36, 42, 44, 47, 48,
  82, 89, 90, 92, 93, 98, 115, 120, 127, 177,
  178, 200, 205, 206, 211, 212–15, 222, 229
space, spatiality 14, 31, 62, 82, 93, 98, 101, 106,
  126, 151, 152, 158, 181, 190, 193, 204, 205,
  219, 225, 236
strife 132
style 1, 5, 12, 14, 15, 20, 41, 44, 46–9, 52, 53, 64,
  65, 67, 70, 86, 89, 125, 126–39, 205, 209,
  212, 216
subjectivity 25, 51, 154, 162, 201, 205, 213

Taylor, Charles 128–30, 180, 182, 195, 233
technology, technological
  devices 166, 167, 188, 189, 200, 209, 210,
    213–15

essence of 152, 153, 167, 186, 188, 198
practices 9, 14, 140, 190, 194, 205, 206, 213
understanding 139, 142, 143, 145, 155,
  165–7, 169, 185, 186, 188–91, 194, 199, 214
temporality 41, 46, 53, 68, 70, 101, 102, 114,
  152, 174
theory 21, 42, 79–84, 86–93, 95, 96, 98, 99,
  102–4, 107, 111, 115–19, 144, 159, 160,
  164, 165, 185
things 1, 4, 8–10, 12–15, 21–3, 29, 31, 37, 43,
  47–53, 56, 65, 67, 74, 78, 82, 83, 85, 86,
  98–117, 120–2, 126, 127, 129, 130, 133–5,
  142, 150, 155, 156, 162, 165–8, 173, 175,
  178–82, 185, 190–3, 196, 199, 200, 202,
  205–12, 214–18, 221, 230, 237, 238
thinkers, thinking 1, 2, 4, 23, 26, 46, 49, 54,
  62, 63, 65, 72, 79, 81, 94, 101, 111, 135,
  136, 147, 155, 160, 169, 175, 186, 198,
  215, 216, 225
transcend, transcendence 10, 51, 62, 82, 83, 97,
  100, 103, 111, 113, 114, 120, 141, 143, 150,
  174, 220, 242, 243
truth 20, 30, 31, 32, 40, 41, 60, 66, 78, 79, 81, 82,
  89, 93, 94, 97, 107, 111, 126, 128, 133–7,
  156, 158–60, 162, 164, 166, 168, 175, 180,
  184, 196, 233, 237, 244, 245

unconcealment, unconcealedness 137, 158
universe 13, 62, 106, 109–11, 113, 115, 116, 118,
  122, 224

values 10, 43, 129, 131, 176, 177, 180, 182,
  183, 190
virtuality 225
virtuoso 33, 35, 37, 38, 40–4
vocabularies 86, 107, 244
vulnerability 60, 65, 66, 67, 69, 70, 72, 74, 225,
  229, 232

White, Carol 45, 74
Wittgenstein, Ludwig 3, 19, 20, 28, 50
world
  collapse 58, 63, 64, 66–9, 71–4
  disclosure 26, 244
  plural 13
  shared 66, 128, 129, 132, 183
  technological 14, 152, 167, 186
  styles 14, 152, 167, 186
  transformation 41, 66
worldhood 51, 126, 144, 145, 151–4
Wrathall, Mark 231

Young, Julian 60

Printed and bound by CPI Group (UK) Ltd, Croydon, CR0 4YY